[the best of]
DEAR
COQUETTE

[the best of]
DEAR
COQUETTE

---

*Shady advice from
a raging bitch who
has no business
answering any of
these questions*

ICON

Published in the UK in 2016
by Icon Books Ltd, Omnibus Business Centre,
39–41 North Road, London N7 9DP
email: info@iconbooks.com
www.iconbooks.com

Sold in the UK, Europe and Asia
by Faber & Faber Ltd, Bloomsbury House,
74–77 Great Russell Street,
London WC1B 3DA or their agents

Distributed in the UK, Europe and Asia
by Grantham Book Services,
Trent Road, Grantham NG31 7XQ

Distributed in the USA
by Publishers Group West,
1700 Fourth Street, Berkeley, CA 94710

Distributed in Australia and New Zealand
by Allen & Unwin Pty Ltd,
PO Box 8500, 83 Alexander Street,
Crows Nest, NSW 2065

Distributed in South Africa
by Jonathan Ball, Office B4, The District,
41 Sir Lowry Road, Woodstock 7925

Distributed in India by Penguin Books India,
7th Floor, Infinity Tower – C, DLF Cyber City,
Gurgaon 122002, Haryana

Distributed in Canada by Publishers Group Canada,
76 Stafford Street, Unit 300,
Toronto, Ontario M6J 2S1

ISBN: 978-178578-095-0

Typeset in Baskerville by Marie Doherty

Printed and bound in the UK
by Clays Ltd, St Ives plc

CONTENTS

Introduction

Dear Coquette,

I've been thinking a lot about your book and how each of us has favorite posts, and how much our favorites say about who we are. Our questions say even more about us, and I cannot wait to read which ones you've chosen.

I've asked you so many questions over the years. Questions about trivial annoyances, self-discovery, heartbreak, and my deepest darkest fears. Sometimes they weren't even questions. Sometimes I just wanted to share with someone who I knew would understand.

Thank you for answering. Thank you for showing us that while we can break, we can also break open, that we are not alone in our fears, our grief, our insecurities, or our ecstasies. I love this tribe of ours.

So tell me, what would you say to us after we've finished sitting at your feet to ask our questions? After we've all been fed and half of us have fallen asleep after a good fuck and the fire has died down and we're just nursing the last of our whiskeys. When we are finally silent, what would you say?

Dear Reader,

I've been thinking a lot about this book too, but I can't quite bring myself to call it *my* book. This is *our* book. It is a token of a shared journey, a memorialization of our years spent growing up alongside one another. We did this together, every last one of us, and I'm honored that you've chosen to be a part of it.

For those of you who've been here since the beginning, you already know what this means. When this all started we were a bunch of delinquent children in a treehouse slapped together in the backyard of the internet. It was a silly game of truth or dare that we played to escape our boring lives and annoying parents and that ex who had broken our hearts. We were fucking around just having some fun, and then somewhere along the way the conversation got deep, the problems became real, and we accidentally stumbled into our adulthood.

It's been a hell of a ride, and this book has been a long time coming. Now that you're holding it in your hands, I hope you feel how much it belongs to you, and I hope you enjoy what we've chosen for this best-of collection. It was a beautiful and brutal thing to sort through all of my thousands of posts and squeeze some order out of the chaos and madness. I think we did a damn fine job. (Shout out to my brilliant editor, Tom, without whom none of it would have been possible.)

The five parts of this book cover everything from love, sex and drugs to philosophical musings on the individual and the greater good. There's even a bit about me. For those of you whose favorites didn't make the cut, please accept my apologies ahead of time. No doubt you'll understand that it takes a merciless form of math and murder to turn 3,500 pages into 350.

For those of you who are new, *welcome*. I hope you enjoy what you discover here. You're a part of this now too, and as you learn more about what we've all been up to, maybe you'll come to love this little tribe of ours as well.

Our tribe – I've never thought to use that word before, but there's something deeply appealing about the idea. It fits. I love that you all have favorite posts. I love that you see yourselves in them. I love the depth and breadth of your countless questions and the connection I feel to each of you as I answer them.

I've had an absolute blast getting to know you all. You've taught me so much over the years. You've made me grow. You've made me think. You've made me proud. You've made me cry. You've allowed me into your lives, and you've been vulnerable in ways that never ceased to amaze. It really has been a fucking pleasure.

And to answer your question (as I always will), at the end of our day after we've all been fed, when the fire has died down and we're nursing the last of our whiskeys, when those of us still awake have finished talking shit and telling stories, when we are all finally silent, then I will raise a glass and say what's in my heart.

Thank you for being a part of my life.

You are all my secret treasure.

PART I

On Love

On true love and a greater purpose

Do you ever wonder why your here? And your purpose? Or if you'll ever find true love? I think about these things every once in a while, and although its great being single and wild, these thoughts come and go. What about you?

As an existential nihilist, I have a problem with folks who indulge in grandiose wonderings about a greater purpose to life.

Anyone with the slightest sense of scale recognizes that nothing we do matters. In a universe so infinitely vast, our lives are entirely without meaning. The trick is being able to laugh at the abyss because you recognize the freedom it affords you.

Pondering your purpose is philosophical masturbation, and the only way you can make yourself cum is by surrendering rational thought to religious doctrine.

No thank you – I don't need god. I already have a clit.

I'm perfectly cozy with the cold hard knowledge that I'll die never understanding the nature of the universe. In the meantime, I've carved out my own little corner of paradise and filled it with all kinds of love, none of which I would insult by deeming any one more 'true' than the other.

That's another thing – I can't stand it when grown-ass women use the word 'true' as an adjective for something so important as love. There is no such thing as true love. Only love.

Going through life with the expectation of some fantastical form of uber-love is childish wish-thinking that would be silly if it weren't so damaging to adult relationships.

Sure, I like *The Princess Bride* as much as the next gal, but fairy tales are lies we tell to children. Still, the myth of Prince Charming manages to sneak past Santa Claus and the Easter Bunny only to worm its way into our romantic expectations.

We don't write letters to the North Pole anymore, but somehow we're still waiting to be swept off our feet.

Again, no thank you – I don't need a prince. I just need a guy who can find my clit.

On the point of relationships

What's the point of relationships? If the initial high is temporary and then you stick together until you hate each other so much that you cheat or break up, then what's the point? Is there ever a time when people find someone they really love?

The human condition is a fun ride, but don't ever forget that we're all just a bunch of talking meat wrapped around a sack of warm shit programmed to eat, sleep and fuck.

We're social animals with a biological imperative to reproduce. That's it. That's all. Love is a neurochemical response with a shelf life long enough to perpetuate the species.

And hey, I don't wanna hear you complaining about it either, because quite frankly, you're one lucky motherfucker to have air in your lungs and the opportunity to be confused by it at all.

The last breath you just took is one more than a hundred billion human beings who came before you will ever get to take again, and one day, the last breath you just took will be the last breath you'll ever take.

That day is the point of relationships, that day when you cease to fucking exist, because it's guaranteed, my friend. This shit all ends, so cram as much love, joy and shout-it-from-the-rooftops happiness as you possibly can into whatever time you can make for yourself.

Meet as many interesting people as you can. Make as many friends as you can. Fall in love as many times as you can. Fuck it if it hurts sometimes. You're one of the lucky ones who's still breathing.

All we have in this world is relationships with other people. At this stage in our evolution, nothing else matters.

On all that matters

So wait, you just said both "We're social animals with a biological imperative to reproduce. That's it. That's all. Love is a neurochemical response with a shelf life long enough to perpetuate the species." and "All we have in this world is relationships with other people. At this stage in our evolution, nothing else matters." I mean, yell at me all you want, but I'm confused. Is love not a relationship with another person? Does that mean it doesn't matter or it's all that matters? I don't get it.

Both. It's both, my friend. Love doesn't matter, and yet it's all that matters.

This doesn't have to be confusing. You just have to be willing to accept the premise that nothing matters. We're all dust. Not just our individual selves, but the entirety of the human experiment. It's all going to be a pile of ashes one day.

Most people recoil at the thought of annihilation. It terrifies them. They invent silly gods and ridiculous myths of Armageddon or eternal life, all to stave off the creeping inevitability of the nothingness to which we will all return.

Don't recoil from your own impermanence. Accept it. Embrace it. Gaze into the abyss, and let the abyss gaze back into you, because if you can let go of your fear while maintaining eye contact with nothingness, the singular importance of love will crystallize right in front of you. It will be an unavoidable revelation.

Love doesn't matter, and yet it's all that matters. The contradiction melts away once you come to terms with not just your but *everything's* eventual annihilation. Sure, love is just a neurochemical response with a shelf life long enough to perpetuate the species, but so what? *It's all we've fucking got.*

On saying those three words

Is it better to tell someone you love them when they say it or leave them hanging until you feel it?

Come on, people. This is Integrity 101. Say what you mean, and mean what you say. If you don't love someone, don't let them guilt you into saying 'I love you' out of some misguided sense of propriety.

You're not leaving them hanging unless they're expecting you to return the sentiment, and if that's the case, then they're not really saying 'I love you'. What they're really doing is committing little tiny acts of emotional extortion.

Don't degrade 'I love you' by surrendering it against your will. Every time you say those three words you should feel it.

On reframing bisexuality

Oh, fuck. If I know I like men and women, how do I decide who to settle down with in the end?

I know this question is just an expression of your immaturity, but it annoys the shit out of me when people frame bisexuality as a false dilemma between genders. It's not.

Go fall in love. Go get your heart broken, and then go do it again. Find out what it takes to be in a long-term relationship regardless of either of your genders. Learn about yourself. Figure out the kind of person you want to be and the kind of life you want to live.

Go do all that shit, and when you've finally grown up a bit, when you've wrapped your head around the wonderfully messy and messed-up complexity of interpersonal relationships, when you've come to terms with how little control you actually have over your romantic destiny in the first place, maybe then you'll realize how ridiculous it is to reduce major life decisions about potential life partners to something as ultimately inconsequential as 'penis vs vagina'.

What is the distinction between loving someone and being "in love" with them? Aren't these just arbitrary constructs?

The classical distinction is between the concepts of Philia and Eros: of brotherly love versus romantic love. The modern distinction tends to be less sophisticated, and pretty much boils down to whether you still want to fuck somebody.

What do you do when you realize you love your significant other more than they love you?

Embrace your vulnerability.

How do I fall in love with my wife again?

Make sure you haven't lost respect for her, and then simply be open to it.

I've accidentally fallen in love with a man who is the single parent of his 1-year-old son. This is not what I had planned out for myself. What do I do?

Get used to life not going according to plan.

I love him. I've loved him for a long time now. I know that he loves me too... why aren't we saying it out loud?!?!

Because you're so desperate for it.

What am I supposed to do when I'm in love with two different people?

That's not a 'supposed to do' situation. What do you *want* to do? Try doing that. (If you're honest with the people involved, and they don't want what you want, then at that point, hopefully you'll know more about what *best* to do.)

On letting go

I'm in love, but we're going to college next year. She to Yale, I to Vanderbilt, so it's most likely too far to keep a relationship in college. Do I just let it go or give a long-distance relationship a shot freshman year in college? It seems like it'd be near impossible, but I want to know what you think about it. Thanks, Coquette.

Let it go. Try to make it as mutual as possible. Your heart will break and you will miss her terribly that first semester at college. Still, if you say your goodbyes and split amicably, you'll end the relationship on a high note.

If you try to stick it out, at best your relationship will die a slow death of long-distance starvation. At worst, incidents of infidelity will destroy your mutual respect. Either way, it ends badly.

It's hard to see now, but the best outcome is that you remember each other fondly in the years to come. Life is long. It's much better to have your first love as a friend ten years later.

On a crush junkie

There's always been a guy in my life who I am completely obsessed with and/or devastated by. It's the same formula each time: great sex, he's aloof and emotionally reserved, I agonize over his text messages. I feel like shit during the entire thing, but I crave his attention/validation so much, contact with him is like a high. What is wrong with me and how do I fix it?

You just listed what's wrong with you. Congratulations. You've correctly identified your dysfunctional pattern of behavior, and that's the first step towards fixing it.

The second step is giving it a name. Some folks like to call what you've got a 'love addiction'. I prefer the term 'crush junkie', because it's not actual love, nor is it an actual addiction.

The third step is breaking the pattern. This is where things get difficult, because it's entirely up to you to change your behavior. Stop obsessing over guys. Stop giving them the power to devastate you. Sure, that's easier said than done, but it's a lot easier to do when you start recognizing that your boy-crazy bullshit – all the attention-seeking behavior and desperate need for validation – it's all just a substitute for having actual self-respect and self-worth.

Find your own internal source of validation, and let it be independent of any relationship. It's not an easy thing to do, but it's necessary for you to stay emotionally healthy, and it will help you to consciously choose not to let yourself get wrapped up in the experience of infatuation.

You can still enjoy the early romantic stages of a relationship, but when you can resist the urge to obsess over a guy because you know in your heart you don't need his validation, you'll also find that you won't feel like shit any more.

On someone out there

do you actually believe that there is a stage in every relationship where you get bored of being with your partner? you don't think that there is someone out there that could entertain your fancies, keep you laughing, and keep you orgasming year after year? i only ask because i have witnessed people with this relationship (namely my parents, i know.. gross, but it's true. and actually pretty endearing now), and i wonder if it's absolutely naive of me to believe that i have any hope of achieving this with someone i'm with ..or if it actually is a feasible possibility.

It never ceases to amaze me how some of you can turn this into an exercise in missing the motherfucking point. Is there someone out there that could entertain my fancies, keep me laughing, and keep me orgasming year after year? Fuck, what an infantile question.

Of course there is. Even if such a person were one in a million, there are literally thousands upon thousands of people out there who could do that shit standing on their heads. Don't you get it?

There is no one magical person out there with the other half of my golden amulet. Instead, there's a metric fuck-ton of beautiful and fascinating boys and girls to play with. Sometimes I even fall in love.

I surround myself with brilliant and witty people. I am responsible for my own orgasm. I am the empress of my own goddamn happiness whether I'm in a relationship with zero, one or several people at any given moment.

Your parents didn't achieve relationship bliss because they found soulmate perfection in one another. They did it because they're a damn good match and shit happened to work out for them. That's commendable, but these days, it's not the norm.

Also, don't kid yourself. Boredom will eventually set in to every relationship. It doesn't have to be a killer, though. Boredom doesn't mean you stop laughing and fucking. Hell, most folks end up taking comfort in consistency. All I was saying is that fireworks always end.

Your naïveté doesn't stem from your desire to be like your parents. That's sweet, actually. Your naïveté stems from an underlying assumption that there is someone – a Prince Charming – who is somehow more perfect for you than all your other potential mates. That shit is ridiculous.

I'm not saying that you won't eventually find someone who you think is perfect and settle down to a marriage very similar to the way your parents did it. Odds are, you will. After all, you were raised in a loving environment, and so the likelihood of scoring a similar situation is that much better.

That's the point really. It's all just a numbers game.

Good luck.

What's left after the being in love phase is over?
Love. Or ennui. Or both. Depends on how you play it.

How do you keep a man in love?
Be cool.

When do I give up on an unrequited love?
As soon as possible.

What is the cure for unrequited love?
Time and distance.

On trying long distance

*I'm trying a long-distance relationship for the first time.
I really care about the girl, but I have always had a hard
time keeping it in my pants. I've never really cheated –
but in this instance I feel like it might eventually happen.
Got any advice?*

You're asking a woman who is at this very moment doing her
level fucking best to execute a dignified and graceful resolution to
a loving and devoted long-distance relationship that has, at least
for now, run its course.

Bad timing, shitbird. I'm about to fuck up your whole world.

A long-distance relationship isn't something you casually try for
the first time like Thai food or anal sex. A long-distance relationship is something you do because you absolutely motherfuckingly
have to, and it's bittersweet and painful and unbearable and you
can't live without it, which I suppose is still pretty much like Thai
food or anal sex, but you get my point.

If all you can say is, 'I really care about the girl', that isn't even
close to enough. You'd better love that crazy bitch with every last
ounce of douche you've got coursing through your veins. Otherwise,
you're setting yourself up to fail.

And what's all this about eventually cheating? Quit planning
to fuck up. Fidelity isn't inversely proportional to distance, asshole.
There are no teen sex comedy loopholes in real life.

Feel free to work out an open arrangement, but if you decide
to go traditional, you'd better have the requisite integrity. Keep it
in your motherfucking pants, or be honest about the fact that you
can't. It's that simple.

I just spent a solid, passionate year loving someone across hundreds of miles of Pacific Coast Highway. It was the loneliest year of my life, punctuated by the most blissed-out orgiastic episodes of heroin-grade happiness I've ever known.

It's an unnatural thing to maintain burning desire at a distance. You've gotta be an emotional athlete to handle the highs and lows. It requires a heart that's pure and strong, and brother, I don't think you're in shape for it.

I'd wish you good luck, but it'd be wasted on your weak-ass shit. Long distance is for hardcore motherfuckers on fire.

You ain't ready.

I'm in love with a married man. Please remind me how big of a piece of shit I am so I can move on from this toxic situation...

You can't help who you fall in love with, and you're not a piece of shit unless you have an actual affair with the guy. Quit punishing yourself. Forgive yourself instead.

True or false: If you truly love someone, being faithful is easy.

False. If you truly have integrity, being faithful is easy. Do not confuse love and integrity. Love is just an emotional state, and regardless of how deeply or intensely it may be felt, it's still not a measure of the content of your character.

I've never been broken up with. I've ended the few serious relationships I've been in. This bothers me, but I'm not sure what to do about it.

That's not what bothers you. What bothers you is that you don't know whether you've ever really been in love.

On prince charming disease

I love my boyfriend in a very warm, comfortable and affectionate way. We are on almost the same page intellectually, and we never fight. Things are pretty much "no complaints" all around. On my end, though, it's not really a passionate love and never has been. He's the best guy I've ever dated, and I do love him, but there is a small part of me that still wants to hold out for at least a steamy love affair before settling down with the safe and comfortable guy (or just find a good guy who also presses my buttons). I'm happy and couldn't bring myself to leave my guy, but I wonder if this desire for something more exciting will rear up one day and make a big pile of relationship-ruining drama. Should I interpret this feeling as a sign I should leave, even though I don't want to right now? Or should I just roll with it and deal with it later, if it really becomes a bigger issue?

At moments like these, I want to drive up to Forest Lawn, find Walt Disney's grave, dig up whatever part of him wasn't cryogenically frozen, and bitch-slap him for infecting generations of American women with something I like to call 'Prince Charming Disease'.

This is a terrible affliction that causes grown-ass women to ruin perfectly good relationships by pining away for a nebulous cartoon fiction: passionate, steamy, 'happily ever after' love.

'*Snow White*', '*Sleeping Beauty*' and '*Cinderella*' are delicious fun when you're a little girl, but fairy tales are lies we tell to children. The myth of Prince Charming has no business sneaking past Santa Claus and the Tooth Fairy and worming its way into your romantic expectations. Do you still write letters to the North Pole? Didn't think so – and yet you're still waiting to be swept off your feet.

You are happy in a stable, healthy relationship built on mutual love and respect with a man whom you consider your intellectual and emotional equal. Girl, you and I should be high-fiving like drunken frat boys at a strip club. Instead, you're writing me about the best guy you've ever dated like he's the winter of your discontent.

You want to hold out for a steamy love affair? You actually used the word 'steamy'? Are you kidding? Sure, you could find a guy who bends you over the furniture, but fresh sexual chemistry is a temporary high, and it isn't gonna scratch your itch.

Your real problem is that you haven't plowed through enough guys to realize that they're all pretty much the same, and so every time the music swells at the end of a chick flick, you think you're missing out on something magical.

Sorry, babe. Nobody is waiting around the corner on a white horse.

If you weren't emotionally, intellectually or physically satisfied, that would be another story – just not this one. You're happy, and nothing is broken except your childlike set of unrealistic romantic expectations, which would be quaint if they weren't so damaging to adult relationships like yours.

On falling in love

Do you think one month is too soon to fall in love? Or 2 months? 3 months? Is there a point where it's just too soon? Or should I just pay more attention to my feelings and less to my calendar?

One month is long enough to be love stoned, but in love? Not unless you're a silly teenager. Three intense months might do it, but it'd still be a raw emotion without the kind of shared life experience that really gets you there.

Ignore the calendar, but take your time.

On learning to love yourself

How do you learn to love yourself? How do you "realize" that in your deepest of hearts you are worthy? I've been trying for years and after every new strategy or life-changing decision I always reach the same conclusion: I'm not. I could give you a list of reasons why I'm right to think that and I could give you a list of reasons why I'm stupid and wrong to think that. My reasoning tells me that the second list is me trying to lie to myself. How do you love the skin you're in? How do you love your personality? How do you, coketalk, do it?

Stop all this 'trying to learn to realize' bullshit. You're tripping all over yourself with lists and strategy and reasoning. This isn't a process for your ego or your rational mind. You're not going to think your way into loving yourself.

Sorry to get all Yoda up in this bitch, but love or love not. There is no try.

The simple truth is that you are worthy of love. That goes for every last motherfucker on the planet. Whether you realize it or not is purely a matter of getting out of your own way.

Seriously, don't you get how amazing it is to be alive? One day you won't be. In the meantime, the skin you're in will wither and age, your personality will ebb and flow, and everything around you will be in a constant state of flux. Ultimately, none of it really matters, except for those moments of joy you carve out for yourself, and you can only experience joy when you forget all the bullshit and remember that you really do love yourself after all.

This isn't about self-confidence. It's not even about self-acceptance really. That's the fucking irony here. Loving yourself isn't about the 'self'. It's a difficult concept to communicate. I've hinted at it before, but once you've had the experience of truly letting go of your ego, you'll understand what I mean. There's a freedom that comes in accepting in its totality both the extraordinary nature and fleeting insignificance of the human condition. For some reason, afterward, it's really fucking easy to love yourself.

Don't worry, I'm not gonna start singing Kumbaya or some shit. You wanted to know how I did it, and that's pretty much it. I guess all I'm trying to say is, it's not that you ever really learn to love yourself. In the end, if you're lucky, you just forget not to.

On teenage love

Can you be in love with someone after only dating them for a short amount of time? Yes I'm a stupid teenage girl who believes in love, sue me.

Sue you for what? Bubble gum and a sense of entitlement?

Shit sweetie, I'm a bitch, but I'm not so nasty a shrew as to slap away the cartoon songbirds that are fluttering around your candy-filled head.

Enjoy the rush. Have a blast. Savor every minute of the experience. Really, I mean it. Young love is the greatest drug on the planet. Just remember, I'll be here after the holidays when break-up season hits.

On Sex

On the real thing

How do I keep myself from feeling jaded and bitter that I've never found anything more than the kind of sex for sale on TV?

The whole reason they're selling that kind of sex on TV is so they can make you feel jaded and bitter about your sexuality. That's how they get you to buy all the other silly plastic things.

Stop letting consumer culture define sex for you. You've never found anything more than the kind of sex for sale on TV because you haven't even stopped to examine for yourself what the real thing might be like.

It's up to you to figure it out. It requires self-exploration and probably a little experimentation. You have to relentlessly ask yourself, 'Why?' You have to be vulnerable. You have to be willing to connect with another human being on terms that you define by and for yourself.

That's the thrilling part, the connection. I'm not talking about love. Hell, I'm not even talking about chemistry. I'm talking about a mutual and momentary annihilation of the ego through a sexual act. It's some spiritual shit. The sex itself is almost incidental, and that's kind of the point.

How you go about finding it is your own thing, but you have to be willing to fucking look for it. You have to recognize that it's an internal quest. Those are never easy, and while it might occasionally leave you confused and frustrated, at least it won't leave you jaded and bitter.

On your virginity

How do you know when to give up your virginity? People talk about how it's a special gift to have but I don't really see what's so special about it or who to give it up to. I'm probably not ready to have sex if I'm still asking these questions right?

Virginity isn't a special gift, because your vagina isn't a commodity. Whether you're gifting it or selling it, only prostitutes treat pussy as an article of exchange.

The irony here is that the same sanctimonious pricks who condemn prostitution are the very ones to tell you that your virginity is something that you should hand over to a man under select circumstances. Those people are full of shit, and you should stop listening to what they have to say about your vagina.

The truth of the matter is that your body is nobody's business but your own. Your virginity is yours to keep, lose, or shrug your shoulders at for as long as you like. You're ready when you're ready. If you're not, just hang tight until it feels right. Despite all you've learned from popular culture, there is no rush to start fucking.

As for virginity itself, it may not be a gift, but that doesn't mean it's not special. You only get to lose it once, and if you bring your heart and mind into the decision, you're much more likely to be prepared for any emotional or physical consequences.

Sex can get sticky. Literally. Sure, there's the obvious stuff you learned in health class. Don't get pregnant, make him wear a condom, and all that. It's important, but really, those are just the instructions printed on the side of the box.

What they don't ever really tell you is that once you start having sex, you're dealing with a sudden increase in the potential depth and breadth of the level of intimacy in your interpersonal relationships. It can be both wonderful and terrible, and it really depends on everyone's level of emotional maturity.

The most important thing for you to have as you make this decision is self-respect. After that, I'd suggest you focus less on how or when to lose your virginity, and more on why.

If you know why you're doing it, and you respect yourself, whatever else you decide will be fine.

On porn

Why do I have a problem with porn? I didn't used to think about it but the more I read about it the more I feel uncomfortable with it, like men are getting off over women being degraded and it makes me feel sick. But then I think maybe I'm just being a bad feminist? It's confusing :/

Porn isn't inherently degrading to women any more than sex is inherently degrading to women. What makes things degrading are patriarchal and misogynistic power dynamics.

Some porn is obviously very degrading to women, but there's also quite a bit of porn these days that is empowering to women. What gets tricky is that some porn is both, depending on where you're standing. You have to pay attention to the power dynamics at play, not just on-screen, but within the larger context of how and by whom that porn is consumed.

As with any aspect of the sex industry (or any industry, for that matter) if there's a situation where you need to do a feminist gut check, just ask yourself, who is profiting? Who is in control? Who has the power? If the answer is men at the expense of women, then you have every reason to react negatively.

Whatever problem it is you have with porn, recognize that it's actually about those misogynistic power dynamics, and adjust your opinions accordingly.

On blowjobs

Is it ever acceptable to use the phrase "you're too big" or is it just a shitty excuse for a job poorly done? I consider myself to be at least halfway sexually adept but I'm no porn star. How can I still maximize his pleasure without getting my throat fucked raw multiple times a week?

Once upon a time, a blowjob was a rare and special gift reserved for birthdays and anniversaries, and if on such a momentous occasion you were capable of suppressing your gag reflex to swallow his cock for even the briefest of seconds, he would crown you a deep-throat queen and throw diamonds at your feet.

Those days are gone forever. I blame the internet.

Our men have been raised on a steady diet of cheap and readily available gonzo porn with an ever hardening core. It's not enough to start out with an oral sex scene any more. Now every run-of-the-mill porn starlet has in her repertoire the ability to unhinge her jaw for a throat fucking so violent she ends up shooting vomit out of her nose.

Expectations have been raised. Standards have been lowered. Having one's face aggressively cock-pounded for twenty asphyxiating minutes is now just an average blowjob.

I respect that you want to maximize his pleasure, but perhaps it's time to change the game.

I suggest you move to a wet two-handed technique where you work the shaft like a traditional lubricated handjob. You only keep the head of his cock in your mouth, which allows you easier breathing and much better use of your tongue.

The trick here is plenty of lube (and/or spit) on your palms so that your hands become an extension of your mouth. As with all good blowjob advice, don't forget to tickle his balls.

The moment's passed, obviously, but any advice as to
what to do when I'm blowing a guy (on and off again bf), I
look up and he's checking his fucking phone, mid-fellatio?
If you're just trying to get him off, feel free to immediately end the
blowjob. If there's something in it for you (like you're getting him
hard enough to fuck, or you simply enjoy sucking dick) then it's up
to you whether to give a shit. In my experience, it's better to find
that kind of thing funny rather than insulting.

I spent the night with someone. Before we went to bed,
I said I was going to get some condoms. She said that I
didn't have to worry, because she takes pills. I'm right
now a bit restless about it. How can I tactfully ask her if
she does indeed take them?
You can't. Now you have to spend an entire month in a constant
state of anxiety praying to a god that doesn't exist that this sloppy
bitch gets her next period. That's what you get for being an idiot.

If you were tied down and blindfolded to a bed and had
a variety of men and women to eat your pussy, do you
think you'd be able to identify the men from the women?
Easily. I know this from experience.

Why do I fantasize about having sex with his friends?
Partly because it's forbidden. Partly because they're within easy
reach for fantasizing. Mostly because it turns you on. (Hey, that's
what fantasies are for.)

How do people really into BDSM go from slapping
and blindfolding and belittling their partners to 'ok we

have to go grocery shopping now'… seems so awkward afterwards.

If things seem awkward afterward, then you're doing it wrong. (And by 'it' I'm not referring to the sex, kinky or otherwise. I'm referring to clear and open communication with your partner.)

Am I bi if I only sleep with women and don't like dick, but fool around with men I feel comfortable with?

I'm not sure whether you're a predominantly homosexual woman coming to terms with incidental heterosexual tendencies or a predominantly heterosexual man coming to terms with incidental homosexual tendencies, but it's entirely up to you whether you choose to identify as bisexual. You can if you want, you don't have to if you don't, and no one else gets to decide but you.

The girl I'm casually seeing just told me no one's ever been able to make her come. What should I do?

Tell her that it's perfectly okay and that there's nothing wrong with her. Tell her that you appreciate her openness and vulnerability. Don't take it as a challenge, and don't put any pressure on her to have an orgasm. In other words, don't make it about you.

What's the point of hatefucks? Like, to take a food analogy, if you hate carrots, why eat some when you can have tomatoes or beets?

Your analogy confuses hatefucking with actually hating to fuck. A better food analogy would be that a hatefuck is like a pie eating contest – it's aggressive, messy, and it requires that you momentarily suspend your dignity, but every once in a while it's fun to gorge yourself without having to give a shit about table manners.

I need ideas for dirty talk in the bedroom. I'm not into 'slut', but 'that feels so fuckin' good' is just getting old...
The trick to dirty talk is using the second person imperative mood to describe the physical action as it's taking place in the moment. When in doubt, just fall back on basic '*verb* (suck, lick, fuck) that *adjective* (hard, wet, hot) *noun* (cock, pussy, ass)' sentence structure.

Why does sex always complicate things?
Because you let it.

Are you still a virgin if you use a vibrator?
You're still a virgin if you have to ask this question.

Why can't I quit masturbating?
You don't have to quit, and you don't have to listen to anyone who tells you otherwise.

Is watching porn bad for you?
It's fine. Just don't let it get in the way of other things.

On taking it up the ass

I love anal play and anal sex, but it always feels a little degrading for me. My boyfriend is super respectful when we do it, but I can't help thinking he – and most men – feel somewhat superior for getting to stick it into my ass. I hate to think he validates his masculinity by fucking me from behind, and him not letting me get anywhere near his region only reinforces the superiority/inferiority dynamic. Is there a way to ever get comfortable and to

change these internalized misconceptions (both his and mine) about anal sex?

Hmm. Sounds like you've got a little cognitive dissonance going on when it comes to your butthole. It's no big deal, really. All you have to do is identify why anal sex feels a little degrading for you, and if I had to guess, there was probably a guy in your past, perhaps the very guy who introduced you to butt play, who also got off on dominating you inappropriately, or who at least behaved in some manner that made you feel degraded, and now you associate those emotions with taking it up the ass in general.

Like most women, I'm guessing you went through your bad boy phase in your early twenties, and while you were expanding your sexual horizons (a good thing) you also spent time in romantic relationships with a dirtbag or two who treated you like absolute shit (a bad thing), and it would seem you're still storing some of that emotional baggage up your butt.

The biggest clue here is that you feel there are power dynamics at play with regard to anal sex, but not necessarily with regard to oral or vaginal sex, because I assure you, the kind of men who feel superior for getting to stick it into your ass are the kind of men who feel superior getting to stick it anywhere.

If your boyfriend really is super-respectful around your butt-hole, and you do in fact love anal sex, then take a hot minute to step back and look at your sex life retrospectively. Identify and acknowledge the source of your degrading feelings about anal sex, and then leave that mess in the past where it belongs.

Now, as for your boyfriend's attitude towards his own ass, there's not really much you can do. If he doesn't want anything up there, then that's his loss, but don't make it about a superiority/ inferiority dynamic when it's really about your boyfriend just being typical and unadventurous. Most dudes are just like that. They go their entire lives not realizing they've got a prostate in there that can do tricks. Poor bastards.

On religion in the bedroom

This guy I'm seeing won't have sex with me for religious reasons but requests to cum on my face while pouring champagne. No shit. Serial killer?

Yeah, this guy seems deeply in touch with his lord and savior.

I love how it's perfectly acceptable for him to blow a load in your face like you're a porn star he just bought bottle service, but the omniscient creator of the universe would suddenly have a problem if you two engaged in even the slightest bit of premarital vaginal intercourse.

Ugh, that's so fucking creepy. Seriously, though. Don't date people who bring religion into the bedroom. Just don't.

On selling your innocence

Hey Coketalk, first time caller here. So I was offered $780 for my virginity from a guy I have never met. Should I consider this? I mean, I just want to lose my virginity and be done with it, but then again I'd be a whore.

You'd be a prostitute, not a whore, and while $780 is an average take for a private dancer doing an hour at a bachelor party in Vegas, it's kind of a low-rent offer for your virginity.

Come on, didn't you see the movie *Taken*? If you're certified pure, that ass is worth a helluva lot more than 700 and change on the black market.

It's also a really strange number. Seven hundred and eighty? Was it gonna be 800, but then he ordered a pizza? What the fuck?

Listen, kiddo. I highly recommend you ignore not only this offer, but all subsequent communication from this creep. He's not just trying to buy sex. He's trying to buy your innocence. That's fucked up. It's predatory and twisted, and you don't want anything to do with someone that unhealthy.

Sure, you want to lose your virginity. It's a natural part of the human condition, but doing it just to get it over with is lazy and dumb.

There aren't that many firsts in life with this much psychic magnitude over which you have total control. For someone with self-respect, it's an opportunity for exploration and growth.

It doesn't have to be double-rainbow special, but don't waste it. Don't sell it either. Honestly, sweetie, if you don't know what something is worth, it's probably best not to put a price on it.

On rape fantasy

I am a self-respecting woman in a happy relationship based on mutual trust & respect. When I masturbate, I fantasize about being treated like an object. Head pushed down into someone's lap; being taken home from a bar and asked to have a threesome; forced to do things I do not want to do. Shit I would be repulsed by/would not tolerate if it actually happened. Sometimes after getting off, I feel dirty for even thinking those things. I've heard the term "rape fantasy" being thrown around; can you shed some light on the issue?

Your first sentence translates roughly into, 'I'm not a freak.' Then your next three sentences break down into, 'but I like to get freaky'.

I know it seems like an oversimplification, but believe me, that's your problem right there. It's called cognitive dissonance, and it's the end result of living in a culture that still shames women for their sexual desires.

We all have a dark and sticky place we go to in our minds

when we're trying to get off. Every last one of us does it, not every time, but we've each got a basement with some dripping nasty shit locked away in it.

Thing is, you feel guilty for it, so your psyche bakes up little Freudian pie filled with repression, displacement and sublimation and serves you up a hot slice of rape fantasy.

It's delicious and guilt-free, because it allows you to experience all that dark sexual desire without owning it. If it's against your will, you don't have to take any responsibility for the shit you want done to you hard and twice.

Of course, after you cum there's that moment of clarity where there's really no denying how you got yourself off, so you catch that wave of guilt.

Quit feeling the guilt. You've got no reason to be ashamed, and quite frankly, you're getting off to pretty garden-variety stuff.

Now, I'm not speaking for all rape fantasies here, just your type where it's more about submission and surrendering free will. There's a whole other level where it's actually about violence and self-annihilation and other horrible shit that stems from unhealthy places.

Don't worry. That ain't you.

Oh, and do yourself a favor. Don't get all brave and ask your boyfriend to try it out on you. Planning out a role play version of a rape fantasy is an exercise in logical paradox that ends up being a punch line to an awkward joke.

Trust me, what you're interested in is called dominance and submission. You're a sub. Start out light. Have fun.

We've been together for 8 months. He wants to have anal. I have never felt comfortable with the idea and really do not want it. Do I give in for him, or stand my ground. I feel so silly asking this.

Whether it's been eight months or eight years, if you don't wanna take it up the ass, don't fucking take it up the ass.

Why do men always want to fold me into a pretzel during sex?
Porn.

The last two guys I've had sex were healthy guys in their mid 20s and both had issues with E.D. Both claimed that it was because of their use of porn they were having issues with impotence and/or delayed ejaculation. Is this becoming a regular trend with young men?
In my completely unscientific opinion, absolutely yes.

Is it wrong or inappropriate of me to ask someone I'm dating to get an std check before having sex with them?
There's nothing wrong with asking, but it does require some tact.

On internet porn

I'm engaged and I love my dude, but I'm pretty sure he's addicted to porn. I know, it sounds fucking stupid, but there's no other explanation for what's going on. I'll wake up in the morning and leave our room to get some water or make lunch for later and he'll be on his computer. As soon as he realizes that I'm in the room, he starts typing quickly and talks to me about whatever website he's looking at. I'm not stupid, I know he's beating off. I watch porn too, so it's not a huge deal for me, but when you have a chick in the room next to you who LOVES to get her bone on, it doesn't make sense to

*be fapping before work. I haven't gained weight, I don't
cry during sex, I know I'm not boring in bed, and he's
for sure not cheating. It's making me feel shitty about
myself and it's pretty much ruining my sex drive (which
was pretty high). I already manned up and spoke to
him about it, but I certainly don't feel any better and I
honestly don't know what else to do about it.*

The good news is, this isn't about you – he's normal and not
at all addicted to porn.

The porn was there before you showed up, and it'll be there
after you're gone. Our pool of eligible bachelors and boyfriends
have been downloading endless streams of progressively raunchier
and raunchier hardcore pornography for well over a decade.

It's really quite remarkable when you consider that by the time
our guys have jerked their way through a single bottle of Jergens,
they've absorbed more XXX action than existed in all the world
at the time of their births.

Try contemplating the breadth, depth and mind-boggling
magnitude of all the porn sites, porn genres and porn stars freely
available for viewing at every hour. Do you honestly expect to compete with just one measly vagina?

You could be a bisexual nymphomaniac fashion model and you
still couldn't hold your own against internet porn, which leads me
to the bad news: *this isn't about you – he's normal and not at all addicted
to porn.*

You couldn't be more wrong in your assumption that 'when you
have a chick in the room next to you who LOVES to get her bone
on, it doesn't make sense to be fapping before work'.

I'm sorry, but ask any straight guy without a vested interest
in boning you, and if he's honest he'll tell you that sexing the ol'
ball-and-chain can be a chore, but getting a good wank in before
work is pure recreation.

In other words, when he's fucking, he's trying to please *you*.

When he's jerking, he's trying to please *himself*. Surely you understand the difference.

I've dealt with this very situation, and if you're willing to put in a little extra effort, I've got a foolproof solution that will have him mounting you in no time.

Next time you catch him in the act, tell him you want to replace his hand with your mouth. Don't let him stop surfing the porn. Go down on him right then and there with no hesitation and make sure he keeps surfing the porn as if you weren't even in the room. Make it about pleasing him, and I guarantee you he'll eventually shove the computer aside and pound you like the porn star he was just watching.

Good luck.

On premature ejaculation

Every guy I've ever been with has came in less than 5 minutes in bed. I'm not exactly sure if I'm just the shit in the sack or I make bad picks, but either way I'm getting no satisfaction. How can I help this?

Not to be a grammar Nazi, but in this context I believe the past tense of 'has came' is simply 'cums'. That is to say, every guy you're with cums in less than five minutes. Now, on to your larger problem.

Based on your conjugation skills, I'm guessing you're a college freshman, which means you're surrounded by guys who talk a big game but haven't logged many hours inside actual pussy. It's not that you make bad picks, it's just that you're bedding inexperienced dudes.

An obvious solution is to start fucking professors, but if you insist on frat boys your best bet is to get their first orgasm out of the way early.

Make them cum right away, hard and fast. The trick is to make sure they know they're not done. Keep the sexual energy high and turn their refractory period into extended foreplay. When erection number two pops up, that's the one you ride.

I promise, the second time around, they'll fuck a lot longer than five minutes.

On a cum slut

I like it when guys cum on my face, so does that mean I'm internally misogynistic?

Not at all, babe. You're a filthy cum slut. Say it with pride.

It'd be one thing if your boyfriend liked to cum on your face and you let him even though you didn't want to, but that's not what's happening here. This isn't about male domination or female objectification. This is just about you enjoying a nice load in the face, and there's nothing inherently degrading about that.

As for internalized misogyny, that manifests itself when other women shame you for taking pleasure in your sexuality. If some bitch calls you a cum slut like it's a bad thing, she's the one with the problem. Fuck that shit. Like what you like, and don't let any one slut shame you.

On threesome date night

How would you go about suggesting and then initiating a threesome? i have a girlfriend that's told me she wants to party one night and "have a lesbian moment." also, her boyfriend is sexy and has stated in the past that he finds me desirable as well, and has made comments about how hot it would be if me and his gf had some fun together (big surprise). i think that with enough liquid courage (and enlightening drugs) that i can play this situation to my favor. your thoughts?

Propose a threesome date night. Let them take you out as a couple. Be playful about it – dinner, drinks, the whole routine.

It'll start out cheeky and kind of innocent, but as the night progresses let things get more and more sexy. Flirt with them. Let them flirt with you.

I know it seems kind of silly, but trust me. A date night lets everyone get comfortable with the reality of what's going to happen at the end of the evening.

Once you're sure that everyone wants it to happen, don't be afraid to act as master of ceremonies. Take them back to your place, crack open a bottle of wine, and start making out with them.

They'll be ready for it.

On small dick

I'm just going to be blunt. My boyfriend has a small dick, and when we have sex it is not as fun as it could be.

What the fuck can do I do, besides telling him that his dick is too small? I dont want to come off like a greedy dick bitch, but still, i have sexual needs that aren't being fufilled.

You're not going to fulfill your sexual needs by crushing his ego, and his dick ain't gonna grow. No good will come from you pointing out his golf pencil.

He's got a tongue and ten fingers, doesn't he? Make him use all he's got.

Otherwise, just go ahead and break up with him. Do him the honor of never revealing why, though. No man deserves that.

On not giving blowjobs

So, my boyfriend wants me to give him a blowjob. I love him, and we've had sex, but they just really aren't my thing. I told him no, and stood by it.

Now he's saying I'm a hypocrite, because he ate me out once.

Am I being a hypocrite? I mean, I don't think I'll do it, even if I am, but still.

Maybe he'll hear it better from you.

Oh, and just so you know, he's 18, I'm 17, we've been together 10 months.

This question is cuter than a basket of puppies. High school sweethearts who had actual sex before oral sex? It's darling.

Listen, sweetie. You're not being a hypocrite, you're just being a bit old-fashioned. That's fine. It's your body. You decide what goes in what hole.

Your boyfriend is showing his immaturity by expecting reciprocity for oral sex, and you should never feel obligated to participate in a sex act.

That being said, you can't expect guys not to want blowjobs. They all want blowjobs. All the time. Always. Nothing will change that, and nothing will stop your boyfriend from getting the blowjobs he wants.

As awful as it may seem, this is the reason your boyfriend will eventually break up with you. He'll never admit it, maybe not even to himself, but once he's sure you'll never give him head, he'll be on his way out.

This is probably more brutal truth than you wanted to hear, but you need to hear it. Better you figure it out now than spend your early twenties wondering why guys keep breaking up with you.

Why doesn't my husband want me to fuck other women?
Um, I dunno. Why don't you ask him?

How is it possible to have amazing sex with a man who doesn't attract me at all intellectually and whose body I find repulsive?
You're just having a little hot ugly pig sex. It happens. Try not to overthink it.

Please introduce me to a new sex position.
Try the one where you make sober, unflinching eye contact with your partner while sharing a deep emotional connection.

Why am I still so attracted to my rapist? He's all I can think about when I masturbate.
You are not attracted to your rapist. You are merely having sexual thoughts about him. Don't mistake those thoughts for an emotional connection. They're just a coping mechanism that allows you to exert control in your mind. It's all a part of your healing process.

What's your opinion on meaningless sex?
Everything is meaningless. Might as well be getting laid.

What is the difference between, "fucking," "having sex," and "making love"?
The kind of music playing in the background.

Do you think sex is overrated?
What's being sold to you as sex is overrated.

Has unlimited access to porn stunted the sexual growth of a whole generation of Internet-having teenage boys?

Stunted is the wrong word. Affected is more accurate, and it's not just the boys.

I've always wanted to lose my virginity in an orgy. Is that a spectacularly bad idea?

It's not so much a bad idea as it is an impractical one. Losing your virginity during group sex would be one thing, but an orgy implies a certain kind of frenzied anonymity that just isn't for beginners.

How do you define "losing your virginity"?

Your virginity isn't something I care to define. Spend some time analyzing the cultural and historical implications of virginity, then decide for yourself whether you think it's still a relevant concept.

On the other orgasm

Who the fuck started the rumor that women can have orgasms from sex without clit stimulation? I'VE personally never met one of these magically orgasmic females...have you? Are they really out there? If it IS a myth (as I suspect) I'm not about to make it worse for all of us by faking orgasms for clueless men. Thoughts?

Oh, you poor, poor woman. This breaks my heart.

Unicorns are a myth. Leprechauns are a myth. G-spot orgasms are not a myth. Clitoral orgasms are great, but if you've never had a G-spot orgasm, I'm really very sorry for you.

Now, I'll grant you that eliminating clitoral stimulation and/or involving clueless men is generally a recipe for bad sex. Still, that should not affect the legitimacy of a good old-fashioned toe-curling, mind-blowing, mattress-soaking G-spot orgasm.

I hope one day you come to know what I mean.

On one-night stands

i'm in college, i got blackout drunk and fucked this really adorable guy last night and he left his socks here. what do i do about that shit. in general, what are the rules on one night stands? sounds ridiculous, may still be a bit drunk, but i think you get it.

Nice.

First things first. It's Sunday morning. Go have a Bloody Mary.

Now, as for the socks, throw 'em in your dirty laundry. Wash them. Start your collection. I guarantee by the time you graduate you will have a respectable number of t-shirts, boxer-briefs, socks, and of course the occasional hat, piece of jewelry, or other interesting shred of evidence.

Over the years, I've filled an entire drawer just with the random stuff I've found on mornings after. I'll spare you the full inventory, but highlights include a full clip of 9 mm ammunition, a pink double-sided dildo, and a La Perla thong that belongs to one of the current stars on the Disney Channel (and no, those items are *not* from the same night).

As for proper one-night stand etiquette, if your adorable guy wants his socks back, it's his responsibility to ask. Most guys consider small items of clothing to be an acceptable loss, especially if they got laid.

Any item above a t-shirt – a hat, jacket or scarf – may have been a deliberate leave-behind as an excuse to call you the next day. Don't get your hopes up with socks, though.

Feel free to keep the collection in rotation. Future one-night stands might need a spare t-shirt or pair of socks – trust me, it happens. When they do, let 'em choose from your collection.

In general, though, one-night stands are best left to just one night. There aren't any hard and fast rules other than being respectful the morning after. That's all you owe each other. Respect.

You don't owe him a morning quickie or your phone number. He doesn't owe you breakfast or a phone call. The fewer the expectations, the less awkward the morning will be.

How's that Bloody Mary tasting? I think it's time for me to go have one now.

Toodles!

Do you think that sodomy is acceptable as an act of love between consenting adults?

Hell yes, it's acceptable. Sodomy doesn't have to be an act of love, either. As long as it's between two consenting adults, it might as well be an act of bravery, an act of business or just an act of mild amusement.

Why do you think people feel forever connected to the people they have sex with?

Do they? I don't know. There are over 7 billion people on the planet. I say any reason we have to feel forever connected to someone is a beautiful thing.

Do you kiss him right after he has gone down on you?

Why wouldn't I? My pussy is delicious.

Great, now I feel bad for having a one night stand to lose my virginity and get it over with.

If you remember the experience fondly you've got nothing to feel bad about.

Every time I'm about to cum with my boyfriend I fantasize of other guys. Is that very bad or just another way of dealing with monogamy?

That shit is so fucking normal. Please stop punishing yourself for being human.

I've recently started having sex. Everyone says that by the third or fourth time, it starts feeling good. But it still hurts like a bitch. What do I do?

Use lube. Slow down. Quit letting your inexperienced boyfriend fuck shit up.

I'm making him wait to fuck me. Bad idea?

Not if it's your step dad.

how rude is it to say "that it?" when the guy comes a few minutes in.

Rude. Hilarious. It really depends on your inflection.

On innocence

I have been with my boyfriend for a little less than two months now. We are both freshmen in college and for both of us, this is our very first relationship.

When I am with him the thought of having sex with him is fantastic and makes me happy, but I'm so so terrified we are moving too quickly. That and terrified of what having sex with both of us being virgins will be like. He says that no matter what, he will wait until I am ready.

I love him and he loves me, yet I don't know if this is BECAUSE neither of us have dated anyone else. I'm just not very sure of myself and I would love to know what you think. Thank you!

You're adorable, that's what I think. First love. First relationship. First time having sex. It's all too precious for words.

Enjoy yourself. Just be present in the moment, and don't worry so much about getting it right. It's not gonna be perfect. Not even close. That's okay, though. You're supposed to be clumsy and clueless and terrified. Enjoy that part too, because as ridiculous as it sounds, one day you'll miss it.

You don't get to be sure of yourself yet, but don't be afraid. Everything has a beginning, middle and end. You've got a lot of beginnings going on right now, and that's a beautiful place to be.

Don't be afraid of any of it.

On pity sex

Is it wrong to have sex with someone just because you know they really want to have sex with you? A literal sexual favor? I know this question makes me sound like a douche, but there's this really nice guy that I'm just not interested in, and he never gets laid and has sort of a low opinion of himself. I feel like having sex with me would be good for him. Thoughts?

If you have sex with this guy, it will confuse him. He is

guaranteed to misinterpret your intentions, and I promise there will be emotional blowback for which you are not prepared. Shit will get messy.

One way or another, you'll end up having to tell him that it was just a pity fuck. Trust me, if you think he has a low opinion of himself now, just wait until that news hits him like a ton of pathetic bricks.

Even if you tell him up front, you're still not doing him any favors. Not really. He needs confidence, not consolation-prize pussy.

Sure, he'll be agreeable to getting laid, but what happens if you're honest about your intentions and then he can't get it up? What happens if he underperforms? Are you ready to deal with the emotional shitstorm? I think not.

I'm just showing you what's at stake. I'm not telling you what to do here, because this isn't about right or wrong. It's your vagina. Fuck who you wanna fuck, but you have to be willing to accept the consequences of your actions, which in this case could very easily be the end of the friendship.

You've been warned.

On promiscuity

I'm a nineteen year-old female college student. For the past three years, I've been getting more and more interested in feminism, and I love the liberation it offers. However, I feel like lately I've been a bit… TOO liberated. I've come out as bi recently, at the same time that my long-term relationship came to an end. I've embraced my sexuality fully, and as a result I've been having a lot of one-night stands and random hookups, and an exponential increase in sexual activity.

I feel like I'm becoming addicted to sex, but I'm not sure if I'm just confusing repressed guilt for compulsion. I enjoy sex, and I've never felt ashamed of it before, but my libido has gotten so out of control recently I don't know what to do. I haven't engaged in any overtly dangerous behavior, but I'm having trouble controlling myself. For instance, I recently solicited sex from a man I know I shouldn't trust—he showed up drunk at my apartment a few weeks ago, refusing to leave and yelling in my face in front of my friend/roommate.

I'm just not sure if I have a serious problem or if I'm just trying to find an excuse for my promiscuity. What do you think?

Yeah. I can see you now, a liberated bisexual co-ed feminist recently out of a long-term relationship burning through your drunk dials at last call, desperate to find some random cock to sit on before the dollar draft specials wear off.

What could possibly go wrong?

Listen, sister: there's nothing inherently wrong with promiscuity, but it's not the same thing as a lack of self-control. Making stupid decisions that involve unsavory dudes is the shit you need to quit. You're trying to find an excuse for your promiscuity when you should be trying to find an excuse for your stupidity.

Please understand, I'm not calling you stupid. I'm saying that you've confused promiscuous behavior with stupid behavior. You've also confused feminism with libertinism, but hey, one lesson at a time.

Oh, and by the way, you did not solicit sex. Don't use that word, college girl. Solicitation has very specific legal implications, ones that you should most definitely avoid.

Sometimes I worry about what my taste in porn says about me as a person.
How do you think the porn stars feel?

Yes, I'm attracted to other women. No, I will never act upon it. Is that wrong?
It's not wrong, but don't let your sexual repression negatively affect others.

I'm a 22-year-old virgin with no real interest in sex or any kind of physical intimacy. Is there something wrong with me?
Nope, you're just asexual. Maybe it's a phase. Maybe it's just who you are. Either way, it doesn't mean there's anything wrong with you. Don't be in such a hurry to judge yourself. You're fine.

Does kissing have a more romantic connotation than sex?
Kissing costs extra for a reason, darling.

how do you suck a dick?
With enthusiasm.

Your feelings on anal? The man-friend is asking for it, and I'm open to it, just not sure what to expect.
Expect a cock up your ass.

How do I know if swinging is right for me?
It won't be right until that question ends with an 'us' instead of a 'me'.

Does my wife have to reach orgasm every time we have sex?

Nope, and guess what? Neither do you.

On sex tapes and honor

I recently broke up with a woman I was with for several years. We lived together, got drunk, did drugs and had awesome sex together. Some of that booze/coke fueled sex was recorded (by her request). Since breaking up she has been a total cunt. Should I make some of those dildo-in-her-ass/cock-in-her-snatch videos public?

There are certain things you just don't do. Ever.

Violating the trust of an intimate partner is right at the top of that list, and yes, for the purposes of those sex tapes, she will *always* be your intimate partner.

I want you to think back to a time when you were head over heels for her. Remember that woman? No doubt, she was crazy beautiful and wild as fuck. You loved the shit out of her. You shared a level of intimacy you'd never before thought was possible, and there were moments when you were sure you'd spend the rest of your lives together.

Have you got her in your head? Do you see her, the way she used to be? *That's* the girl you'll be betraying if you make those videos public, the one you loved.

Don't do it, man. You can never get your integrity back.

Trust me on this. I have a whole hard drive full of compromising pics featuring exes and former lovers whom I detest, motherfuckers I wouldn't cross the street to spit on today. Some of that shit would be on the six o'clock news if I posted it on this blog, but I would *never* do that, not in a million years.

Be a decent human being about this. It's a matter of honor.

No matter how much of a total cunt your ex is being, *you still have honor*. This is one of those things that determines whether you're a good person.

I hope you never make the wrong decision.

On getting what you deserve

After checking my boyfriend's browsing history on his laptop (I know I shouldn't!), I found out that he likes to look mainly at picture of girls with "big naturals." And by that I mean BIG—like 36FFF and shit like that. I'm a typical B cup. He says he thinks I'm sexy, my tits are great, and we have great sex. But I can't get this out of my head! What should I do?

Stop checking your boyfriend's browsing history.

On spanking it to porn

I used to masturbate to porn pretty regularly, but I've recently been making an effort to stop because of the extreme feelings my long-distance girlfriend harbors about my looking at other women. I'm having some trouble totally kicking the habit, though, and it sucks that a few minutes of horniness and no girlfriend nearby can lead to an hour or two of having to listen to her get upset—and pretty angry, depending on her mood. (I usually figure that if I can't keep from looking at porn, I at least owe her the honesty of telling her that I did.)

What do you think? Do I just need to do a little more thinking with the upstairs head, or do you think she's not giving me enough credit for genuinely trying here? Do

you have any miracle solution that'll make this easier? I
need some coke-fueled wisdom, here.

This is a joke, right? You're not really so emasculated that you confess to your nagging long-distance girlfriend every time you jerk off to a little porn. Tell me this is a joke.

Come on, man. You don't deserve credit for genuinely trying. You deserve a smack in the head for putting up with her shit in the first place.

You want a miracle solution? Here's an idea. Don't sign up for a long-distance relationship with a ball-busting cunt who's so insanely hypervigilant that she refuses you the privilege of a pornography-assisted spank session.

Too late for that, you say? Well then, maybe you should grow a pair of fucking balls. Tell the bitch that you'll jerk off to whatever you damn well please, and if she doesn't like it, she can fuck off. If it offends her delicate sensibilities so much that it ends the relationship, consider yourself lucky.

I don't care what Dr Phil says, masturbating to pornography doesn't qualify as infidelity. In this context, porn is just another tool to get the job done. It would be like you getting all pissed off at her for using a vibrator. It's not cheating. Don't let her tell you otherwise.

Of course, that's when she'll pull the gender card and fall back on the argument that pornography is degrading to women. She'll cross her arms and say, 'I simply won't stand for it.'

When she says this, what she really means is, 'I am a hypocrite who is terrified of raw sexuality, and I prefer my degradation in easy-to-swallow form such as women's magazines and Lifetime miniseries, so instead owning up to my petty jealousies, I'm gonna cram this unreasonable ultimatum down your throat.'

It's all bullshit. The simple fact of the matter is that she's threatened by other women to such an insane degree that she's punishing you for thought crimes. I'd say it's Orwellian, but even he had the good sense to include porn in *1984*.

Seriously, you don't have to stand for this.

If a guy routinely screws me from behind, does he not respect me?

Only if it's a metaphor. Also, you're an idiot.

What if everybody could have sex with anyone at any given time? What do you think would happen?

You still wouldn't get laid.

What does it mean if I'm 21 and I'm still not ready for sex?

It means absolutely nothing, except that now you can worry needlessly about your virginity while enjoying a cocktail.

I can't help but feel like sex is degrading to women.

That's because you secretly hate both.

Why do I feel guilty when I masturbate?

Because you're ashamed of your sexuality.

Is fisting creepy and unnatural, or just taboo experimentation?

Fisting is when you use your fist. Quit assigning value judgments to consensual sex acts.

What does it mean to be "sexually unprincipled"?
It means you've compromised your integrity with regard to your sexuality. The most common example is cheating on a sexual partner.

How can you tell if a guy is using you for physical gratification or if he actually cares for you?
If I'm having consensual sex with a guy, it's not possible for him to use me, because I accept personal responsibility for the decisions I make with my own body.

On not getting used

Okay. I've recently begun fooling around with this guy from work (we're both college kids, so it's not like I'm fucking the boss or anything). We have a lot of mutual friends, who seem to really get a kick out of spreading everyone's gossip around. Anyways, he and I have told no one that we are sleeping together, so it's very hush-hush. Now. I just don't want to get used, I feel like the whole "let's not spread this around" kind of thing could potentially enable him to go out and sleep with other girls as well (which I suppose is okay, he and I aren't officially dating or anything). I would rather know what's going on with him and his potential other girls, because quite frankly I do not want to waste my time with him, if I'm just one of 15 girls. You know? So, I want to find a way to bring it up, without being awkward, as I have to work with him, and I still like the guy. Any ideas of how to bring it up? Or any key phrases to say/AVOID saying? Thank you!!

How is your time with him suddenly being wasted if he sees another girl? I'll never understand that mentality. Then again, I'll never understand the mentality of a woman who grants a man the power to 'use' her. Fuck that. I'm not some inanimate object that dispenses refreshment. My pussy isn't a vending machine.

If you don't want to get used, then be present in the relationship and accept personal responsibility for the decisions you make with your own body. Do that, and he won't be able to use you. At worst, all he'll be able to do is lie to you.

As for your dilemma, just be straight with him. Tell him what you expect. Say something like the following:

'I'm not asking for a formal relationship. I'm not telling you that you can't see other women. All I'm doing is letting you know that I'm not comfortable having sex with you if you're also having sex with other people. Therefore, out of respect for me, it's your responsibility to tell me if and when you start having sex with someone else. It's no big deal either way. It's not going to fuck up our friendship, because I like you, and I like what we've got going on.'

It's a perfectly reasonable request that not only respects his boundaries, but also your feelings. When he agrees (and he will), then the burden of integrity is on him. He's the one who has to communicate with you before sleeping around, otherwise it's a violation of your friendship.

It's a solid way to get him thinking about the progression of your relationship without feeling trapped. You'll seem like the cool chick, and if the day comes when he chooses not to sleep with another girl because he'd rather keep sleeping with you, he'll think it was his idea.

On how not to get used

"If you don't want to get used, then be present in the relationship and accept personal responsibility for the decisions you make with your own body. Do that, and he won't be able to use you. At worst, all he'll be able to do is lie to you."

Can you just explain that a bit more? I love it, but I'm having a hard time grasping it in those words.

I mean... I understand not letting yourself be used to an extent, but what if you're not even aware of it? Does that make sense?

Anyway, I'd just like more of an explanation.

Whenever I hear a girl complain of being used by a guy, I instantly lose respect for her. It's evidence of a victim mentality, one of the most unattractive traits anyone can have.

'He never really liked me,' she'll whine. 'He never really wanted to be with me. All he really wanted me for was sex.'

That kind of shit drives me crazy.

What she's actually saying is that she entered into an unspoken contract where she would provide him with access to her vagina in exchange for some combination of affectionate attention and emotional security. He then failed to deliver on that unspoken contract, and now she's pissed.

All I hear is a prostitute complaining that she didn't get paid, and you know what? Tough shit. If you're going to be a prostitute, the first rule is always get the money up front.

That's what this all comes down to, really – girls who don't know any better because they're raised to think that sex is a barter currency in their romantic relationships.

Fuck that. If you insist on treating your pussy like a commodity, then you're an idiot if you trade it for anything but cash.

It's your body, and it's your relationship. Do what you want with both, but be adult enough to accept personal responsibility for the decisions you make.

An unspoken contract is no contract at all. A man doesn't owe you anything for sleeping with you. If he does, accept your role as a prostitute, and recognize that you're kind of an idiot for expecting payment in affectionate attention and emotional security.

Now, here's the part that always blows my mind. Some of you

reading this right now are saying to yourselves, 'I'm no prostitute, but how am I supposed to get affectionate attention and emotional security from a guy without fucking him?'

If that's you, go sit in the corner. You don't get to play any more.

The rest of you probably get my point, even if you think it's a bit unsavory. It boils down to this: if you don't want to get used for sex, get the money up front, or don't expect payment at all.

All I'm saying is that sex shouldn't be treated like a commodity in traditional romantic relationships. Once you've internalized this notion and really put it into practice, then you'll find it impossible for a man to use you for sex.

He can lie to you. He can deceive you. He can be a total douchebag asshole, but he can never use you.

How do you separate sexual desires from real feelings?
Sexual desires *are* real feelings.

Why do I keep giving people head?
Either because you enjoy it, or they pay you. Otherwise, quit it.

The sex was so good he said, "I love you," even when he didn't mean it.
He meant it, but he was talking to your pussy.

How do I get myself to orgasm?
By using that thing between your legs.

How can you tell when a woman is faking?
If you knew how to tell, she wouldn't be faking.

Is honesty cruel when it boils down to "I am no longer sexually attracted to you"?
It can be. Cruelty isn't a product of the honest words. It's a product of how, when and why you deliver them.

The second I am done "hooking up" with a girl I immediately find her unattractive, its awful because I would like a meaningful relationship but once something sexual happens I am no longer able to view her in a romantic way… what is wrong with me?!?!
You hate yourself.

What is the difference between being promiscuous and being slutty?
Your vocabulary.

Tell me why I'm 58 and I have never been fucked or kissed.
Because you put them in that order.

Why is sex always something a man has to win from me? Why is it wrong when I give it because I want to?
It isn't, and it isn't.

I'm bored with sex. Any suggestions?
Fuck more interesting people.

On Drugs

On the drug war

What are your thoughts on ruthless violence of the drug cartels in Latin America? That shit is almost entirely funded by our greedy demand for and mindless consumption of cocaine. I just spent two weeks down there and got a much better sense of how grave the crisis really is. I've now decided to kick the habit and stick to good ol' California-hippie-grown pot from now on and I think you should hop on board.
Just sayin'...

Two whole weeks? Wow, you're like an honorary Latin American or something. I guess I should really listen to you. You're like an expert. I bet you even know how to ask for bottled water in Spanish.

Listen, when you're done patting yourself on the back for supporting your local pot farmer, maybe you could set aside your smug sense of self-appreciation for going on a field trip and take a hot minute to learn the basic principles of a black market economy.

When it comes to cocaine, it's not our greedy demand nor our mindless consumption that's causing the ruthless violence. It's prohibition. The law is to blame. The illegality of cocaine is what vastly inflates its price above the cost of production, creating an artificial price bubble worth hundreds of billions every year. That money is the ultimate cause of all the violence.

If the United States ended the war on drugs tomorrow and the DEA became strictly a regulatory agency, the market price of cocaine would collapse and the cartel violence would end almost immediately. Not only that, but the demand and consumption of cocaine wouldn't really change all that much. It's not like the drug war actually keeps people off drugs.

You're an idiot if you think there's any moral superiority in saying no to blow for political reasons, because as a citizen of a country waging this kind of war on drugs, you'll always have blood on your hands.

Just sayin' …

On cocaine

You are one of my two favorite blogs. Your writing is brilliant. You should know that I lead a completely different lifestyle from yours- I live in the midwest, I don't know much about the opposite sex, I have never done a drug "harder" than weed, and I was raised Catholic.

Your blog has made me reevaluate my feelings on a multitude of issues, and I thank you for the mental stimulation.

My main question is: Why cocaine? You say things like "when I die, I want my ashes mixed with glitter and cocaine, and shot up into the sky from behind the Hollywood sign."

What is it about cocaine that gets you through the weekend? How does it expand your mind? Is there anything you don't like about it?

Friends get me through the weekend, not cocaine. New experiences expand my mind, not cocaine. I'm a party girl, not a drug addict. Sure, sometimes we'll lay out a few lines and ramble on into the wee hours, but that's never the point.

Listen, there's plenty I don't like about cocaine. It can turn people into gibbering idiots, it has the tendency to amplify anxiety, and it has the potential for serious abuse. There's plenty I don't like about glitter too, but fuck, most things get messy when you use too much of them.

I'm not here to glorify drugs. If you think that, you've missed the point entirely. It's all just a pile of chemicals. Strip away the bullshit, and cocaine is just another medicinal plant extract no different to caffeine.

It's only through a series of unhappy ethnobotanical and geo-political accidents that caffeine is the primary active ingredient in the can of extreme soda some thick-skulled police officer slurps down for a cheap rush right before he commits some horrible injustice against a citizen for possessing a mere gram of powdered cocaine.

A drug is a drug. The rest is all politics and culture. I know at first glance it may seem like I'm constantly blowing rails, but gimme a break, this whole silly experiment was born out of one night of coke talk with my friends last summer. At the time, I didn't know I was creating a goddamned personal brand.

The decadent shit I do on any given weekend may or may not include recreational substances, but the glorification is owed to incredible experiences with fabulous people. I can't stress enough that it's never about the drugs.

Try cocaine if you want. Or don't. It sounds like you might want to smoke a little more weed and sit on a rock-hard cock or two before you start thinking about the California booger sugar. Whatever. Move at your own pace.

Just remember, cocaine isn't the enemy. Human weakness is.

On acid

My friend and I finally have an acid hook up, but I'm really nervous about it. I've tried robotripping which has been good, but i imagine this shit will be really intense, and I don't want some 12 hour panic attack. So, to drop or not to drop?

Your only frame of reference for LSD is fucking cough syrup, so yeah. What do you want me to say?

I'm not going to make this decision for you. No one else should either.

I will say that with LSD, the best way to end up with a twelve-hour panic attack is to expect a twelve-hour panic attack. Being in a good state of mind is key, so whatever you do, chill the fuck out.

You may want to consider asking yourself what you want to get out of it. You have the opportunity to expand your mind a bit, or you have the opportunity to giggle at MTV for a few hours. Don't waste it.

Do a little spring cleaning in your head before you drop. Read some poetry or listen to some classical music. Consider it the equivalent of stretching before a workout.

You don't have to be serious, but take LSD seriously. Especially at first.

On meth

So tomorrow I'm suppose to go and try meth with my friend for the first time. The problem is I've never really done any sort of drugs like this before (marijuana once). Obviously I'm out of my depth; I was just wondering if you could pass some judgement before I submit myself?

Please, don't go. I'm not kidding.

Weed, blow, ecstasy, ketamine, whatever. You know I'm all for expanding your mind. I'm all for experimentation. Just not meth. That shit will steal your soul. Meth is not a healthy chemical. Trust me on this.

You are, indeed, out of your depth. Getting high on meth is sucking the devil's dick. I promise, whatever immediate pleasure you may feel will not be worth the days of brutal sleepless hangover, and I assure you, the kind of people who do meth are the skankiest among us.

If you know enough to ask me this question, then you know I'm not fucking with you. That shit is filthy. Don't go there.

On prescription drugs

Ok, so I've done drugs before. I'm not necessarily naive. I've had lots of fun doing K, E, and blow for a long time now but for fear of sounding lame I feel like taking my drug habit a bit more legit. How do I go about getting Oxycontin or Dexedrin or something along those lines?

No, no, no. Just because a doctor writes you a note, it doesn't make getting high legitimate. Don't fucking kid yourself. Oxycontin and Dexedrin are just smack and speed with a college degree.

If you think your choices are any more appropriate because your dealer works at Walgreens, you are missing the point.

If you're an adult who understands personal responsibility, feel free to get fucked up and accept the consequences. Trying to shift that responsibility to a pharmaceutical company is bullshit.

A drug is a drug is a drug. Pretending that an addiction is okay because your health insurance covers prescriptions is the worst kind of hypocrisy.

(Just to be clear, my reaction here is based on two words that are red flags: 'habit' and 'legit'. If you were just talking about experimenting with something new, my answer would have been completely different.)

On smoking

When did you start smoking cigarettes? Do you think 14/15 is too young to start? If someone starts (well, me) at 14 (already started), is it possible to keep it under control or should I stop altogether? How do you smoke? Are you addicted? Please map this ground out for me because I'm lost.

I had my first cigarette in a church camp bathroom, not coincidentally on the same night that someone's finger other than my own first found its way inside my vagina. All in all, a pretty wild night for an eighth grader.

I never really started smoking, though. Much like getting fingerbanged, it was just something that happened every once in a while when I was sneaking around with high school boys.

In college, I would smoke with friends who smoked, but I never actually bought cigarettes myself. These days, I keep a pack of Parliaments laying around like I keep beers in the fridge. They're on hand for when I have guests, and occasionally if I'm in a particular mood.

I guess you could say I'm a pack-a-month smoker, which means on an average day I could call myself a non-smoker and no one would know the difference.

That's just it, though. I'll never become someone who needs a cigarette every day. I won't ever let it become a habit. As habits go, cigarettes are fucking disgusting. The dry cleaning bills alone make it a stupid idea.

Of all the shit I put into my body, cigarettes do the most damage and leave the most lasting negative effects. Sure, when I'm high as fuck, I'll smoke like a chimney, but that doesn't make it any less gross.

Not to start sounding like a Public Service Announcement, but a couple of my crazy party friends happen to be doctors. These guys have shoved ecstasy up my ass, and I've done cocaine off their cocks. They know their way around every recreational poison you can imagine, and they've told me the same thing every time: smoking is the worst thing you can do to your body.

So there it is. Maybe it's a bit of a mixed message, but I hope you understand that I'm not holding myself out as an example. Sure, I smoke a little, but I do all kinds of whacked-out shit that I obviously shouldn't do.

You're only fourteen. If you've already started smoking, you're fucked. You should absolutely quit. Never let yourself get addicted to anything, especially something so damaging as cigarettes.

Is there such a thing as casual heroin use?

There's such a thing as experimental heroin use, perhaps even occasional heroin use, but the word casual implies drug use that is both controlled and non-problematic. Given heroin's ridiculously high potential for physical dependence and the lifestyle typically associated with its users, I'd have to say that genuinely casual heroin use is a damn near impossible feat, especially over time, and even more so if needles are involved.

I smoke weed everyday, is that too often?

You've probably crossed the line from smoking recreationally to using it as a coping method. Don't let that shit become a crutch. Get your life in balance.

Sex on ketamine?

A kitty party? Fuck yes. Dangerous, though.

Isn't coke a bit of a waste of time?

Quit looking at your watch, asshole.

I fucked my drug dealer and now he refuses to take money from me.

See how that works?

is it okay to use addiherol to lose weight .. ?

Sure. Then again, it's not okay to use drugs you can't spell.

What do you recommend as a stylish alternative to the pacifier when you're on a massive ecstasy bender? I chain smoked all night last night and I want a way to control my grinding teeth without waking up with vocal chords that feel like breaded, fried spaghetti.

Higher quality drugs and some chewing gum, you numbnard.

How does one deal with post-ecstasy depression?

5-HTP supplements and enough presence of mind to know that the funk will lift in a couple days.

How do you cure a hangover?

Water and time.

On day drinking

Is it okay to start drinking strawberry and lime cider at half 9 in the morning because im bored?

Strawberry and lime cider? Am I big in Sweden or something? Are you fucking twelve?

If you're going to get hammered for breakfast, at least have the dignity to do it with real alcohol. Whiskey. Vodka. Beer if you must.

Unless you're poolside with Truman Capote, no self-respecting day drinker would ever tie one on with a fizzy drink where more than one fruit is involved.

On self-medicating

I suffer from BED and my weight gain has been out of control lately. I have tried to lose weight the old fashioned way, but all my diets fail because I lack will power and can't control my binges. So I'm considering using coke as an aid to suppress my need to overeat and take my mind off food. (It's either that or black market bupropion.) Any advice on that? Do you think it would work?

You're a binge eater who wants to trade up to a coke habit. What could possibly go wrong?

Listen, sweetie. You have deep-seated psychological problems, impulse control issues and a lack of will power. Cocaine will fucking destroy you.

Self-medication by a person inherently incapable of self-regulation does not work. It may seem effective in the short term, but it always makes things worse. All you're doing is switching substances. You're not addressing the underlying addiction.

By the way, did a medical professional diagnose you with Binge Eating Disorder, or did you just look that shit up on Wikipedia? And what's all this talk about black market antidepressants?

I have a sneaking suspicion that you've never actually talked to a doctor, and you're just a fat chick with an internet connection who's full of shit. It's bad enough to self-medicate, but you sure as hell don't get to self-diagnose.

Go to a doctor, preferably a psychiatrist specializing in eating disorders. Get some real help.

62 [the best of] Dear Coquette

On unreasonable demands

I'm 16. I've been dating this guy for 10 months, but I can tell we're going to last for at least a while. It's not love, but who, at 16, even knows what love IS? I've never been addicted to any substance, but I had partaken in smoking weed about half a dozen times with a trustworthy girlfriend of mine, and he knows. Now, he is asking me to never smoke again, and never to drink, even though I have never been drunk, and the last time I smoked was months ago. Nothing happened to spark his demand this of me. He just decided. I have been wanting to smoke again with that friend, but I'm not sure how to confront him about it. I refuse to lie and act like it never happened after I have done it. What should I do?

He just decided? Excuse me, but where does he get off making decisions on your behalf?

Never smoke? Never drink? Fuck that guy. Never surrender your free will, and never put up with an ultimatum.

It'd be one thing if he had genuine concerns about your health or well-being, but this sounds like some tight-ass moral objection to getting a little stoned. You don't have to obey him. Simply tell him no.

You're fucking sixteen years old. Boyfriends are fruit-flavored candy at that age. If he does anything but respect your wishes while following you around like a puppy dog, end the relationship so fast that his pointy little head spins.

Why is it so easy to make painfully stupid decisions when it comes to love and relationships, even for people who generally display decent judgment elsewhere?
Because drugs impair judgment, and love is one helluva drug.

I can't remember the last time I was sober for more than two days.
Yes you can. What changed?

So, I have a problem. I can only hook up with guys when I am drunk. The prospect of hooking up sober scares me. How do I solve this?
With self-respect and maturity. Short of that, quit drinking.

I can't sleep unless I'm completely toasted. I know this probably means I'm an alcoholic. I think I'm admitting it for the first time right now. What in sweet hell do I do next?
You might be an alcoholic, but this also sounds like you're self-medicating a mild but undiagnosed anxiety disorder. Go see a shrink.

On cautionary tales

I was around for the 80s wave of cocaine fun. It fucked up more people in my personal circle of acquaintances than any other drug. When I say, "fucked up" I mean: driven to suicidal despair because they couldn't kick. So, they committed suicide. This, unfortunately, happened more than once as you will no doubt deduce from the use of the third person plural. I also mean: death by overdose. I also mean: careers and lives ruined, as well as collateral damage on an operatic scale.

I know ex-junkies of various stripes, including booze, heroin, and cigarettes. The heroin kickers, in my experience, often make it through, along with the others.

I don't know any ex-coke heads. They all died.

Now, I've done some white lines, and was able to draw some lines. So yeah, you can be all "Trotsky did it, and Freud did it" (along with a lot of other annoying, teeth-grinding egomaniacs). Many of them survived, and perhaps enjoyed some especially wonderful insights and very deeply satisfying sex.

But to be so cavalier and defensive about raising the issues of its dangers is beneath the general level of intelligence you offer up here (often accompanied by your rebranded Dr. Laura tough talk. (Seriously, are you Jewish, or what?)

I find your touchiness about marital infidelity quaint and charmingly Victorian; I guess that same Victorianism applies to your attitude about cocaine as well.

You find me quaint and charmingly Victorian? Wow. That's about the nicest way anyone has ever come off as a condescending prick. Normally, I'm one to respect my elders, but I don't appreciate being compared to Dr Laura, so if you wouldn't mind, please go fuck yourself.

That being said, I understand where you're coming from. It's the same now as it was in the eighties. The chaos you describe is the hallmark of drug abuse in any decade, and it's brutal shit. Still, drug use is not the same as drug abuse. I've always been clear about the distinction, and when it comes to addiction, you'll never catch me being cavalier.

Also, I'm gonna call bullshit on you not knowing any ex-coke heads. I appreciate your dramatic flair, but who are we fucking kidding? Pretty much everyone you know from that era technically qualifies, yourself included.

Oh, and in all seriousness, I'm very sorry to hear about the people in your life who didn't make it. I know how horrible it feels to bury someone who died too young, and I've seen the kind of havoc suicide wreaks on a circle of friends.

Thanks for reading, and feel free to write me back about your mid-life crisis.

On respect

so, you are very clearly pro-drugs and all that. but i'm curious – would you respect someone's personal decision to stay clean or hold them in contempt?

Live how you wanna live, babe. I don't give a fuck. Oh, and just to be clear, you're the one holding me in contempt for thinking that you're somehow more 'clean' than I am.

On getting away with it

isn't cocaine illegal? then how do you do drugs, openly advertise the fact that you are taking an illegal narcotic on the internet, and get away with it?

Get away with it? Fuck you. May no vehicle in which you travel ever go faster than the posted speed limit. May you be audited by the IRS every year. May you live your entire life and never break a single rule or law, be it for sodomy, loitering or walking on the grass.

I wish that for you and everyone like you who thinks that in a free society, someone like me should have to be getting away with it.

What would you do if all recreational drugs, including alcohol, disappeared off the face of the earth tomorrow?
Ridiculously stupid thought experiments like this only demonstrate your gross misunderstanding of chemistry, biology and human

nature. The fucking tragedy is that this kind of idiotic thinking has been shaping US drug policy for years.

Are drugs bad?

Nope. Addiction is bad. Human weakness is bad, but drugs are just a bunch of chemicals, and chemicals are morally inert.

Is it wrong to use drugs to fill emotional voids?

Wrong is a moral judgment. If you want one of those, I'd need more context. I will say that using drugs to fill an emotional void usually leads to negative consequences. Do with that what you will.

I got sober. So now what?

Keep your shit together and don't make a big deal out of it.

PART II

On Dating

On goal-oriented dating

I'm in my last year at a good university, enjoying life and getting excited about heading out into the professional world. My biggest insecurity is that I've never had a relationship that's lasted longer than a month. In high school, I was a late bloomer in the dating scene and never even hooked up with someone until the summer before Senior year. Most of my "relationships" (if you want to call them that) have been with girls whose company I enjoy but the chemistry just never seems right. I just can't seem to find the right girl that I'm both attracted to and has a personality that matches mine. I'm an attractive, social guy, and I don't put out the desperate vibe – I feel like it's just circumstance that I haven't found anyone. But it's gotten to the point that it really bothers me. I feel like college is a time when I am surrounded by people my own age and of similar intelligence – if I graduate without having had a single meaningful relationship, I'm going to be pretty unhappy. Am I being overly analytical? Should I be less picky?

You don't need to be less picky. You need to be in less of a hurry. Your problem isn't that you're being overly analytical. It's that you've got a ridiculous master plan for your life that includes charts and graphs and a timetable.

I know your type. There's a voice in the back of your head constantly reminding you that you're supposed to be married with 2.5 kids and a golden retriever by the time you're in your mid-thirties. This voice says you're supposed to date around for a few years before you find the perfect girl and settle down. It says you're supposed to be in a stable, long-term relationship for a couple years before you get married, and it says you're supposed to be married for a little while before you start having kids.

This voice in the back of your head (which sounds suspiciously like your mother) has already done the math, and quite frankly, it's a little disappointed that you didn't find your future wife during college. Well, guess what, skipper? You need to tell that voice to shut the fuck up, or you're gonna end up leading a miserable life.

You're wrong about what will make you unhappy. It isn't the fact that you might graduate without having had a single meaningful relationship. It's that you're blind to the fact that regardless how long they've lasted, all of your relationships have been meaningful.

Every random hookup, every super-cool chick you weren't really attracted to, every potential girlfriend that fizzled after the third date – all of them count as meaningful relationships, especially during your college years.

Your single biggest mistake is that you think you have to find the right girl and spend a predetermined amount of time in a relationship before it counts as meaningful. (I'm guessing with you, it's probably three months.)

Do yourself a huge favor and throw the timetable and your 'right girl' checklist out the window. Stop being so damned goal-oriented with your dating. Come on, man. You're in your early twenties. Smell some fucking roses already.

On nice guy syndrome

I'm a 21 year old guy with one more semester of college left. If there was a textbook of "nice slightly geeky guy," it'd have my picture there. I'm not fat, I'm not pimply, but I'm not cut or super-hot either… just a slightly above-average looking guy who knows how to treat a girl.

All of that introduces my question: why is it that I always get thrown into the friend zone? To clarify, I get put into the "gay best friend" zone. I'm straight as the day is long, but I'm the one who gets to hear about new shoes, shopping, cute boys, shitty boys, assholes who stood them up... you get the drift.

Is it because I listen too much? Am I too nice? Should I not offer a shoulder to cry on, tell her the shoes are cute (when they are), or that the dude she's dating is a douche who's probably fucking someone else too?

Can you help me? I'm asking because there's a gorgeous, intelligent girl I'd usually say is out of my league that has expressed lots of interest, and I don't want her to turn me into another "gay best friend" style friend, where I get to hear about her day, her shoes, and her boy problems.

Ugh. Nothing rolls my eyes into the back of my head faster than a 'nice guy' who whines about being in the friend zone, and quite frankly, if it weren't my job to try and smack some sense into you, I'd tell you to go fuck yourself for the ignorant 'gay best friend' remarks. (Not cool, dude.)

Let's be clear, you are not a nice guy. You are actually a magnificent douchebag with a raging case of Nice Guy Syndrome. (Yep, it's a thing. Look it up.)

While we're at it, let's be clear about something else. You don't know how to treat a girl. You say you do, but you don't have the slightest fucking clue. If you really knew how to treat a girl, you wouldn't bitch about listening too much, and you wouldn't act like a shoulder to cry on is only something to offer if it's in furtherance of getting you laid.

That kind of thinking is glaring evidence of the underlying issue with guys like you. You don't actually respect women. You pretend as if you do, and you may even believe that you do, but it's not real.

It's outrageous and downright insulting that you think a girl has the ability to turn you into a 'gay best friend'. You're doing that to yourself, because you aren't really being a friend in the first place. You're just acting like one with the ridiculous expectation that platonic behavior on your part might somehow transmogrify into romantic behavior on her part.

Sorry, but it doesn't work that way. Platonic relationships are different to romantic ones. They begin differently, they progress differently, and they sure as hell end differently. You'd better cozy up to that fact pretty quick, because you simply cannot continue to behave like this with the new relationship. If you want a romantic relationship, you have to be emotionally honest from the get-go.

You have to put yourself out there, and if she rejects you as a potential romantic partner, you have to move on without thinking platonic behavior will eventually entitle you to something romantic.

On being easy

Some advice: if you fuck on the first-date, he probably won't come back for a second. If the sex was hot and he does come back enjoy becoming fuck-buddies, because by fucking on the first-date, you've essentially told him by your actions: "I'm easy and definitely not the type of girl you'll be wanting to take-home or marry, because anyone who I find attractive and who picks up the bill, I'll let fuck me."

I can appreciate the brass balls it takes to offer someone like me unsolicited advice, but honey, not only are you in way over your head, you're also wrong about life. I fuck who I fuck when I fuck because I wanna fuck, and I don't give a flying fuck whether the people I fuck think I'm the marrying type. That doesn't make me easy. That makes me hard.

I am the one in command of my own sexual virtue. I am the one who defines that virtue. No one else gets a say in it – not you, not the world, and certainly not some guy I allowed the privilege of fucking me on the first date.

Everything you believe to be true about sexual virtue is a tragic lie instilled in you by a misogynistic, patriarchal culture that is fundamentally terrified of female sexuality, and that bullshit needs to be systematically unlearned. I'd feel sorry for you if you weren't making yourself part of the problem by spreading around this kind of ignorant, regressive poison.

On doing what needs to be done

My friend-with-benefits sent me a text saying "You need to back away from me until you can control and handle your emotions. You're being clingy, obnoxiously attached, and irrationally upset for no goddamn reason. Until then, please do something constructive instead of sending me a text." He just sent this straight out of the blue and I'm about 5 seconds from kicking his ass to the curb. I can't keep giving him second chances. I need advice. Help. Anything.

You can only give somebody one second chance. After that, 'giving him second chances' is just code for putting up with more of his bullshit.

And let's be clear, he didn't send that text straight out of the blue. You may not want to admit it, but you know damn well why he thinks you're being clingy, obnoxiously attached, and irrationally upset for no goddamn reason.

I'm not saying he's right. I'm just saying quit acting all surprised. Even if he is right, he's still behaving like a gigantic asshole, and you shouldn't tolerate a lack of respect like that from a friend, with or without benefits. It doesn't sound like a healthy relationship, so you should probably take your five seconds and then go ahead and kick his ass to the curb.

Now, here's the real question. Can you do what needs to be done, or are you just in this for the drama?

On flirting

How should a male feminist flirt? (I get the impression that a little guide to this might help ease the symptoms of Nice Guy Syndrome sufferers...)

Oh my god, no. It is definitionally impossible to be a male feminist who suffers from Nice Guy Syndrome. The two couldn't be more mutually exclusive. If you really are a male feminist, whatever social awkwardness you might be suffering should never be confused with something so gross as Nice Guy Syndrome.

What bugs me even more about this question is the assumption that courtship rituals are somehow different for male feminists than they are for other dudes. You're not special because you identify as a male feminist. In fact, that's not a label you get to claim for yourself, especially in this context. I'm sorry, but your behavior has to speak for itself.

How you should flirt as a male feminist is no different than how any dude should flirt, and quite frankly, there's nothing I can tell you about flirting that shouldn't be patently obvious to someone who claims to be a male feminist. But hey, since you asked, here's my two cents:

First and foremost, be situationally aware. Ninety percent of the awkward moments in the known universe could be avoided if guys would just pay attention to their surroundings before hitting on a girl.

Is it an appropriate time and place for you to flirt? Do you have any indication that your advances might be welcome? Is there anyone who might be made to feel uncomfortable if you started flirting? If you don't have clear and positive answers to all of these questions, then any move you make will be a one-way ticket to awkward town.

If you do have a handle on the situation, then it really just comes down to being respectful and not saying stupid shit. The goal is merely to telegraph a little bit of romantic intent through non-verbal cues.

Please note, I said romantic intent, not sexual intent. Leave your dick out of the equation. Communicating the idea that you find a woman attractive is not the same thing as communicating the idea that you want to fuck. If you fail to comprehend this simple distinction, then I assure you, you are not a male feminist, and for the sake of all womankind, you should probably never go out in public again.

Good luck with the flirting. Oh, and did I mention? Don't say stupid shit.

On a dick tease

What was supposed to be a no biggie fling has turned into a brain exploding headfuck with a guy who has suddenly decided he doesn't want to sleep with me because he "respects me as a human-being" and even though he finds me "extremely sexually attractive" doesn't want to use me like a "toy" and is afraid sex will lead to "feelings".

The misogyny embedded in his dick-teasing explanations for not wanting to fuck make me want to put my head through a wall. Last time I was single, this city was a casual sex fest. I haven't yet encountered this shit and I'm really confused.

I'm pretty butthurt I didn't get laid cos, apparently, I'm a "woman" and I have "feelings" and those "feelings" are activated through my vagina. How should I process this stupid shit?

He just didn't want to fuck you. It happens. Get over it.

It's okay, though. I know his type. The sex would have been terrible, and he'd have been calling you a cab while you were still wiping his cum off your tits.

Of course, that's what he was trying to tell you with all that coded 'nice guy' bullshit. You just have to know how to read between the lines. When this guy said he's afraid sex would lead to 'feelings', what he meant is that he's afraid sex would lead to 'you being needy'.

And he doesn't find you 'extremely sexually attractive' any more than he 'respects you as a human being'. That's just him being patronizing. After all, for him to think that casual sex would be 'using you like a toy' pretty much sums up his internalized opinion of women as sex objects.

I get that rejection sucks, but not getting laid by an emotionally crippled douchebag ain't the worst thing that'll happen to you this week. Hard dick is good to find, but good dick is harder to find than you think. Keep looking. You'll get some soon enough.

On the harm in flirtation

does instant messaging with a man twice my age who's married to a wife i really admire and who just had an adorable baby make me feel nervous and guilty because i know he and i mutually think one another are awesome and even though i would never never never do anything, this is the way people who do things start out, or is it because i'd just like to tell myself i wouldn't but I really would?

You'd never never do anything? Bullshit. If the two of you have to hide the instant messages from the wife, then you've already crossed the line.

A little flirtation can be harmless. Hell, a lot of flirtation can be harmless, but if it becomes a thing she would be hurt to discover, then you shouldn't be doing it. The betrayal is in the secret, not the act itself.

Of course, you already know that, which is why you feel nervous and guilty.

How do I date my best friend?

Carefully, only once, and with the full knowledge that it could easily destroy the relationship.

What does my poor choice in men tell me about my self-esteem?

I dunno. Choices only become poor with hindsight. You chose those men for a reason, and those reasons satisfied a short-term emotional or physical need at the expense of your long-term happiness. What are those needs? Are they linked to your self-esteem? Are there patterns of behavior that you can identify and learn from and not repeat? You're the one who has to answer this question for yourself. I can't do the work for you.

I've been out with a new guy on about 4 dates. He recently told me that he has never been in a relationship. We're both 26. Red flag?

Depends on what he considers a relationship. If it means he's never been in love, it's not a red flag. If it means he's never been exclusive, it's a yellow flag. If it means he's never gone on a 3rd date, it's a red flag.

Casual guy told me I was too smart for him/ he couldn't keep up. Then we fucked one last time and he ghosted. It's just an excuse cause he's not into it, right? What the fuck

The whole 'he's just not that into you' thing implies that it actually had something to do with you in the first place. In a casual world full of narcissists, y'all need to start getting used to the fact that it wasn't ever about you to begin with.

Why does it bug me so much when guys call me a tease?

Because not only are they implying that you use your sexuality as currency, they're also suggesting that they're owed some of it.

What does it mean when a guy doesn't want to get into a relationship with you because he doesn't want to disappoint you?

It means he doesn't want to be in a relationship with you.

I have had numerous men tell me in so many words that I'm unlovable. It's clear they think I'm smart, fun, pretty, etc, but I don't evoke an emotional response in them. How do I interpret this? How do I not let it (continue to) ruin my self-esteem?

Nope, nope, nope. Unlovable is your word, not theirs. You are not unloveable. You simply have a pattern of picking emotionally unavailable men. Pick better men, and while you're at it, stop letting their faults inform your self-image.

On rejecting an older man

There's a man in my life that I've known for almost six years now & our relationship is complicated. He's older than me by 20 years exactly (I'm in my 20's), & until recently we were just good friends. Two years ago he said he was in love with me & has told me so several times since, as well as buying me various expensive gifts. We've never been sexually involved & we live on separate sides of the country, so we don't see each other more than once a year. I do care about him as a friend & a person but I'm not in love with him & don't have any desire to be with him. I've told him I don't love him but he says that doesn't matter & he loves me anyway. At this point I don't know what to say, & I feel guilty that I don't return his feelings. Any advice?

Both his age and the fact that you feel guilty for not returning his feelings are evidence that he is emotionally manipulating you. You need to take a step back and recognize that you are being inappropriately pressured.

You are in no way obligated to return his feelings. If you've made it clear that you don't have any desire to be with him and he says it doesn't matter, that means he is showing you disrespect. Fuck that shit.

Stop allowing him to give you romantic attention. Definitely stop accepting gifts from him, and if necessary, return the gifts that he has already given you. I know it's nice to get gifts and attention, but you can't let that shit happen if you just want to be friends.

Be kind, but be firm. Let him know that you are not romantically available for reasons that should be plainly obvious. Your age, your distance and your unrequited feelings make a relationship impossible, and if he can't move on, then you may have to sever the friendship.

(Oh, and while you're at it, stop using a damned ampersand when it's just as easy to type the word 'and'. Don't be fucking lazy about the details.)

On dudes losing interest

I can't detach emotions from sex. I'm single and dating but whenever I try to hold off on the sex until I'm ready, dudes get impatient and lose interest. When I've gone ahead with the sex on the first few dates, I feel gross and used. I try to date all different kinds of men and I like to think I can weed out the douchebags but apparently something is amiss. What can I do?

Keep doing what you're doing. Nothing is amiss. You're on one end of a spectrum where dudes get impatient and then lose interest. Women on the other end of that spectrum fret just as much as you do, because they have experiences where dudes get laid right away and then lose interest. Either way, dudes lose interest, and women find every way to blame themselves without recognizing the broader pattern.

Dudes are gonna lose interest. It's what dudes do. Occasionally you'll find one who's legitimately looking for a long-term relationship, and if it's for healthy reasons and you two have chemistry, you might become a thing for a while. Whether that happens or not has nothing to do with your ability to detach emotions from sex. Don't scapegoat that aspect of your personality. It may be the reason dudes get impatient, but it's certainly not to blame for why dudes lose interest. That's on them, not you.

If sex before you're ready makes you feel gross and used, don't do it. If a guy you're dating gets impatient, tough shit. If he loses interest, fine. Good riddance. Dating should never be about keeping someone's interest at the expense of your own emotional well-being.

On a selfish cheating asshole

*I drunk fucked a guy I work with. I'm 24 and he's in his
late 30's. He's married and has a kid, I have a boyfriend
I moved states for. Its an all around bad situation .
The sex was amazing, but it was just sex. Theres no
chemistry on either side that is anything close to how
it is with each of our SO's. But I'm worried its going to
happen again ... The sex was so good. I don't want to
lose everything but I am young and I want to have good
sex while I can. Am I going to hell?*

There is no hell, you selfish cheating asshole. What you did is
wrong. Don't fuck your married coworker ever again, and don't use
alcohol or your youth as an excuse for your shitty behavior. If you
need a more adventurous sex life, then either be honest with your
boyfriend and open up your relationship, or break up with him and
start fucking some non-married non-coworkers.

Have some fucking integrity, bitch.

*Is it morally reprehensible to seek & be flattered by
male attention even though you don't have the slightest
interest?*
Attention seeking can be a bit shallow, but it's not morally reprehensible unless you're also engaging in deception or dishonesty.

*I fucked a guy with a wife and baby on the way. He just
got married but he's been living with the girl for more
than 5 years. I don't even know if I like him. It's just I
want – SO BADLY – for him to like me. It's the lowest I
have ever GONE. And I need some slaps in my face to
snap out of it.*
You know what you did was wrong, so let's set aside your shitty
behavior for a moment and help you recognize a deeper truth: the

worst thing about you is that you believe you need to fuck a guy in order to get him to like you.

Your thoughts on a guy who counts his sexual partners and boasts with his number?
Don't fuck him. He's terrible in bed.

What exactly characterizes the border between pursuing a love interest and being creepy/obsessive?
Putting your wishes ahead of theirs.

Why am I attracted to arrogant dudes?
Ask your dad.

Nothing makes me feel smaller or uglier or more like a piece of shit than someone I care about showing romantic interest in me, and I don't know why. I wish I could get people to stop.
The reason it makes you feel small and ugly is because you consider romantic interest to be an unsolicited sexualization of a platonic relationship. It's a shift in how you think a person values you, one that degrades your own self-worth. It doesn't have to, though. The trick is in realizing and fully accepting that you're not doing anything wrong. You're not the one betraying the fundamental nature of the relationship. They are.

If someone openly says that they are not a good person, and also includes that they don't know what it means to love someone, would it be stupid to date them? Is it stupid to even ask?

They are either telling the truth, and you shouldn't date them, or they are playing games with you, and you shouldn't date them.

On not getting hit on

Why won't guys look at me? I'm 30, pretty, smart, well-educated and have a good career. I like to think I'm a strong woman (or at least appear to be strong, since I'm whining here). Yet when I go out with friends, all of whom are in relationships, guys hit on my friends, never on me. It's like I don't exist. True, I'm not very good at hitting on guys, but my friends get hit on without doing anything. Damn, sending this question feels weird.

Either you're wrong about being pretty, or you're wrong that guys never hit on you. Take your pick. It's one or the other.

If you're willing to jump right in and call yourself pretty, I'm willing to give you the benefit of the doubt, which means that unless you're an insufferable bore or a big pile of awkward, you're probably just clueless when it comes to being hit on.

Odds are, you have a selective memory. You remember all the guys who hit on your friends, and you remember all the guys who didn't hit on you when you wanted them to, but you don't remember any of the poor bastards who tried hitting on you when you weren't interested.

Of course, pointing this out doesn't solve the real problem, which is that you secretly think all your friends are much more attractive than you. It doesn't matter whether this is objectively true. What matters is that you believe it to be true.

Yes, that's really the problem. I didn't need to know that all your friends are in relationships, but you thought it was important enough to tell me. It bugs you. That's the tip of your iceberg of resentment.

This entire question is a head-fake towards male attention when at your core you have issues with female competition among your friends. You start out with, 'Why won't guys look at me?' when what you're really asking is, 'Why are guys looking at them?'

That kind of indignation is poisonous to female friendship, especially when you don't recognize that it's there. You need to acknowledge some of your underlying feelings about your friends, and deal with them before your negativity starts to fester.

On a lazy idiot

ive been dating this girl for over a year now and have found over time that she has slept with way more dudes than i thought. she also took my virginity. i cant help but feel like this imbalance is eating away at me. got any words of advice?

I've got plenty of words of advice, but you're an idiot and nothing I say will stop your male ego from eventually destroying your relationship so that you can add a few notches to your bedpost. That's fine, though. She can do better, and you need some time to fuck around and figure out what's important.

In the meantime, start using capital letters. Your shit is lazy.

On boundaries

There's a woman at my office (the receptionist), who's really attractive (duh, receptionist). In my professional capacity I don't have much interaction with her but

I'd really like to find a way to create some without being another creepy dude making contrived moves(I know that's what I'm doing, hopefully with less creep). Who knows if we'll even click… this isn't about trying to fit where I can't, but I'd like to give it a legitimate try without boning my chances by being a typically awkward guy.

Pen, company ink. I get it. I'm adult enough to not let that kind of shit get to me if it doesn't work. Aside from not dating someone from work, what should I do?

Aside from not dating your receptionist, you should also not hit on your bartender, you should not ask out your waitress, you should not proposition your stripper, and you should not kiss your prostitute on the lips without permission.

Listen, jackass, this isn't about being adult enough to not let shit get to you if it doesn't work. It's about being adult enough to respect the boundaries of professional relationships.

On not seeing the point

He's trying to get to know me, but I just want to fuck. Why do guys insist on going through this phase? I just don't see a point unless you're looking for something serious.

Oh, I don't know. Maybe it's because you're a beautiful and interesting human being worth knowing beyond your vagina who somehow doesn't quite grasp that the delicious complexity of interpersonal relationships can't be reduced to a binary state of 'something serious' or 'I just don't see the point'.

Or maybe he's just a dildo with a dude on the end of it.

Which do you think it is?

On going out with a bang

I've been dating this guy for the last week, but right now I'm just not emotionally available. I feel like I should break things off, but I wanna have sex with him first. Is that a really dick thing to do? I feel like it is... Should I do it anyway?

Shit, it's only been a week. Just be honest. Make plans to see him one more time. Look him in the eye and say, 'I'm not emotionally available right now and I don't think I can keep seeing you, but I'd really like to have sex with you tonight.'

It's a win-win. Not only are you shooting him straight, but I guarantee he'll bring his hair-pulling, ass-smacking A-game just to see if he can change your mind.

At the end of the night, just give him a kiss goodbye.

Good times.

How do you say no to someone who continuously asks you out and refuses to stop, even upon request?
Tell the creep to fuck off. Be rude. Be loud. Embarrass him for not respecting you, and when he acts all butthurt and calls you a bitch, don't feel the least bit bad about it.

Why am I attracted to guys who always have one foot out the door?
So that you can experience all of the emotional drama without taking any of the emotional risk.

Any tips on how to tell if a married man is lying about being in an open relationship, without asking his wife?
Look him in the eye and say, 'Tell me about how you and your wife decided to open up your marriage.' You'll immediately know if he's full of shit.

My fuck buddy wants a relationship. What's the least awkward way to tell him that I'm not looking for a commitment?

Use whatever words you'd like, but the least awkward way is to immediately stop fucking him.

Is it okay to talk to and fuck someone who is ugly when you are not?

I dunno, you sound pretty ugly to me.

I hate every man who starts to like me after I've slept with them. How do I stop?

It's not hate. It's a reflection of your own self-loathing that you use as a clumsy defense mechanism to protect yourself from vulnerability.

I am relatively sought-after, but my high standards have made me lonely. How do I fix this?

Your high standards aren't the problem. It's your unreasonable expectations that are keeping you lonely. There's a difference.

Is sleeping with your teacher morally wrong, even if their not married?

Is it your English teacher? Because you need to learn the difference between 'their' and 'they're'.

On making a move

So I've got a mad crush on this girl who lives on my hall. We've been hanging out and stuff, probably to the point where she thinks I'm just her friend. And I'm bad at picking up signals, but I get the feeling that there could be something here. (This is coming from a guy with zero, zero, zero experience. But I've already complained about that for years. It's time to make a change.)

We went to Harry Potter last night and blazed together. Unfortunently we were with a bigger group as well of mostly her friends so I couldn't try anything. That sounds stupid to me because I have no idea what I'd 'try'.

So what's the best option for me right now as far as making the next move? Remember...I am a total loser who hasn't had any experience with girls and somehow I made it to college a virgin, because I'm that cool. I'm not solely out for sex, though; I like her.

Dude. You're fucking precious. I just wanna tussle your hair and pinch your cheeks and shit.

Listen up, this isn't about 'trying' anything. Don't make this about your virginity. Nobody gives a fuck about your lack of experience except for you, and trust me, you're surrounded by virgins.

I can't tell you how to make a move here, kid. That shit is on you. Accept your vulnerability, accept the possibility of rejection, and then just be brave and fucking do it. Making a move is an organic, in-the-moment kinda thing, but I will say this, if you think there's a romantic spark between you and this girl, you're the one who's gonna have to acknowledge it.

Be sweet about it. Be honest. Use whatever words or actions that come to you naturally in that moment of bravery, but the gist of it doesn't have to be any more complicated than, 'Hey, I like you, and I think you like me too. Here we go!'

Do it with a kiss. Do it with your own words. However you do it, get it fucking done. Don't worry about what happens next. For better or worse, the heat of that moment will become self-sustaining once you get it started, unless of course you fuck it up by overthinking shit.

Whatever. You're gonna do what you're gonna do.

Tell you what, though, you're not a total loser. That much is for sure. You just need to get out of your own head. Quit complaining, and savor the experience you're about to have.

Learning this shit is ten times more exciting than already knowing how to do it.

Fucking enjoy yourself.

On hesitation

Whenever I think I like someone, I always put up walls. Half the time I'm scared to commit because I don't think people will be able to handle me. I always end up convincing myself I don't like them, but I don't like seeing people get hurt...What's your opinion on this?

Oh please. You're the girl standing in the freezer section of the grocery store staring at the ice cream like her head is about to explode.

It's fucking ice cream, bitch. It's creamy and delicious. You know you want some. Quit making lame excuses for yourself and pick a damned flavor already.

On a complicated dilemma

I have a dilemma and i need your advice. my best friend's roommate and i are totally into each other, and the best friend is pissed and is begging me not to hook up with her. In addition, the roommate is currently in a relationship with this really nice guy who's pretty chill. I don't want to be a relationship breaker, nor do I want to fuck up my friendship with my best friend. What would you do? Hook up with the roommate asap, wait for the roommates current relationship to end, or not hookup with the roommate at all?

You seem to have way more experience with complicated relationships than I, hence why I ask you.

Here's what you should do. Go get a dictionary. Look up the words 'dilemma' and 'complicated'. Note that neither of them should be used to describe what's going on with your pathetic excuse for a lack of self-control.

You're a piece of shit for even considering this. Seriously, dude. You're willing to drop a live grenade of hot messy drama into the middle of your best friend's home so your dick can get wet for ten, fifteen minutes tops? Fuck you.

This is only a dilemma if you're an emotionally crippled tool.

On sixteen

I'm sixteen and have never had a real relationship, just a bunch of mild drunken hook-ups. I don't want to put time and effort into someone I'm not crazy about, but I'm afraid that when I actually have relationships, I'm always going to be the person who likes the other slightly more. Also, I have crushes on people I don't know very well, so I can construct their personality into something I like better. And then I always find out that they're assholes. Fix me?

You're not broken. You're sixteen.

All that shit you're feeling is right on schedule, and the fact that you're self-aware about it means you're ahead of the game.

Don't worry. One day, you'll be able to spot assholes before you crush on them.

In the meantime, try not to think in terms of relationships. Just enjoy the company of interesting and respectful boys and/or girls.

On all there is to say

I'm 19 and i'm seeing this guy, but all we do is fuck. We've been dating for about a month and he knows nothing about me. Whenever we hang out all we do is have sex and then he sort of ignores me until I have to leave and then begs me to stay. The fucked up part is that he told me that he loved me about 3 weeks into the relationship (I don't believe him). What's this guys deal?

He's an emotionally crippled piece of meat. Then again, so are you.

Stay off television and on birth control.

On secret affairs

Here's my dilem. I'm having a secret affair with this guy. This certain guy has hooked up with my best friend a few months ago. He confessed to me that he actually likes me and could see us being more than fuck buddies. My best friend still isn't over him even though they never actually dated (she gave him a bj and he was high and barely remembers it). I like him so much and really do want to be with him. But my best friend would be crushed if I dated him.

So, do I put my happiness in front of hers? or go the chicks before dicks route?

A secret affair? Don't be so dramatic. This isn't about love. Nobody's married. You're just sneaking some dick behind your best friend's back after she tried calling dibs on it.

The whole thing is just a half-assed love triangle, the heightened circumstances of which are fooling you into thinking that this guy is more than a fuck buddy.

Don't kid yourself. It's a summer fling, one that's going to ruin your relationship with your best friend when she finds out.

Yes. She will find out. It's inevitable, and unless you're the one who steps up and tells her what's going on, she'll never be able to trust you again.

This isn't about your happiness. It's about your integrity. Seriously, is your summertime fuck buddy worth your best friend's trust?

Didn't think so.

Why do I scare guys I like away, and attract the ones I don't?
That's just your confirmation bias talking.

How long is the "normal" amount of time to be single?
That's good. The first step is putting it in quotes. The next step is realizing that there's no such thing.

No matter what, whoever I date starts to look ugly to me after a while. Is this normal? How do I stop this from happening?
You're confusing what they look like with what they are like. Even worse, you're probably confusing what they are like with what you are like.

I want to be in love with someone who is kind, witty, and sexually attractive, and have them love me back. Why does it this seem so impossible?
Because you're confusing kindness, wit and sexual attraction with long-term compatibility, and you're confusing love with infatuation.

How do I stop feeling guilty about casual sex?
Stop believing casual sex is wrong.

Why am I so scared of committing to a nice, sweet guy who I regularly hang out and sleep with? What's stopping me from making it official?

You still think you can do better.

I'm really great at finding hot, fun guys to fuck and having a hot night of sex. Not so great at turning it into either a regular fuck or a relationship. Any advice?

Yeah, stop trying to turn one-night stands into ongoing relationships. Going out for a hot night of sex and going out to meet guys are two completely different rituals with completely different codes of etiquette. Separate the two in your mind, and understand that you can't do them both at the same time.

On dating in los angeles

I'm having trouble dating, specifically dating in Los Angeles, the land of superficiality. I'm a med student and I've been in Maxim, so I'm surrounded by nerds & get hit on by douchebags, neither of which I want to date. I keep getting wrapped up in men who are smart & successful but more interested in their jobs than me. What's a girl to do to find an honest, hardworking family man in LaLaLand?

Honest, hardworking and a family man? This is Los Angeles, babe. Unless you wanna marry a Mexican immigrant, you can only pick two out of the three.

You're a soon-to-be doctor, former model living on the west side of paradise. Don't tempt the fates by also expecting Ward Cleaver to fall out of the sky. You're asking for too much.

That's not to say you don't deserve happiness, but is this really an honest assessment of your criteria for a man? It all seems a bit simplistic – no nerds, no douchebags, smart and successful – I wouldn't go so far as to call you superficial, but your lists of pre-requisites don't seem to have any depth.

That's not your fault. You're young, and you've been too busy overachieving. You simply haven't taken the time to do the kind of serious personal exploration necessary to figure out not just who you're looking for, but why you're looking in the first place.

Self-exploration is a tough thing to do, and I would imagine you come from a family that considers that sort of thing an indulgence. Still, and I've said it before, you need to look inside yourself instead of using an external set of guidelines handed down from your mother.

I'm not saying that you won't find an honest, hardworking family man in Los Angeles, but you're not going to find him with a grocery list. You'll find him once you find yourself.

Good luck with the search, sweetheart.

On why you even bother

First, I'm going to say what everyone says: you're great and I need an honest opinion, no holds barred. I was in a very long term relationship that ended a couple years ago. I've never been much of a dater – I'm one of those annoying people who just sort of fell into relationships when I was younger. However, I've been trying my best to get myself out there and meet guys, which seems so fucking impossible in New York (totally cliche, I know, but it's true).

My real problem is that I've met a few guys that I've had a good few months with and then they start the disappearing act. You know, less frequent phone calls/ texts, distancing themselves, and behaving badly. In some cases, they've ended it, in others I have, but always because of their actions. They've all been fairly normal, good guys. I'm a smart, fun, good-looking laid-back woman and I don't see what the deal is.

For the sake of full disclosure (because I want the most honest opinion from you), I've slept with all of these guys within the first couple weeks (which I don't think is a bad thing) and I tend to give people the benefit of the doubt. If a guy shows a serious interest in me and I like him, I don't play hard-to-get. I'm usually very up-front and I don't like game playing to get the "upper-hand."Is this bad? Are these guys thinking I'm too available?

Am I just having a run of bad luck? Should I re-evaluate my judgment on the men I'm choosing? Or should I just stop "giving away the milk for free?"

D. None of the above.

Your real problem is that you think you have a problem. You're not experiencing bad luck, you don't need to re-evaluate your judgment, and you're not a fucking dairy cow.

Perhaps you should start questioning the underlying notion that you exist in a binary state of either couplehood or singlehood, and that the former is somehow superior to the latter.

After all, you're the type who 'just sort of falls into relationships'. It seems like you're long past due for some introspection into why you even bother.

Why are you looking for a man? Do you need a man to feel safe? Happy? Fulfilled? Do you want a best friend? A partner in crime? Someone to pay the bills? Do you want kids? Come on, why are you even out there dating? Let me guess, because that's just what you're supposed to do.

You have no idea why you're out there engaging in the courtship ritual. All you've got is some nebulous set of external relationship guidelines that you've pulled from popular culture and whatever your mother taught you. None of it is relevant to your core self, because you haven't taken the time to reflect on what it is you want out of a relationship.

Now is as good a time as any to start figuring it out. The cool thing is, there's no wrong answer here. Just be honest with yourself. What do you want?

Not to get all Cheshire Cat up in this bitch, but until you know where you want to go, you're wasting your time wondering why you're lost.

On being hard to get

Does playing hard-to-get (in order to get a guy) actually work?

Playing hard to get works on boys. *Being* hard to get works on men. In either case, don't confuse hard with impossible.

On playing vs being

I'd appreciate it if you could elaborate on your perspective on playing hard to get vs being hard to get.

1) What practical difference is there between consciously holding back to stoke interest in a lover, and unconsciously holding back if they both serve the same ends?

2) Is playing/being hard to get even a legitimate tactic in romantic relationships? Isn't appealing to someone's desire for what they can't have just a matter of ego rather than a substantial bond between two people built on mutual affinity?

3) you can't be naturally hard to get AND consciously making sure you're not too hard to get. You've contradicted yourself.

Everything about your question – all of it – falls squarely into the category of playing hard to get. You have yet to even grasp the concept of being hard to get.

Being hard to get isn't a tactic. It has nothing to do with conscious or unconscious action. It just fucking is.

Stop thinking about it. Let it go. I know you want me to elaborate on the distinction, but until you start getting zen about this shit, it's only going to frustrate you.

(Sometimes I wish I could end these things with the sound of a gong.)

Either way, just enjoy yourself. We're lucky to live in an era where our livelihoods no longer depend on it.

On whether to text first

I hooked up with this guy I have liked for a while last friday. It is now Sunday and he has not texted me or tried to make any communication. I dont want him to think I like him even though i do.

should i wait for him to text me, or should i text him first?

Wait a few years until you mature into an emotionally honest woman who has enough self-respect not to play silly mind games with her cell phone, and then call him.

On bitterness

Best way to start dating again if still bitterly single from last meaningful relationship? And don't say tequila, xanax or drunken sex.

How 'bout you lose the attitude?

It doesn't matter how much of an asshole your ex was. You are responsible for your own emotional state. It's your own fault if you're bitter. Get over it.

If you're packing all this emotional baggage, don't even bother dating. It's a waste of everyone's time.

(Especially without tequila, Xanax or drunken sex.)

On just doing it

It has literally been over 12 months since I last had sex. Right now I'm contemplating ruining my friendships by having sex with them at a party and then having shit get awkward and whatever. So far as I can see it's either that or continue my steady diet of abstinence. What should I do?

Is it really so hard to fuck a stranger? Quit acting like you're married and go have some filthy, no-strings-attached, 'What was your name, again?' sex.

On poaching boyfriends

it seems i always have a thing for guys with other chicks, so my question is… is that bad? i can't help it if i'm better looking then their girlfriends.

You can't help being better looking, but you can help being a cunt. Don't poach guys. It's incredibly selfish and disrespectful. Do I need to remind you of the golden rule?

As hot as you think you are, there's always somebody hotter. Would you want that bitch stealing your man?

On naughty pics

Here's the deal. I met this guy not to long ago, over the internet . Blahblahblah to that, I have no problem with meeting people online. He is hot. Damn good looking And I usually go for the nerdy lanky boys. HOWEVER, this boy is gorgeous. On with the story. We talked for the first time last week on the phone, around tuesday or wednesday. We ended up having phone sex. I have NO idea how it even got to that point but it did. And I feel kinda weird about it because I do not do that with guys I have just started talking to. I like to keep some kind of respect for myself. He wants pictures of me sans clothing now. And I don't know how to say no. Because let's face it, I phone fucked the guy the first time talking to him. And after that, how do you say no to something as simple as pictures? Part of my thinks I wouldn't mind, but part of me would like to save some kind of whatever dignity I may have left. I'm not quite sure what to do here.

Ah, the perils of 21st-century whoredom. Every last one of us has a few naughty pics floating out there in the digital ether, and nowadays the American teenage experience includes making your first sex tape before getting your driver's license.

Billions of little red record buttons, so simple and ubiquitous, make it far too easy for boys to do what boys like to do – point and shoot. It desensitizes girls like yourself until you're asking ridiculous questions like, 'how do you say no to something as simple as pictures?'

Simple as pictures? Are you fucking kidding me? The legal and emotional consequences of turning a camera into a sex toy can be staggeringly complicated and more permanent than an STD.

If every iPhone shipped with anal beads instead of a camera, would you still be asking how to say no to something as simple as assplay?

You're not sure what to do here because you seem to have devalued this part of your sexuality. Take a moment to reflect on the levels of trust and intimacy that are required to safely share naked photos with someone, and hopefully you'll see that I'm not being facetious when I compare this to taking it up the ass.

Posing for pics can be incredibly hot, and shooting a wildly creative sex tape can be one of the most intimate things you do with your partner, but the decision to let anyone other than yourself control that content is a serious one.

Don't kid yourself – the second you email naked pics to a phone-fuck buddy you met online less than a week ago, you've effectively posted those pics to every amateur porn site this side of Chatsworth.

Just tell the guy no. If he presses you, turn the tables on him – insist that he be the one to send raunchy pics. If he backs down, that's the end of it.

If he follows through and sends you pics, tell him they aren't raunchy enough and that he has to send more. Never promise to send any in return.

Demand that he send you dirtier and dirtier pics of himself until he either backs down, grosses you out, or gives you so much blackmail ammunition that there's no harm in sending him a naked pic or two.

If you do ever decide to send him something, make sure he's familiar with the doctrine of mutually assured embarrassment, and let him know that you'd go nuclear on his ass if he ever stepped out of line with your pics.

Be wild and have fun, but take this shit seriously.

On begging to differ

after reading all your posts, i realized that your typical answer to questions like "how do i tell someone i want to fuck them?" is plain and simple: just fuck them. i beg to differ. it is not that easy, especially for people who are a bit shy and conservative. i am one of those.

i want to fuck this college senior who is probably going to become my graduate student supervisor. i guess it would be an awkward thing to do since it is likely that i will work with this guy for 2 years or so...but that still does not deter me from wanting him. would you please be so kind to give me some steps before actually getting to the just fuck him step?

You beg to differ? Okay, fine. Keep doing whatever it is that you're doing over and over again until you get a different result.

Also, keep missing the point. Keep letting life experiences pass you by. Keep making excuses for yourself, as if anyone gives a fuck that you're shy and conservative.

If you want something, go get it. It's not my job to give you strength. All I can do is point out that you're an idiot if you think any of this shit is supposed to be easy.

How do I tell the girl I like that I'm interested in her without being awkward?

What's your reason for telling her that you're interested? Are you trying to date her? Fuck her? What are your intentions? Has she done anything to lead you to believe that she might have feelings for you too? Hell, is she even available? If you don't have clear and immediate answers to all of these questions, there's no hope of you not making it awkward.

If he's under police investigation, he's not at all boyfriend material, right?

If you have to ask this question, you're not girlfriend material either.

Is there even a point in being in a romantic relationship between the ages of 18 to 21?

No, but that shouldn't stop you from trying.

If a member of the opposite sex with whom you're kind of friends asks you to go with him to a party, how can you know whether it's a date or just two people attending a thing together because they're kind of friends?

You do realize that you're the one who gets to decide whether it's a date, right? Yep, it's completely up to you. (Relax, you can change your mind at any point throughout the evening.)

Why is it that when I'm dating a guy and I start showing more interest, they decide to disappear?

Because you don't know the difference between showing interest and acting needy.

I'm 16, he's 32. Legal where I live, but what are your thoughts?

One day, when you're an actual adult, you'll look back and realize how creepy it was for this dude to be having sex with you at 16.

Why when I think I like a guy do I always over analyze everything and then end up convincing myself that I don't like him?

Because you don't know yourself.

What's the point in being hard to get? I don't understand why it's better than being easy. Why are harder to get people more deserving of respect?

The point isn't to be hard to get. The point is to have high standards. You don't understand because you don't know the difference.

How can you tell if a guy likes you or if he just wants to fuck you?

Fuck him and then see if the phone rings.

Why would a guy that likes a girl ignore her over the phone, yet, clearly show that he's head over heels in person?

Proximity to your pussy.

What's your idea of a nice date night?

I prefer a genuine human connection followed by a healthy round of athletic sex. The rest is just window dressing.

Do I message a guy I found on OK Cupid when I joined just for laughs?

Sure. Then date, fall in love and get married. You know, just for laughs.

If I have to question whether he's flirting or not, that means he's not flirting, right?

Maybe, or it could just mean that one of you isn't very good at it.

On a fucked-out cliché

There's an asshole who doesn't give a shit about me except for when we're fucking, who I'm a little bit in love with. And then there's the super nice guy who cares for me a lot, who I don't feel anything for. Help me break out of this, Coquette.

I can't do shit for you if these are the choices you bring me. Have some fucking self-respect and get rid of them both. Go be something other than a fucked-out cliché from the first act of every teen romantic comedy.

I mean, how hard is this? Once you've established that a guy is an asshole, stop fucking him and move on. Once you've established that you're never gonna have feelings for a guy who's romantically into you, set firm boundaries and don't lead him on.

It's bad enough to get either one of those things wrong, but to fuck up both at the same time and then bring it to me like it's some kind of dichotomy? Honestly, get your shit together.

Don't act like you're trapped between anything here. You created this triangle, and you maintain it for a reason. You can walk away from it any time you want, but you get something out of it, so don't come whining to me like it's beyond your control.

This is some silly girl shit. Start acting like a woman and handle your fucking business.

On a contender

He's a twenty-nine year old business owner with an enormous personality, well traveled, well read too. He's incredibly nice but he's ring leader of his wild circus of asshole friends.

I'm a twenty-three year old college dropout who's back in school and just came through the tail end of my

depression. I'm nice, I read, but am a very good (boring)
girl who over thinks everything.
   Please just tell me why it's not going to work out
before I fall tits up in love with him and his Ewan
McGregor smile? I want to think that in time I can
become a contender but that seems…unrealistic. Give it
to me Coquette; hurt me so he can't.

If you need me to point out a bunch of red flags and tell you
why a particular relationship is doomed, I can do that, but that's
not what you're really asking me. You just want me to say the magic
words that will protect you from emotional vulnerability. Sorry,
kiddo. There's no such thing as magic.

Pain is inevitable. Relationships end. You are going to get hurt
– maybe by this guy, but definitely by someone you care about, and
there's nothing you can do but accept it. If you live your life trying
to avoid the possibility of future pain, you will end up a numb and
timid creature without any stories worth telling.

Go ahead and fall tits up in love. Enjoy the feeling while it
lasts. Just promise me you'll quit thinking of yourself as a contender. That mindset is poisonous. You are worthy of him. Timing
and circumstance might prevent you two from ending up in a
relationship, but no matter what else happens, you are fucking
worthy of him.

Confessing feelings to a guy. Good idea, bad idea?
Why are you confessing? What do you want to have happen? If you
don't have quick, rational answers to both questions, it's a bad idea.

A one-night stand told me that I hide behind sarcasm.
What does that say about me?
It says you let your one-night stands talk too much.

Why is it that the more guys hit on me, the less attractive I feel?

The more guys hit on you, the more conscious you become of your own physicality, and any positive male attention is far outweighed by your negative self-image.

Do you have to date tons of people before you know you've met the one?

You might have to date tons of people before you believe me, but there is no such thing as 'the one'.

Why am I significantly more attracted to a guy knowing that he's dated a fuck ton of hot chicks?

The same reason all your clothes have logos on them.

What do you say to a 26-year-old man who claims he might never be able to love again?

Say, 'Lose my number, douchebag.'

Why do I always fall for guys that I barely know?

Because they're a blank slate onto which you can project your fantasies.

I just want to date myself. Or at least someone very similar to me. I know it's narcissistic, but is it wrong?

You only think you want to date yourself because you're blind to the fact that you're insufferable. (I promise, you wouldn't put up with your own bullshit.) What you really want is to date someone who allows you to be yourself, despite the fact that you're an asshole. Good luck.

What is a socially acceptable amount of people to sleep with before you get married?

You know what's socially unacceptable? A preoccupation with how many sexual partners you or anyone else might have had.

If he's the right guy but it's the wrong time, is he the wrong guy?

He's just a guy. The rest of it is all silly bullshit.

On a dirty whore

I'm a stripper, and I recently had a guy I've been sleeping with say I can come over after work, but only if I "shower off all the lapdances first." I ride my bike a lot, sometimes to work, and I asked if it was about being sweaty (just to absolutely clarify) and he said that my sweat in his bed was encouraged, but that other men's was not. What the fuck is his problem? That doesn't even make sense. Why does me showering make him feel like somehow I didn't just get done lap dancing for money?

Here's some brutal truth. The guy you've been sleeping with is an ignorant misogynist who likes the idea of fucking a stripper, but doesn't respect you or what you do for a living.

He asks you to take a shower because he secretly believes that you are an unclean woman. Not literally. Figuratively. He thinks you're a dirty whore, and making you shower off after your job is his weirdo way of keeping you as his whore but getting rid of the dirty part. It's outrageously disrespectful and more than just a little bit creepy.

Don't put up with that kind of negative bullshit for one damn second. Call him out for being disrespectful, and if he gives you even the slightest bit of attitude, stop fucking him.

Say it with me now: good dick is never worth disrespect.

Good dick is never worth disrespect.

On proto-exclusivity

Found out my guy was sleeping with somebody else in the first few months we were dating. We weren't calling it a relationship but it was exclusive (or so I thought). It was a year ago but I've only found out now. I'm devastated but I love him. Fight or flight?

If you weren't even calling it a relationship yet, then it certainly wasn't exclusive. Like you said, you just thought it was. That doesn't mean it was acceptable behavior, but it does put it in a gray area. Here's something to ask yourself: are you devastated that your boyfriend's dick was entering another vagina contemporaneously with yours? Or are you devastated that your boyfriend may have engaged in willful deception early on in your relationship? One is a manifestation of petty jealousy, and you should just get over it in time. The other is a legitimate concern for what may have been a breach of integrity.

Ultimately, the question you need to answer is, do you trust your boyfriend now, within the context of your long-term relationship? If you think you can trust him, then stick around, be pissed for a little while, and then get over it. If you don't think you can trust him, either find a way to repair that trust, or get the fuck out of the relationship.

Don't make this about some girl your boyfriend used to fuck. Make it about your boyfriend's integrity as it applies to your current relationship.

On bad dating advice

I'm no Mensa material, but I'm smart; not hot, but pretty and fit; well-educated (medicine graduate next year) and open-minded (thanks to traveling, mostly). I am also a yoga teacher and know 4 languages. Now, I'm no ideal and I'm not looking for an ideal man either; neither do I want a copy of myself. I just want somebody equal, a partner. My grandma has recently told me that, with my brains and confidence, I probably scare men away, and I should lower my expectations (and pretend to be less smart and versatile, basically). Is she right? Is it that men I'd consider equal are not interested in women like me because they can, as a rule, "do better"? Thanks.

Listen up, everyone: STOP LISTENING TO DATING ADVICE FROM YOUR GRANDPARENTS. Yes, they love you very much, and you love them too. No doubt they are adorable and wise and they have your best interests at heart, but that doesn't mean they have the slightest clue what it's like for those of us trying to find a life partner in this century.

Everything your grandmother told you was wrong. You don't scare men away. You scare boys away (and that's a good thing). If your expectations really are just to find an equal, then they are perfectly reasonable, and you shouldn't lower them. Don't pretend to be less smart or versatile. That's insane. (Sure, playing dumb can come in handy every once in a while, but it's not something you do with a man you respect.)

A man who is your equal *by definition* won't be preoccupied with 'doing better' than you. I think you may be in a mindset where you believe there is a certain tier of men that are your equal, that it's something you can identify based on a list of skills and accomplishments. That's your real problem. You're looking for a guy who looks good on paper.

I get that you're a box checker. It's obvious that's your style, and there's nothing wrong with that, but try not to define your equal by matching up résumés. That kind of dating profile mathematics is an exercise in pure frustration.

After he describes how I'm attractive and intelligent, what does it mean when he says "I'm not in a great place right now?"
It means, 'Fuck off and die.'

I currently like a guy, but we're both too shy to do anything about it. Are we doomed to just being friends?
Invite him over for movie night. Watch *Paper Heart*. It's all about love and being doomed by shyness. It's also incredibly boring, so after the first twenty minutes I suggest you go down on him.

Sometimes I think if I weren't such an independent woman, maybe I'd have a boyfriend once in a while...
Sometimes I wish I could spray my inbox with weed killer designed specifically for shitty voiceover from *Sex and the City*.

Five days is too long to not call a girl after cuming on her face, right?
A classy guy like you? I doubt she's counting.

I don't want to date him, but I don't want him to date anyone else. Thoughts?
Um, sucks to be you? Did you remember to take your pills? Put down the knife? I dunno, take your pick.

What's a classy way of rejecting guys that try to pick you up at a bar?
Six little words. 'I'm flattered, but I'm not available.'

So, oh wise one, how would YOU get a boyfriend?
First know why, then the how will follow.

How do you tell a flirt from one who actually likes you?
If she licks your balls, she actually likes you.

Should I call him back?
Do you have anything to say?

When's the best time to make a move?
The second before you start wondering whether you should.

On paying attention

I assume you are a beautiful girl, and obviously confident and full of spunk (spunk?). Are you flattered, interested, or just pissed and annoyed if a guy in a coffee shop / restaurant / bar asks you out? Should I say something when I see a girl I'm attracted to in these situations, or just keep my fucking mouth shut?

Dude. You should be able to tell whether I'm flattered, interested, or just pissed off and annoyed within a fucking microsecond of approaching me.

Women are walking symphonies of non-verbal cues. Eye contact. Body language. Facial expressions and gestures. Are you fucking kidding me? It's not even something we can consciously control. We drop a million hints a minute whether we like it or not, but most of the time you idiots are too blunted by alcohol or blind lust to notice.

If you walk up to me in a public setting, you'll get a flood of information about what I think of you long before we exchange a greeting. Just pay attention, man.

Was that an extra half-second of eye contact or did I just think your hair looked ridiculous? Am I wondering if you're going to talk to me, or am I wondering if the guy next to you went to high school with me?

These aren't difficult questions. You should instantly know the answer to them. I know conventional wisdom says otherwise, but come on, we aren't that fucking mysterious.

Now, if your larger question is whether you have the balls to approach me in the first place, that's entirely up to you. Just do us both a favor and have your exit planned in advance. Trust me, you want me wondering where you went, not wondering why you're still talking to me.

On vulnerability

Long story short, my usual pattern of meet a guy, hook up once, part ways forever changed when I met a guy, hooked up once, and then kept hooking up, drunk and sober. We never had a "talk" about "where things were going" because initially, he was more into me than I was into him. But once I started liking him, I felt like he could almost smell it, and he became less interested. We went from seeing each other every other day to once or twice a week—is it ending and I'm too dumb to realize

it, or is this just how things are? I'm afraid to be the
vulnerable one in this situation—I wanna know if it's
over so I can move on before he does.

Oh, grow up.

God forbid you should have enough self-respect not to play silly games, but since you insist on acting like a small woodland creature, you might as well scamper away now.

Then again, maybe you could stick around, accept the fact that you're already vulnerable, and practice your relationship skills like a woman instead of a girl.

Quit treating him like an opponent and start treating him like a partner in crime. Celebrate the fact that you might like him, and don't fear letting him know. If it doesn't work out, it'll hurt for a hot minute. So what.

Vulnerability is not the same thing as weakness.

On Relationships

On cheating

What exactly do you classify as cheating?

Willfully participating or conspiring to participate in an act of intimacy with the foreknowledge that your partner would reasonably consider that act to be a breach of the mutually understood and agreed upon terms of the relationship.

On tough shit

I cheated, came clean, and after some work, he forgave me. We've been together for over a year and shit has been fantastic. He's my dream dude, so why am I the one having trouble trusting him?

You're the one having trouble trusting him because you're the one who cheated. Cheaters are always plagued with trust issues. It's a little slice of karmic retribution I like to call cheater's irony.

I'd tell you I'm sorry, but I'm not. You cheated, and now you're worried he'll do the same to you. Tough shit. That's just how it goes.

On more tough shit

I've been with this man on and off since middle school. We have an eight year old daughter, which is the main reason why I'm still with him. He is a great man, but I am not truly happy. We have built a home for our daughter together, and I feel wrong to end it and have to put her through the heartbreak and mess. What the hell would you do?

It doesn't matter what the hell I would do, because I wasn't stupid enough to get knocked up by some guy I met at recess. What the hell you should do is continue putting your daughter first, and get ridiculous notions of being 'truly happy' out of your head. 'Truly happy' doesn't exist. It's just another bullshit manifestation of the 'happily ever after' fantasy.

You've built a home for your daughter with a great man. Nicely done, but you don't get to fuck it all up over a mild case of existential ennui. I'm sorry that you're bored, but tough shit. It's not your daughter's fault that you regret settling down with your first pre-teen crush. She's eight, so for at least the next decade, her best interests come first, and your best interests come second. That's what it means to be a mother.

Now, as for becoming happier more often in your current circumstances, take a hot minute to examine what exactly you feel is missing in your relationship. Do you want more passion? More excitement? Or do you just want a shiny new dick to sit on every once in a while? There are any number of obvious solutions to all kinds of unfulfilled needs, but if your problem really boils down to a bunch of 'this isn't how I thought my life would turn out' angst, then please just shut the fuck up and go do some yoga like all the other listless housewives.

On a certain kind of life

My boyfriend and I have known each other for 5 years, and we've been together for the last year and a half. He's 27 and I'm 23. We're in the process of leaving our respective apartments to move into one together. I

assume this means he'll propose sometime afterward,
and he's alluded to it several times after a couple beers.
However, that whole "I've never found anyone greater!
You're my soouuulmate!" (shit everyone thinks when
they start a new relationship) got thrown out the window
like a big gulp on the highway a pretty long time ago.

We've had our fair share of break ups and make ups,
and what I'm simply learning is that we're alright with
each other. We spend majority of both our time with
one another, we're best friends, we're good room-mates,
we have good sex, and he's head over heels for me. I
think we're practical, but I'm worried maybe I could be
settling just because it "makes sense."

Doesn't every couple eventually get this way? Or am
I just being an asshole?

Yes, every couple gets this way, and yes, you are settling. Then again, yes, it does make sense, and yes, you've got it pretty much as good as it gets.

What do you want me to tell you? You two are best friends who have good sex and can live together without climbing the walls. That's a fucking marriage right there, with bonus points if you can stand being around his family.

Thing is, do you want that life? If you do, great. Go get a dog, squirt out a couple of kids, and start wearing ugly jeans.

If not though, be strong enough to admit it. This isn't about your boyfriend. I'm sure he's fine, but he's also as interchangeable as a side item on an Applebee's menu. This is about a certain kind of middle-mind, middle-class, middle-of-the-road American experience that you're signing up for at a relatively young age.

Again, if that's what you want, cool. There's nothing wrong with eatin' good in the neighborhood, but I get the sense that you really don't know how to feel about any of it.

Be careful. You don't strike me as self-realized enough to be content with what's being handed to you, but neither are you dumb enough to be happy leading an unexamined life. That's a recipe for disaster.

I don't mean to freak you out, but if you follow the path of least resistance without some honest self-exploration, you're just setting yourself up for a miserable seven-year itch followed by a tacky mid-life crisis.

Good luck figuring it all out.

On long term and long distance

I can't stop thinking about the person my partner dated before me. They only dated for a few months but I know it was really intense and even though we've been together for ages it keeps cropping up in my mind. I never used to be jealous before, why is this happening now, so far into our relationship? It's completely irrational and it's driving me fucking crazy. I don't know what to do anymore.

Let me make the problem obvious for you by translating some of your bullshit:

When you say, 'I can't stop thinking about the person my partner dated before me', what you really mean is, 'I can't help projecting my own relationship insecurities onto the nearest available target.'

When you say, 'I know it was really intense and even though we've been together for ages it keeps cropping up in my mind', what you really mean is, 'I'm terrified that they had better sex than we do, especially now that things are getting stale between us.'

When you say, 'It's completely irrational and it's driving me fucking crazy', what you really mean is, 'I'm not self-aware enough to recognize self-destructive patterns in my behavior.'

And of course, when you say, 'I don't know what to do

anymore', what you're really saying is, 'I've never really known how to handle the inevitable ennui that sets in with every long-term relationship I've ever had.'

I love my boyfriend but when he's really drunk he's kind of a dick to me. What do I do?
Don't put up with it.

In your opinion, is it ever acceptable to marry/spend the rest of your life with your very first boyfriend?
Sure. Even in marriage, your first doesn't have to be your only. (And I hope you understand that 'marry' and 'spend the rest of your life with' are two very different things. It's naïve of you to conflate them.)

In a weird series of events, I found out my boyfriend's old fling had an abortion. He doesn't know. He's religious and it would upset him. I'm allowed to keep this secret to my grave? Yes?
Definitely, yes. (It's really not your place to tell him.)

What does "I want to be with you, I'm 100% committed to this relationship, and if you asked me to marry you I would say yes, but a wedding is a whole big thing" mean? I kind of feel shitty for wanting to get married, now.
Quit feeling shitty. (That's one of your most annoying personality traits.) Your potential fiancé is rightfully terrified of having to plan and pay for a wedding. You obviously have no idea how stressful and expensive that shit really is.

I sleep with guys to feel a little less lonely because no one wants to commit to an actual relationship. WTF is wrong with me?

Nothing is wrong with you. Stop having sex to fill an emotional void, don't confuse loneliness with being alone, and don't let your relationship status have an effect on your self-worth.

We've been dating for 4 years. He wants to get married in another two years, I wanted to have been married like yesterday. It feels shitty to give in to his timeline of events and yet – if we both agree on the end goal – why can't I just be happy and enjoy the wait?

Because deep down you know damn well he's just stringing you along. (I mean, come on. Is there even a ring on your finger? I didn't think so.) If he wanted to be married to you, he would be married to you. Clearly, he doesn't. Hell, it doesn't even seem like he wants to be engaged to you, so unless there's some super-obvious reason for waiting two years, you should really consider the possibility that he's only agreeing to marriage on some far-off, theoretical horizon just to shut you up.

Why am I so afraid to be mad at my boyfriend?

You *are* mad at him. You're afraid of something else.

On four years as the other woman

I've been fucking someone with a girlfriend for four years. Apparently, he loves us both. It's fun when we're together until we're not, then I'm left to think of him with her. How do I regain control of my emotions? I don't want to care anymore. I don't want to care about him.

Regain control of your emotions? Fuck you. It's not like you got drunk one night and accidentally fucked a dude who wasn't single. You've spent nearly half a damn decade as the other woman. Quit acting like you lost your free will and take some responsibility for your shitty behavior.

If you don't want to care about him any more, step back and recognize this dude for the duplicitous piece of shit that he is. Start caring for your own emotional well-being, and have some fucking self-respect.

You're better than this, aren't you? Come on, at least admit that you deserve more than being a mistress. Who gives a flying fuck if he says he loves you both? Do you have any idea how slimy that sounds? You're nothing but a runner-up piece of ass to a douchebag capable of long-term deceit and emotional dishonesty.

This guy has zero integrity. You don't want his love. It's not worth it. It never was. Cut your losses and fucking end it.

On age differences

I'm 20 going on 40. He's 30 going on 20. Does this work? Or am I just fooling myself into thinking our respective stages in life won't get in the way of a serious relationship?

You're fooling yourself, but not about what you think. You're not going on 40. You just think you're way more mature than you actually are. He's not going on 20. He's just an emotionally stunted man-child more comfortable dating a girl than a woman.

Yes, you're still a girl. Quit making that face.

The good news is that your respective stages in life won't necessarily get in the way of a serious relationship. You're not gonna live happily ever after, but hey, sticking it out for a year or two at your age definitely counts for something.

On not feeling guilty

*I cheated, but I don't feel guilty. I really like the guy
I'm with and I wasn't looking for something more or
different than what I already have. I'm not sure why
I did it, but I feel like I probably will again. Is there
something wrong with me? It seems everyone else is
so sure cheating is wrong. I understand in theory, but
I wouldn't be upset if my guy messed around with
someone else, so I guess I just don't get what the big deal
is. Help?*

You're so full of shit.

You cheated because it felt good, you'll do it again because you
have no impulse control, and you don't feel guilty because you have
sociopathic tendencies.

If you don't care whether your guy messes around with someone else, that's fine, but this isn't about the sex. It's about the lie.
Would you be cool with it if your guy repeatedly and maliciously
lied to you? Didn't think so.

Feel free to be in an open relationship, but you have to establish
that *before* fucking other people. Have some fucking integrity.

On the seven-year itch

*I'm 37 and feel like I'm married to the wrong man. He's
a great provider and loves me unconditionally. We don't
have kids yet, but he wants to. Should I risk leaving
him to try to find "the one" even though I'm no spring
chicken?*

You're 37? Jesus, lady. Put down that Chardonnay-stained copy
of *Eat, Pray, Love* and back away slowly because that nonsense has
you talking like a doe-eyed teenager.

I'm sorry that you don't wake up every morning blissed out with a raging ladyboner for your husband, but that doesn't mean you're married to the wrong man, and it sure as hell doesn't imply the existence of the right man.

It's sad to see a woman your age still suffering from the delusion that there is such a thing as 'the one'. Get that Prince Charming crap out of your head. There are just a bunch of men out there, any number of whom could be perfectly compatible life partners for you. Sure, there's a slim chance you could meet someone you think is better and, over time, build a more intimate connection with him than your current husband. Probably not, though. You don't strike me as the type with realistic expectations of the men who are available to romantically unfulfilled 37-year-old divorcées.

The real problem here is that you've got a nasty little case of the seven-year itch, and you're trying to scratch it Oprah's Book Club style. All that suburban housewife ennui is combining with your massive sense of entitlement, and before you know it you'll have an ex-husband paying spousal support so you can go on some scented-candle journey of self-discovery. Ugh.

I wish we could just skip to the part where you get a little taste of enlightenment, but you're still seeking contentment in the silly fiction of a perfect mate, in spite of the fact that you've already said your vows to a great provider who loves you unconditionally.

Sorry, lady. Your husband isn't the problem. You are. As long as you're of the belief that someone else can be the source of your happiness, you're doomed to wallow in this minor state of existential crisis.

There's no chance of you finding what you're looking for if you keep looking outside yourself. Leave your husband. Don't leave him. Whatever. In the end, just take some personal responsibility for both your actions and your own happiness.

Good luck finding a clue.

*At what point, if any, is it okay/right/appropriate/
required to tell a new partner that you were raped a
few years ago? Honest by nature, but also terrified of
opening up.*

It's never required. It's okay if you want to, and it's okay if you
don't. Appropriateness depends on the context. It's perfectly appropriate to tell your new partner in the natural course of growing
intimate, but it might be inappropriate if you use it as some sort
of relationship test. In your case, maybe wait until you're not so
terrified. A little anxiety is normal, but too much might mean it's
too soon to share.

*Is it possible to ask for more communication and/
or more time together in a relationship while still
remaining casual?*

Yes. Ask for what you want. Know what it is and be specific, but
just fucking ask.

*If a guy cheats on you once, why does it mean he'll cheat
again? What if he learns his mistake and regrets it?*

Regret is a very poor indicator of whether someone will repeat the
same mistake. When it comes to behavior, look for patterns, not
promises.

*She cheated on me a year ago. We broke up. She begged
me to get back together. We did. Why? Because I've
fucked up in the past and I believe in second chances. We
are doing okay and 95% of the time I trust her. Why can't
I get rid of that last 5%?*

Because she cheated on you a year ago.

He cheated on me and we're trying to make it work, but it's just not the same anymore. Will it ever be okay?
Sure it will, just not with him.

On getting over an abortion

I recently had an abortion. My partner had a bit of a tough time dealing with my emotional wreckage afterward so he talked to his mum about what he was feeling. She's now visiting both of us and cannot stop talking about how excited she is about becoming a grandmother (her step-son and his wife are having a baby). She keeps asking me my opinion on names for the baby, if I want to go shopping with her for toys and clothes. I told her that I am happy for her but I can't participate in all the baby stuff at the moment but she won't let up. My boyfriend thinks I should "just get over it". Am I being oversensitive?

So let me get this straight.

You're over here trying to deal with the emotional trauma of terminating a pregnancy, and your pathetic weakling of a boyfriend can't handle it, so he runs off crying to his mommy.

Then the crusty old bitch shows up, and in a mind-boggling display of self-centered thoughtlessness starts rambling on relentlessly about babies, which understandably upsets you, and your boyfriend's response to this whole ordeal is, 'just get over it'.

Sweetheart, the question isn't whether you're being oversensitive. The question is whether you should castrate your boyfriend before or after you kick his mother in the face.

He does not get to utter the words 'just get over it' ever again. Do you understand me? Not once. Ever. You are entitled to as much time, love and support as you need from him to deal with your emotions over that abortion.

Be strong, sister. Don't put up with his punk-ass shit, and don't ever let him forget about his culpability in that abortion. Never hesitate to remind him that however tough he thinks it's been for him, it has been infinitely worse for you.

Also, don't be afraid to tell his mother to shut the fuck up.

On a manwhore

My boyfriend has had sex with 53 people before me, and admitted to doing lots of cheating before me. Obviously I care about him and I'm not gonna end things over his past, but I'm kind of worried ... Does once a manwhore mean always a manwhore?

I know you won't take my advice, but I'm gonna give it to you anyway. Break up with this guy *immediately*. It's not because he's a manwhore, nor is it because he's admitted to past infidelities (although neither of those things bode well for your relationship).

No, the real reason you should break up with him is because he knows (or pretends to know) the *exact number* of people he's slept with in the upper double digits. It's not about him having sex with a lot of people. It's about the fact that he keeps a running tally.

Trust me on this. Once a dude's exploits fall outside the realm of easily remembered single digits, keeping a precise set of sexual statistics is more than just a little bit creepy. It's also a red flag that says he's got something really unhealthy to prove.

I know staying with him is your mistake to make, but I promise that you're making one.

On fucking up big time

I cheated on my boyfriend with my best friend, who is married.

As much as I hated to, I ended it with my boyfriend and I ended it with my best friend. Because what I did was fucked up.

I know I deserve it, but now I really have no one. I'm totally lost. I don't know what to do.

Find yourself.

You hit the self-destruct button on your life. Why? There's a reason you fucked up this big. Figure it out.

It takes a lot of self-loathing to show so little respect for the people you love like that. Where is it coming from? Identify the source of all that mess and deal with it.

It's not good enough to just shrug your shoulders and acknowledge that you hate yourself. You have to put in some serious introspection here. The goal is to gain enough self-awareness so that you won't feel the need, consciously or otherwise, to go nuclear on your interpersonal relationships again.

Oh, and while you're at it, you also have to forgive yourself. Good luck with that.

On some trifling shit

My boyfriend has pictures of his ex-wife and ex-girlfriend still on his phone. He's explained the situation that he hardly talks to either of them anymore, although he was involved very deeply and completely in these former relationships. The pictures bother me (example: his ex-wife in a sexy maid halloween outfit; his ex-girlfriend making that goddamn kissy face in a recent picture she sent him). Without seeming like a jealous

control freak (which I am not), how do I get him to
remove the pictures?

Um, you *are* a jealous control freak. You're just not any
good at it.

Not only are you in denial about your jealousy, but you lack
the basic manipulation skills to convince a boy to delete pictures
from his phone. Pathetic.

Your best bet is to slow your roll and hope you wake up cool
tomorrow.

Good luck.

i don't feel like a partner, i feel like a trophy
Get the fuck out of that relationship.

Do or don't tell my boyfriend, who I love, that there was
a short period a few years ago when I was having sex for
money?
If you have to ask me, then you aren't prepared to tell him.

He makes six figures. I'm a student with no income. I
had to get an abortion (very hard, I'm pro-choice but
come from a religious background) and he only paid for
half. Is it wrong that it bothers me?
It should bother you. It speaks volumes about his lack of character and how little he values what you had to go through. Demand
he pay for the other half, and then cut him out of your life
completely.

I'm dating a guy who is a selfish asshole 60% of the
time and a genuinely enjoyable person 40% of the time.
I'm not sure if I'm dating him because I like the 40% so

much or because I'm scared of the turmoil dumping him will bring to my life.

You aren't dating a guy. You're being held emotionally hostage by a selfish asshole with mood swings. Big difference, kiddo.

Every time I tell my partner they're doing something that upsets me, they take it as a personal attack of me reminding them how "fucked up and terrible" they are. What do I do?

Stop putting up with manipulative bullshit from an insecure partner.

Am I terrible for thinking my girlfriend is really ugly when I wake up in the morning next to her, seeing as she has no makeup on?

Yes.

On a boring marriage

You've probably already had this one (a million times) but I'm annoying and lazy so I'll ask it anyways. What should I do if I'm bored in my marriage and have two small kids. Wait it out because we're *both* boring and fat now? or let him know and deal with the consequences?

Wait it out? You're in a marriage, not a line at the grocery store.

Get your shit together, woman. Children are no excuse for being fat and boring. If your husband isn't doing it for you, feel free to tell him, but don't be surprised if you aren't his idea of a hot time either.

Sure, you've got kids to raise. Those little buckets of obligation are your first priority, but after that, you should both feel free to chase whatever excitement you can handle.

Presumably, you and your husband have something in common other than your offspring. If so, go find some fun together. If not, go find some fun separately.

Either way, have a fucking honest conversation with each other about your emotional conditions. Get that shit out on the table.

Otherwise, all that boredom is gonna fester into resentment and anger as you lead a life of quiet desperation. You'll end up damaging your kids with your loveless marriage, and they'll move to Los Angeles to pursue dreams of acting.

Trust me, you don't want that to happen.

On what's inappropriate

I have an ex-wife. We get along all right. I see her once every few months and we have lunch and talk about our work and families and so on.

I have a girlfriend. The girlfriend (who is otherwise not even remotely neurotic or whiny) seems to think that my amicable relationship with my ex-wife is inappropriate.

What do you think?

Inappropriate. I hate that word.

It's used by persnickety little bitches who are inevitably trying to cover up some negative emotional response they won't otherwise admit to having.

Go ahead. Make her confess to it. It's as simple as asking your girlfriend, 'How does my amicable relationship with my ex-wife make you feel?'

If she's emotionally honest, she'll admit to being jealous,

embarrassed, resentful or ashamed. That gut-level response is the real problem.

Maybe you can fix that shit, and maybe you can't, but once the underlying negativity is addressed, you'd be amazed at what's suddenly appropriate.

On new levels of stupidity

i am currently dating a few guys, and have been proposed to by two (one, i think because the other one did). guy#1 is my best friend, but he is a little small in the undies department. he has never left me unsatisfied... HE is the one who has a problem with it... and trust me, he knows how to use it. he is even willing to let me have other "friends" to make up for his inadequacies.

guy#2-makes more money, is adequately sized (although he claims he is "bigger than average" which he is NOT). He and I have been friends for a long time, and I am not sure if he only asked me because he feels that is what i want because the other guy proposed first.

what do i do? you will tell me straight.

I think you should finish getting your PhD in astrophysics from Caltech.

Really, I don't know what the guys at the Jet Propulsion Lab would do without you if you decided to give up your budding career as a rocket scientist just to marry a man with a slightly less-than-average penis.

I know, at the moment nothing seems more important than choosing your life partner based on the size of his genitalia, but have you considered what a blow this will be to the scientific community? A mind like yours, wasted on a man who is 'a little small in the undies department'.

Please, I'm begging you, for the sake of humanity, don't allow yourself to be distracted by suitors of middling girth like some common shallow whore.

A genius of your caliber deserves nothing less than to marry a man with a truly massive cock. We're talking two coke cans stacked end to end. Flaccid. Your research is too important to mankind for you to settle for anything less.

On being emotionally involved

I feel like I'm getting too emotionally involved in my relationship. I've been dating this guy for a while now, and I literally have never felt so, I don't know, caught up in it all. I'm only 20 and I literally want to marry him. I think about it all the time. I shouldn't be thinking of marriage, I should be out getting drunk and hanging out with friends. You know what I do instead? BAKE. I'm dreaming of a little domestic life and I don't know how to handle it. How do I get out of this terrible, terrible, slump I'm in Coketalk?

First of all, stop using the word *literally* as an intensifier. Also, spit out your gum.

Listen, cupcake. There is nothing wrong with daydreaming about wedding days and white picket fences. You've got a crush on this guy. That's great. Enjoy it, but don't worry. It'll pass.

You're getting all freaked out because you think you're in a slump. Nope. This is a peak. You're at the top of the fucking mountain right now, babe. The slump comes later when Mr Abercrombie & Fitch decides to dump you for another sorority girl because you got too drunk one night and started absent-mindedly throwing around the M-word.

This is the first time you've ever been emotionally involved in a relationship, and you're over here complaining that your bicycle has training wheels. Trust me, you need them. You're still a child who doesn't yet think for herself. That's fine, but I'd be wasting my time expounding on the virtues of vulnerability and owning your emotions.

For now, just keep baking and do what feels good.

so are you totally opposed to the idea of long-term romantic relationships or what
No. I prefer long-term romantic relationships. I'm just opposed to staying in unhealthy or imbalanced ones.

He is perfect for me and treats me amazingly well, but he is also a workaholic. How do I get more time with him?
You don't. Learn to deal with it, or move on.

Sometimes I just want to ignore the guy I'm dating even though I really like him. Why?
It's one of the ways you exert control over the power dynamics in your relationships. (Remember how your mom used to give your dad the silent treatment? Yep, there you go.)

How do I stop feeling lonely when I'm with him?
If being with him makes you feel lonely, take the fucking hint.

I treat my boyfriend badly for no reason. Why?
Because he lets you, so you don't respect him, so you treat him badly, and thus repeats the cycle until you both hate each other.

My wife is fit and attractive, but her c-section scar is a total turnoff for me. What should I do? Tell her? Ask her to look into scar removal treatments? Just keep the lights off?

You should become less of a shallow, insensitive asshole.

On your tan and your respect

im gay and ive been dating my boyfriend for ten months now. we broke up like a week ago. why? because i went tanning!!! who in their right mind does that? weve always had a disfunctional relationship, but i really did love him. even pasyt the physical fights and petty little arguements. the sad part about all of this, is tht he cheated on me and i forgave him, but he breaks up with me because of a few U.V. rays? I cant figure it out, so can you tell me why im still in love with this asshole?

Your tan isn't the reason he broke up with you. Quite frankly, tanning is just a symptom of the larger problem that caused him to break up with you.

He broke up with you because you're a queeny little bitch.

Yes, you are.

You know how I know? Because of that sound you just made. Also because you forgave him for cheating on you, and because you're an adult male who uses multiple exclamation points for emphasis.

He doesn't respect you, not even enough to tell you the real reason he dumped you. Instead, he just pushes your buttons by telling you it was something as stupid as tanning.

That's why you're still in love. He pushes your buttons, and you're the type who thrives on chaos and drama. Fuck that shit. It's not healthy, and it makes for an awful pattern of relationships.

Have some fucking dignity and move on.

On finding yourself in an affair

*I've been "dating" this guy for a couple weeks casually.
It's more like we get together for dinner and then fuck
like rabbits, but I have absolutely no problem with that.
He's a no strings kind of guy that's still genuine and
fun to hang around/party with. It's kind of the perfect
"relationship" for me. Then, the other day, he forgot to
take his wedding ring off. First time I ever saw it. I don't
necessarily enjoy it when women sleep with married
or taken men, and now I feel like shit. I somehow feel
like I shouldn't because I didn't know (and, like an ass,
never noticed anything that would indicate that he was)
but I can't help it. I've cut off contact for now, but I don't
know how to get rid of the guilty feeling. Any advice?*

You cut off contact for now? Fuck that. Confirm that he's married, and if he is, cut off contact *permanently*.

The guilty feeling exists because you haven't done the right
thing and actually ended it yet. Finish the job, sweetie. Up to this
point, you haven't been complicit in an affair, but if you continue
seeing him, you will have a reason for the guilt.

It's not worth it, by the way. Consider this a learning experience
and move on. Don't waste your energy or your emotions on people
who lack integrity. A man who engages in that level of calculated
deception doesn't deserve one more second of your time.

On the ex-girlfriend stash

*I'm dating a 28 year old who kept all of his ex girlfriends
weird-ass sex toys in a dresser drawer after 4 months of
being apart. Do you think he's just lazy or waiting for her
to come back so they can have some kinkysexytimes?*

Relax.

All single guys have a drawer in their closet filled with ex-girlfriend shit. It's a universal truth, just like all guys have a bedside stash of condoms, and all guys have a secret collection of porn.

It was bound to be something – a leftover piece of jewelry, some lingerie, an old t-shirt, or in your case, a few sex toys. Big deal. Nothing to worry about.

Most guys go to the trouble of hiding the ex-girlfriend drawer. It's actually a good sign that your man doesn't give enough of a fuck to bother making it a secret.

Oh, and here's a little parting gift for you: don't refer to them as 'weird-ass' sex toys when he's around. It sounds negative and judgmental, and you probably don't want him thinking that you're any less wild in bed than his ex-girlfriend.

On how to beat an xbox

How does a girl compete with the XBox 360?

My boyfriend ignores me all the time. We get home from work and he immediately heads for the couch and stays on it long after I go to bed.

We had a daughter about 2 years ago, so in the beginning my libido was none existent, but that's changed. I'm back in my size 2 jeans, you can barley see any stretch marks and I'm not ugly.

I try to initiate sex, I try to get him off the XBox and his response is "Babe! Your making me die" Seriously WTF is that?! Mastubating is not as good as the real deal. So what's a girl to do?

Stretch marks and an Xbox addicted babydaddy? You are living my nightmare.

Listen, you picked this guy. Normally I'd tell you to suck it up and deal with the consequences of your stupid life choices, but for the sake of your daughter, I'm gonna ignore my bitchier instincts and throw you a bone here.

In situations like this one, your daughter is what's known as 'leverage'. As long as your boyfriend wants to be a part of her life, you have positional advantage to affect his behavior. I suggest you use it.

For your daughter's sake, for his sake, really, for America's sake, I want you to take that Xbox out to an empty field and smash it with a fucking baseball bat. Remember the fax machine scene from *Office Space*? Yeah. Do that. Go crazy.

Your child will *not* be raised in a house with video games. It's as simple as that. Never forget, you are well within your rights and duties as the mother of the house to lay down the motherfucking law.

Sure, he'll be pissed. He'll be furious, but what's he gonna do? *Not* fuck you? Right. You're already used to that. Let him throw a tantrum like the child he obviously is. Too bad. It's time for him to grow the fuck up.

And don't listen to any of his man-of-the-house bullshit about 'after a long, hard day at work…' He's not out grabbing a beer with the guys to blow off a little steam. He's a lazy sack of shit parked on the sofa playing video games instead of spending time with his family.

If he wants to be the man of the house, then he needs to put away childish things, and you know what? Now that he's a father, he's *obligated* to grow up.

That's how you compete with an Xbox. You don't even allow it a place in your home.

Is it always a bad idea to forgive a cheater?

No, it's actually a good idea to forgive a cheater, but that doesn't mean forget, and that sure as hell doesn't mean give back your trust.

What does it mean when a guy says that he doesn't deserve you? Red flag?

Yeah. It's a bullshit way of saying that he appreciates the things you do for him, but he's not quite into you enough to commit to a relationship.

Why do all the married couples I know seem so unhappy?

Because unhappiness is the resting state of marriage.

If unhappiness is the resting state of marriage, what's the resting state of being single?

Loneliness.

What's worse: Marriage or loneliness?

Thinking those are your only two options.

What do you think of people that are in happy relationships but break up to "see what else is out there"?

Don't kid yourself. Those relationships are either shallow to the point of worthlessness, or they aren't really happy.

On girl meets boy

Here's the story: girl meets boy. girl likes boy. boy is out of her league. girl and boy become friends. better friends. best friends. girl falls in love with boy. girl overanalyzes everything that boy does. this causes drama. boy eventually walks away from friendship. girl and boy get back in contact. girl tries not to be passive agressive this time and just asks him what's going on. boy calls girl out for overanalyzing the shit out of everything again. girl and boy talk. girl gets upset and asks boy to call her. says she misses him. boy tells girl he will. boy never calls or anything. girl texts him a week later about something else. they talk. what the fuck is going on with the boy?

Boy likes girl. Boy doesn't love girl. Boy will *never* love girl. Girl doesn't want to deal with reality. Boy doesn't want to deal with girl.

On a girlfriend in the wings

I met this guy three weeks ago and he's really great: kind, great in bed, attentive... and he has a girlfriend. WELL, it's more complicated than that. He dated a girl that graduated from our school last year and she high-tailed it to another country and will be there until February. Thus, they're in an "open relationship" until then. Should I drop this guy ASAP? I feel like our relationship/tryst/whatever has an expiration date on it and that he's only using me for sex. But another part of me likes spending time with him. We're not only hook-up buddies either, so it's not like I'm getting the "booty-text" every night at 2 AM. What do you think?

He's respectful? Open? Great in bed? If it were me, I'd fuck him silly through New Year's and when the girlfriend comes back in February, I'd offer them a threesome for Valentine's Day. Why? Because I know I could handle it.

Every relationship has an expiration date, so don't fear it. Just enjoy your time with him and be cool. The girlfriend's return doesn't have to be sticky or awkward. In fact, by being the cool chick, you can take away a lot of the girlfriend's power to affect that expiration date.

In other words, don't try and steal him. Don't get possessive. Just rock his world, and more than likely she'll be the one who has to steal him back.

Actually, that's where the threesome comes in. I'm serious about that. Offering up a Valentine's Day threesome will checkmate the entire love triangle. Here's how it works:

If you offer a threesome and she's not into it, then you've forced his hand without being possessive. He has to pick either you or her.

If he picks you, you win.

If he picks her, the threesome offer will burn a hole of regret through his male ego within a month, and you will have sabotaged their relationship by being the cool chick. Not the best outcome, but satisfying nonetheless.

On the other hand, if you offer a threesome and she's into it, then suddenly you're the one setting the agenda.

Give them both orgasms, and at that point, you can pretty much take the relationship any direction you want. It doesn't matter if you're sharing him, because you're the one in control.

I know this sounds a bit devious, but it's not. This isn't black magic. None of it will work if you're malicious. It's all just a complicated variation on the 'kill 'em with kindness' method.

Of course, my plan requires that you at least be willing to eat a little pussy. I don't know. I guess I kind of take that shit for granted these days.

Whatever. Just have fun.

On teenage sweethearts

I've been in a relationship for four years off-and-on with the same guy. How practical would it be to move in together? Both of us have steady jobs, he's already moved out with room mates at the moment, but I'm still living with my parents so that I can save up more money for the possibility of us taking things to the next level.

Red flag number one: 'four years'

Red flag number two: 'off-and-on'

Red flag number three: 'but I'm still living with my parents'

Do you really want me to answer this question? My advice has nothing to do with practicality, and I promise you will not like it.

Here's a hint: as much as sentimental conservative types may disagree, I feel strongly that settling down with your teenage sweetheart is a recipe for a mid-life crisis in your early thirties when you realize that the only cock you've ever seen is attached to a man who resents you for stealing his youth and won't fuck you because you've got short hair and stretch marks. Not that it matters to you, because you fell out of love with him years before and now you subsist on fantasies about the personal lives of pretty people on daytime television.

So, are you sure you want my advice on this one?

On getting out of the closet

Ok here goes, I cheat on my wife with random hook ups with men. I usually just get blown. I fucked a guy twice. I just do it for the release since I get nothing at home.
   Your thoughts?

Listen up, Congressman. Stop cheating on your wife with anonymous dudes. It's super creepy.

If you're trapped in a loveless marriage, get the fuck out – in this case even if you have kids. You'll do more psychological damage to your offspring as a self-hating closeted homosexual than you will as an openly gay divorcee.

Also, stop voting Republican.

To what extent should a partner's romantic past matter in a relationship?
Only to the extent that either of you can't leave it there.

What do you think about marrying your first love? Does everyone have to go through heartbreak?
Do what makes you happy, but you're a fool if you think marrying your first love is any kind of protection against heartbreak.

What if you're not sexually attracted to your soulmate?
There's no such thing as a soulmate. If your partner doesn't turn you on any more, I suggest you both evaluate your sexual needs and then re-evaluate the terms of your relationship.

Why am I obsessed with my boyfriend's ex?
Because she used to touch your boyfriend's penis.

What's the best way to deal with emotional infidelity?
Honest communication.

How do I reconcile the fact that I have an awesome boyfriend whom I love dearly, but who is lazy beyond belief and won't get his act together? I want to conquer the world, but I feel anchored by his laziness.
Substitute 'ex' for 'awesome'. Boom. Reconciled.

Why do I want my boyfriend to stop loving me as much as he does?
Because romantic obligation makes you uncomfortable.

Is it worth it to try to change anyone?
Is it insanity to believe that you can?

Is the one you love supposed to piss you off like no other creature on this planet?
It should be possible but not probable.

Is it OK to flirt when you're married?
It's fine with me, but you might wanna ask your wife.

How much bullshit is it worth putting up with for true love?
Please do not put the word true in front of love. Love is love, and you are not the Princess Bride.

What's the most important quality in a relationship?
Mutual respect.

My wife says my shoes need to be put away. Do I have to do this?
What are you, twelve? Go ahead and substitute the word 'mommy' for the word 'wife' in this ridiculous question. Notice how the tone didn't change? Grow up, dude.

The man I'm fucking is in love with my best friend. He treats her with respect, and he treats me like nothing. Guess this is what I get for fucking him, right?
No, this is what you get for thinking your vagina is a hole through which respect passes.

*Negotiating an open relationship because your partner is
a mediocre lover – coping or cop out?*
It's coping if you're honest with him about why you're not satisfied,
otherwise it's copping out.

*Why do smart, beautiful women get stuck in abusive
relationships (physical and emotional)?*
Because brains and beauty ain't got shit to do with crazy.

When is it okay to lie to someone you love and respect?
A good rule of thumb is that if you have to ask yourself this question, now is not the time.

*Why do you think most people are so against 'open
relationships'?*
They find it threatening to what is ultimately a false sense of
security.

*At what age should a man stop looking for the perfect
partner and just settle for someone half way attractive
with a job that you can stand to share a place with?*
A man would know better than to expect perfection in the first
place. A man would also understand what it really means to settle.
Grow the fuck up.

How do you know when to give up on someone?
When they've shown you who they are, and it isn't enough.

My boyfriend cheated on me and is now dating the girl
he cheated on me with. Yet, I would still take him back if
he asked. What is wrong with me?

A complete lack of self-respect.

Relationships are difficult and don't work out, what's the
point?

Relationships are the point. They're all we've got. Quit whining
and get back out there.

On boredom and chaos

I've been with my boyfriend for three years and I love
him so much. He's truly my partner in everything. We
adopted a dog recently and we're moving into our own
place in a few months. Everything is sort of gliding
effortlessly forward and that scares me for some reason.
I've never had a relationship last this long that didn't
have some serious red flags by now. He is so supportive
and reliable. Since I met him my life has become much
more calm and stable, but sometimes that also seems
boring. It's like we're too comfortable with each other,
which I know sounds like complaining that my jewels
are too heavy. How to I keep from becoming ungrateful
for this life we have together? How do you keep this sort
of thing fresh?

The relationship isn't boring. Life is boring, and you're just
now noticing for the first time as an adult because you aren't being
distracted by some youthful flavor of chaos.

If you want to keep from becoming ungrateful, do some serious
soul-searching and identify exactly what's missing in your life now
that you're in a stable, healthy relationship. 'Things aren't fresh

any more' isn't a good enough answer. Be very fucking specific, and very fucking honest with yourself. Remember, fresh isn't the same thing as exciting, and excitement isn't the same thing as chaos.

If you can't come up with a specific and valid problem other than the mild state of boredom known as everyday life, then guess what? This is as good as it gets. Take that as good news or bad. Either way, you'd be wise not to go searching for a taste of chaos. That shit isn't a spice.

On bringing too much to the table

I make 80 percent of the money and do 75% of the housework. I'm tired. I'm also doing feminism wrong somehow. Help.

Don't ask me for help. Ask your lazy, good-for-nothing partner for help. Better yet, *demand* his help. Realign the inequitable gender roles in your relationship with the unilateral force of someone who brings home the fucking bacon.

Why isn't he the one taking care of the house? What, is that women's work? No. Huh-uh. Fuck that shit right back to the fifties. That's not how the game is played any more, and folding the laundry before you stick it in the drawer ain't that hard a trick to learn.

Give him an order, and expect it to get done. You know you can do that, right? You're in charge, even if you don't wanna be. Don't put up with one ounce of whiny prideful bullshit, and if he doesn't step up, then he can fuck right off.

Honestly, what does this guy bring to the table? Is he a fitness model? Is he making you cum three times a day? Is he as emotionally supportive as a therapist and two best friends? He'd better be all those things, because if he's just some basic bro kicking in beer money and the occasional light bulb change, then I gotta ask what the fuck are you still doing with him?

Unfortunately, I already know the answer, and it's as ugly as it is obvious: relationship inertia. You're used to his lazy ass, and it would take time and energy to either whip it into shape or kick it to the curb.

Well, tough shit. You picked him, and you spoiled him by bringing too much to the table. Now you gotta deal with him, and if he's not worth the effort, then you gotta deal with that too.

My husband annoys the fuck out of me.
Of course he does. He's a daily reminder that you've given up.

Why is it so hard to quit a jerk?
It's hard to quit anyone once you've fallen for them. The more important question is why you pick jerks to begin with.

We had fire, I told him I liked him, now we have smoldering embers. But sometimes it sparks up again and we both get kind of lost in the smoke. What the hell is going on?
What's going on is a situation where a dude isn't that into you, but still wants to fuck you on occasion, so you let him, which leads to confusion in the form of overextended fire metaphors.

I love him, but why don't I trust him?
I have no idea, but you'd better fix that shit or your relationship is fucked.

My boyfriend has gained some weight and I feel like a shit person for being less attracted to him now.
Yeah, being shallow sucks. Sorry your boyfriend is gross.

How do I ask my boyfriend if he's cheating without
making an accusation?
Quit being a doormat.

How do I tell my boyfriend that I cheated on him with
my best friend and her girlfriend?
I think you'll be surprised how easy it is to confess to your boyfriend
that you had a lesbian threesome.

On an open marriage full of lies

My husband's been cheating on me. We are supposed
to have an open marriage, and the agreed terms are
that we know what each other has been up to. Not that
he hasn't denied doing anything until he has to bring
me antibiotics from the clinic because he's caught
something.

I don't mind the sex, I mind the lying for I don't
know how long, at least a year. Not just not telling, lying
when asked. I'm not possessive or weird, but we had an
agreement about how this was supposed to work. If one
of us wants to change the terms, it's a negotiation, not an
unilateral change.

We've been married for nine years. We both want an
open marriage, but this whole time he has had trouble
actually admitting that he is doing it with anyone else.

If it matters, we're both bi, and he's mostly hooked
up with men, though I just learned there was one
woman 10 months ago, maybe more, I don't know. Now
what?

It's entirely up to you.

First, you need to make a rational and realistic assessment of your husband's character, and then decide whether his potential for infidelity is enough of a glaring flaw to end your marriage.

You need to take into account that an open marriage isn't enough for him, and it probably never will be. Cheating itself is obviously part of the thrill. He'd rather tell lies and keep secrets than put in the minimum amount of effort required to keep an open marriage healthy, and that's not something you can easily remedy.

It's a terrible thing to learn that your husband can't be trusted, and I'm sure he'll come up with a long list of bullshit reasons why he lied, but at the end of the day, the fundamental reason is that he just couldn't be bothered to be honest.

In an open marriage, he was morally lazy. It was simply easier for him to lie – and perhaps even more fun – right up until the moment it wasn't. The question you have to ask yourself now is, can you see yourself ever being in a position to trust your husband again? Better yet, do you want to even bother?

Nine years is a long time. Maybe you want to try to make it work. Then again, nine years is a long time. Maybe you're ready to move on.

What do you want to do?

Sure, it's a tough decision either way, but if you do a gut check, you probably already know which way you want to go. Don't be afraid if you have an answer. Even if he can't be honest with you, you still have to be honest with yourself.

On being unreasonable

I just told my boyfriend it bothers me that he is constantly either on his computer, his iPad (which I bought him) or watching TV. And his answer was that he's like that because he's constantly seeking knowledge and that

I'm basically asking him to choose between me and knowledge. I know he's not playing games but even if he is doing it for a "noble cause", I don't think I'm asking for a lot. He said that if we get to a middle ground, I'm going to keep asking for more. I feel like I'm in a never ending argument. Am I being unreasonable? For the record we only see each other weekends because we live an hour away from each other so he stays with me Fri-Sun.

I'm constantly amazed at how often I get questions that are some version of a girlfriend asking me, 'Am I being unreasonable?' because the outrageous nonsense coming out of her boyfriend's smug fucking face is so utterly ridiculous that it makes her question her rationality.

Let me assure you, and all the women out there like you, that you have not lost the capacity for reason. Your boyfriend is simply a self-centered douchebag who has so little respect for you that he won't stop staring at a screen long enough to look you in the eyes and tell you to fuck off.

It's bad enough that he can claim to be 'constantly seeking knowledge' with a straight face, but do you have any idea how condescendingly rude and totally full of shit he has to be to create a false dichotomy between spending quality time with you and feeding his casual internet addiction?

Please do not believe for one solitary second that you are somehow asking him to choose between you and knowledge. All you are asking for is a bare minimum of togetherness, and if he's not willing to give it to you, *then you should kick him the fuck out of your house.*

Your boyfriend is a gigantic gaping asshole for talking to you that way, and I honestly don't know how you put up with it. Fuck his middle ground. Send his ass home for the weekend, call up all those friends you haven't seen in a while, and go have some fucking drinks.

Motherfucker hasn't even *seen* unreasonable.

I constantly feel it's only a matter of time before one of us cheats. Should I just end it?
Perhaps, but ending it won't fix your trust issues.

How do I know if my girlfriend loves me?
Dude, she'll tell you with her actions and her words exactly how she feels about you. If you're not paying attention to what she's telling you, that's a minor communication issue you can fix by being present in the relationship. If you don't believe what she's telling you, that's a major trust issue you need to address or it will ruin everything.

I'm caucasian and attracted to a brilliant, attractive Asian woman. There's long-term potential, but when I think about having kids, everything stops; I want kids that look about half like me. Is this some strain of racism? Pride? If not, what the hell is it? And how do I overcome it? Thanks.
Your kids will still look like you, dipshit. That's how it works. And yeah, for the record, your reaction is good old-fashioned racism with a little dash of narcissism thrown in for good measure. Overcome it by pulling your head out of your ass.

My boyfriend and I have been dating for four years and have never lived together due to his inability to find a full-time job. Are we screwed once he does? Will he ever?
Stop kidding yourself. Your boyfriend is a loser, and you aren't living together because he doesn't want to live with you.

I'm attracted to my boyfriend's sister. How do I deal with this?
Whatever you do, don't suggest a threesome.

On unexamined monogamy

My girlfriend and I have been together for six months, and it's a great relationship. She had to travel overseas for three months for work purposes, and I'm stuck at home without enough money to travel. She's been gone for more than a month already, and it was all fine up until recently.

She was caught out by an overseas friend of mine being kind of flirty in public. Every day for the last week or so, my girlfriend tells me she's so horny and doesn't think she can last the length of her stay without cheating; it's "so hard" and "the distance is getting to me, so hard." She tells me how guys approach her in clubs and try to sleep with her, but also makes it out that I should be proud of her for saying no to them.

She has a history of sleeping around while over there and not in a relationship, and saying "no" to guys is something new to her. I give her credit for that. I also admit she's one to usually get what she wants, when she wants, thanks to a rich mother and forgiving father, and now's a time where she can't get all of that without hurting me.

However, it still messes with my head. I've spoken to two of her friends that have since became my own, and they're disappointed in her. I'm sorry if this is long, but you seem great with advice. What options are available for me? Is she doing a normal thing? Am I right to be so cut up by it?

This isn't about you being right or her being wrong, and this certainly isn't about doing the normal thing. This is about coming to terms with your petty jealousy, addressing her potential lack of integrity and recognizing that you're in a self-made prison of unexamined monogamy.

Having sex with other people while you're in a relationship

doesn't always have to be cheating. So many people are in a constant struggle – to cheat or not to cheat – and it never occurs to them that in order to cheat, they have to accept a set of rules before they can break them.

Why accept the rules? Why not make your own? It's so much healthier to simply reject the underlying assumption that monogamy and fidelity are interchangeable concepts. They're not.

Yes, that's right. Monogamy and fidelity are not the same thing.

It's such a simple statement, but there is so much freedom in it. Being true and faithful in a relationship has no inherent connection to how many sexual partners you have. The connection is self-imposed.

Why do you care if your girlfriend has sex while she's overseas? Why should she care if you do the same? What are you proving to each other by not having sex for three months? That kind of behavior isn't strengthening your relationship. All it seems to be doing is building resentment and mistrust.

What am I suggesting here? Well, it's not all that salacious. Really, it's about integrity and strength – the integrity to be totally open and honest in a relationship, and the strength to allow yourself and your partner to pursue happiness wherever it may be found.

Obviously, your girlfriend shouldn't be having any love affairs while she's away, but physical and emotional intimacy are completely different than getting your rocks off. Come on, dude. You're not a doe-eyed grade schooler. I shouldn't have to tell you this.

Take some time to re-examine your romantic fundamentals. Lust isn't love. Flirting isn't intimacy. Sex isn't passion. As long as you two keep the love, intimacy and passion to yourselves, do you think you can handle letting her have a little lust, flirting and sex when you're not around?

If not, that's fine, but understand that the reasons matter. You aren't talking to me about your girlfriend being undignified, unsafe or disrespectful. All I'm hearing from you is petty jealousy. You are jealous and insecure in the relationship, and that's not healthy. Jealousy is a symptom of larger trust issues and fears. Throw in the long distance and a girlfriend with a healthy sex drive, and that's a recipe for things ending badly.

And come to think of it, this advice goes for all couples, gay or straight, in any combination of girl or guy. There is no double standard here. Fear-based monogamy is a terrible foundation for exclusivity in any romantic relationship. Instead, exclusivity should be based on physical and emotional intimacy.

Of course, sex can be a beautiful expression of both physical and emotional intimacy, but that doesn't mean it always is. Is your girlfriend looking for intimacy while she's overseas for work, or is she just looking to get laid? Be honest. You know the difference. Are you being jealous out of deep insecurities? Again, be honest.

Listen, I'm not saying you should give your girlfriend an international hall pass. That kind of thing is entirely up to you. All I'm saying is that you need to take a step back and open up a dialog with your girlfriend about fidelity, and focus on being true to one another where it really matters.

On Breakups

On why you weren't good enough for him

Why wasn't I good enough for him?

Life will be miserable if you think like this.

In one simple sentence, you've managed to cram together an invalidation (why wasn't I), a value judgment (good enough) and a personalization (for him). Let me help you see it another way.

First, you can't take this personally. It's not even about you. I know this is difficult to accept, but you have nothing to do with what he wants or doesn't want. His personal preferences do not speak to your quality in any way whatsoever.

While you're at it, stop judging yourself. This has absolutely nothing to do with you being 'good enough'. Your value as a human being is not connected to his romantic whims.

Finally, don't invalidate yourself. This isn't a failure on your part. There is no reason to frame this negatively. I know it hurts. Believe me, I know how much unrequited feelings suck, but don't let the pain trick you into believing you deserve it.

Strip away the invalidation, the value judgment and the personalization, and 'why wasn't I good enough for him' becomes simply, 'he prefers something else'.

That's it, really. He prefers something else, and it's not a reflection upon you, nor is it under your control.

Accept that. Learn to think this way. You'll still feel the pain, but it won't be agony. It will be bittersweet instead.

On someone better

My boyfriend of 2 years just broke up with me. Besides the emotional turbulence, which I know will pass, I'm pretty sure rationally that I don't have great chances of ever finding someone better for me.

Actually, that's pretty much the opposite of rational.

Getting dumped sucks, and right now it's perfectly understandable for you to feel like you'll never find someone better. It may even seem like a logical conclusion, but it's not.

The fault in your logic is that you aren't going to stay the same person you are today. Yes, the emotional turbulence will pass, but more than that, you're going to continue growing and changing, so it's perfectly okay if you never find someone better for the person you are at the moment, because that's not who you're always going to be.

Whatever you do, don't set this guy up in your mind to be 'the one that got away'. He isn't, and that's not really a thing. That kind of thinking is just a bullshit excuse people use to let themselves stay emotionally paralyzed.

Keep your shit together, and start moving on, because the point isn't to *find* someone better. The point is to *be* someone better, and if you do it for yourself, I promise that one day, you'll look back on the boyfriend who you thought was perfect at the time, and all he'll seem like is a quaint exercise in early love.

On moving the fuck on already

My ex-fiancee just got engaged to the guy she cheated on me with. After 3 years I thought I was over her, and yet one stupid Facebook notification through a friend of a friend and I'm a goddamn wreck. Apart from drinking myself to sleep for the next few nights, how the hell do

I get past something like this? I know it's stupid and childish to cling to the past, but she was the first woman to break my heart. Compounded with the breakup I had about a month ago, I'm almost turned against the whole relationship thing entirely.

I know I'm being reactionary and selfish, but beyond that I have no idea how to cope with this shit. Coquette, help?

Dude, put down the bottle of cheap Scotch and log out of Facebook.

So you had your heart broken. Good. It's one of those necessary experiences that are all part of having a full life, but three years is long enough. Quit your damn wallowing. It's fucking pathetic.

She wasn't your one great love. You two weren't meant to be together. The guy she cheated on you with didn't win any prize by getting her to say yes. Hell, you got her to say yes. Big fuckin' deal.

You didn't lose anything here. They didn't get one over on you. It only feels that way because you've concocted a bullshit fantasy about the way things coulda shoulda woulda been if only … if only … if only what exactly?

Please. You were in a shitty relationship that ended badly three years ago. Quit romanticizing it. You should be laughing at this news. He's a fool for getting engaged to a cheater, and you're a mope every goddamned second you don't see it that way.

Get your shit together, man.

What do you do when the man you love is marrying someone else?

You do what it takes to fall out of love. Step back. Reframe him. Let it hurt for a while, and then move on. He's just a man. One day you'll see that.

Why did I only feel comfortable telling him I loved him after I broke up with him?

Because after you broke up with him, there was no emotional risk.

I'm thinking of sending a letter to my ex boyfriend. Even though we love each other, we broke up because our relationship wasn't realistic on the long run, and it feels like this letter would be the final closure for me. Is it a good idea to sign it with "love" then my name?

Yes. Write the letter, sign it with love, and then *don't send it*. Trust me. Stick it in a drawer for at least three months. If you forget about it, great. If you don't, pull it out and read it. If you still wanna send it, send it. If not, even better.

Chère Coquette, I'm 40 years old, divorced 5 years ago and just starting to feel better after a long grief of having become a broken family (fuck you, ex-husband) and a depression related to this event. I have an amazing 11 years old daughter, I love my job and own a great apartment in the coolest part of Montreal. Why do I feel stalled, stuck and unable to start the next chapter of my life?

Because you still feel the need to say 'fuck you' to your ex-husband.

I thought I was fine, but he found someone else and now I'm losing my shit. I've been with a few dudes since him but haven't been able to catch any feelings. How do I poise myself against something that unexpectedly hurts like hell all over again?

Yeah, you gotta let it hurt. Fresh pain after your ex falls for someone else is a pretty standard break-up aftershock. Learn to expect that shit, especially if they catch feelings first.

I miss him so much that I cry myself into a half-sleep every night. But it's been a month since we broke up, and I have shit to do. How can I speed up the process?

You can't, but that's no excuse not to get your shit done.

On how to break up

I have a boyfriend of 3 months and am not happy. I try to break-up with him, but every time he cries and whines that he'll do better. He's a bad liar and a cheap date. How should I break up with him?

Pick up the phone. Dial his number. When he answers, say the following:

'Hey asshole, we are broken up. I don't want anything to do with you any more. Lose my fucking number.'

That's it. You're done.

Hang up the phone.

Ignore him.

On your ex's horny friends

Cut to three months after a three-year-long heartfelt and soul-deep relationship ended. I'm on pretty good terms with the ex; we both still have residual feelings for each other but are keeping a little bit of distance (mostly my request as the ex-to-friends transition hurts like a bitch). That's not the problem. The problem is that now his friends are trying to get at me.

I make no effort to seem even remotely available to these people. We've interacted only a handful of times through Facebook, all amounting to more-or-less pleasantries and those stupid-ass game invites.

While this most recent friend hasn't been explicit in his efforts, it's still smelling kind of fishy. I want to do the right thing by my ex, and let's face it, I'm still loyal to some degree. Also, I have a little thing called integrity. I'm in no way interested in my ex's friends. They were out of bounds the second I started dating my ex (though I honestly wouldn't be interested in them anyway.) I'm just trying to figure out the most graceful way to navigate the situation. That's where you come in, hopefully.

Thanks, Coquette. It's times like these I wish I could call you up for whiskey sours at a dive bar until 3 am.

Sweetheart, the first thing I would do is wean you off of whiskey sours. (If you insist on adding anything other than ice to your whiskey, that list ends at vermouth and bitters.) The second thing I would do is give you a big hug and tell you that you are not alone in this. It happens with such frequency that I'm surprised there's not a formal name for it.

There will always be a few acquaintances of your ex who come sniffing around after a breakup. It's inevitable, especially now that they can do it so easily on Facebook and still maintain plausible deniability. After each relationship, I pretty much expect to play a game of post-breakup whack-a-mole with a horny handful of my ex's douchebag friends who suddenly find a reason to poke their heads into my business. (And yeah, the really sneaky ones wait a few months.)

The most graceful way to handle this is just ignore them. Unless you have a good reason to be exchanging pleasantries, don't even do it. You are not obligated to respond to these guys, and you shouldn't be afraid of seeming rude. Don't make it your problem that they don't know any better. Shut them down hard and fast the moment they start hitting on you, and feel free to unfriend them if they make you uncomfortable in any way.

Unless one of them gets aggressively creepy, don't get your ex involved. The only thing worse than telling your ex that his friends are hitting on you is actually hooking up with one of his friends. Leave that kind of tacky behavior to the attention whores and drama queens.

Good luck with the broken heart, babe. I'm sorry you have to deal with a few jokers along the way.

What's the protocol on sending an ex an email? Is the answer just don't do it?
If you're having even the least bit of doubt, definitely don't do it.

I'm 38 and about to get divorced. Any advice? Shouldn't I be sadder?
Fuck no. Congratulations. You're getting out just in time for your mid-life crisis. It'll be wonderful and terrible all at the same time. Do your best to grow as a person. Save your money. Don't rush into anything.

I just broke up with my boyfriend and it was seriously the hardest thing I've ever had to do in my life. Does that make me soft?
You're soft now, but doing hard things is what hardens you.

I just got out of a pretty serious relationship. Hurt, but ultimately OK. Problem: before the relationship, I enjoyed having casual sex with various people. It was awesome. Now, however, I find the vast majority of people fairly gross. How do I get past this and start having fun again?
Time. It just takes time. Your heart is still sore from breaking, but don't worry, you'll have fun again. (And for the record, the vast majority of people have always been fairly gross. You just have a selective memory from the last time you were single.)

First real, long-term, "I love you" relationship; first breakup. General tips and pointers?

Step back and see the relationship as a whole, as something with a beginning, a middle and an end. Be sad for a minute, learn what you can from it, and then move the fuck on.

Is emotional closure a lie?

It can be. Usually it's just an excuse to try and fuck you one last time.

On getting the fuck out

I tried to break up with my boyfriend a few days ago, and after yelling at me and throwing the things I was trying to pack, he physically barricaded the front door with his body (after bolting and locking it). He broke down crying and told me that he won't let me leave and threatened self harm. He has openly told me that he attempted suicide multiple times as a teenager. I stayed because I am genuinely concerned for his safety but every instinct inside of me is screaming to get out of this. I love and care for him deeply, but I am well aware our relationship is toxic. I know I can't control what he does to himself, but I just would like to know how you'd navigate this situation.

Pack up all your shit and get the fuck out. Do it as quickly as possible, preferably when he's not around. The relationship is already over. You didn't 'try' to break up with him. You *did* break up with him. Now he's just using emotional blackmail to hold you hostage.

Quit worrying about his safety. He's not going to kill himself. Even if he did hurt himself (which he won't) it's not your fault. He's just saying fucked-up shit like that to manipulate you, which is all the more reason for you to run for the hills and never speak to this motherfucker again.

Set whatever feelings you have for him aside and simply leave. You don't owe him an explanation or any further communication, and you are not responsible for his behavior.

Gather your strength and just fucking go.

On actually breaking it off

My boyfriend of 2 years told me he couldn't marry me and we broke up. But now he still wants to talk to me everyday and still stop by my house. I know too that we were not a right match, but part of me just wants to cut him off so he understands what he is missing. Petty?

Not petty. Necessary.

He doesn't get to break up with you and still creep around at his convenience. Fuck that. Tell him to lose your number and forget where you live.

This isn't about him understanding what he's missing. Don't make it about him. This is about you moving on and enjoying whatever's coming next.

On breaking up with a fuck buddy

I've been fucking this guy who's a lot older than me. He's a great fuck buddy and all (he was my first casual sex experience) but there's also this guy I've been long-term flirting with and have real feelings for and am about to start an actual relationship with. So what's the best way to say goodbye to my fuck buddy? I don't want it to have to end like "Hey babe, why don't you come over

tonight?" "Oh sorry, I have a boyfriend now." I just feel like that's a little too crass.
I'm so going to miss the way he fucks though, ugh.

Tell him just like that. Say, 'I'm going to miss the way you fuck.'

Don't wait for a booty call. Give him a ring and invite him to lunch. That'll probably be unusual enough for him to ask why, and you can either choose to tell him over the phone or wait and do it in person.

Either way, he'll understand. He's older. He's a fuck buddy. He knew it was inevitable that you'd move on. He'll act happy and be respectful.

After all, he'll want to be at the top of your rebound list when you break up with the new boy.

On apologies, and letting go

I've just realized that I treated one of my exes very poorly during our break-up. I feel terrible about it and it was never my intention to be cruel, and I want to apologize. I understand this is just me trying to get rid of the guilt I'm suddenly feeling, but do you think it could be mutually beneficial? Should I try a short and direct call or email or just forget about it?

If you genuinely believe that an apology might have a positive effect on your ex, then it's something to consider. If an apology will have a negative effect on your ex, and you're just trying to get rid of the guilt, then don't do it.

The whole point of an apology like this is that it's not about you. It's entirely about someone else's feelings. The goal should be closure for your ex, and any benefit you derive from that is incidental.

On your first heartbreak

*I'm currently going through my first heart break.
And, christ, does it hurt. I'm 18, about to graduate as
valedictorian and recently got accepted to my dream
school, NYU. Last week I was living in ecstasy, and this
week I can't think of anything worse than getting out of
bed in the morning knowing that there's a 65% chance
of seeing my ex (what a fucking awful term, 'ex'). I've
literally studied/worked my whole life to get to where I
am now, so why should I be preoccupied by thoughts of
sorrow caused by some asshole who thinks he can make
do without me?*

I shouldn't, I know.

*But it's hard, Coke, I loved the shit out of that boy
and I've never felt so lost and subordinate in my life.*

*Do you have any tips for a pitiful heartbroken teen
who's lost her sense of direction?*

You're preoccupied by thoughts of sorrow because you're a
batshit teenager. It doesn't matter if you're one of the smart ones,
that's just the way it goes.

Don't worry, you'll be fine. You haven't lost your sense of direction. Losing your sense of direction is some shit that happens over
time as life wears you down. You're just a little dazed because
you've had your ego shattered. At your age, that's something you
can recover from by listening to shitty music for a month.

Not that you want to hear it, but being dumped right now
might be the best thing for you. Heartbreak sucks and all, but it's
better to learn what that process feels like now. You have plenty of
time to get back up, dust yourself off, and head over to NYU with
a bit more emotional maturity under your belt.

Trust me, in New York, having had this experience will be a
helluva lot more valuable than the fact that you were valedictorian, so, as fucked up as it sounds, congratulations on your first
heartbreak.

I just dumped my long-term bf who has depression and anxiety. I'm 100x happier now. Am I horrible person?
Nope. You should've dumped him sooner.

Can exes be friends?
Exes can be friendly. There's a difference.

How do you deal with a relationship that has ended but the person just throws shit at you because their perception is that you abandoned them?
If you still have to deal with the relationship, then it hasn't really ended, now has it?

When someone says, "I've fallen out of love with you," does it really mean, "I think I can find someone better?" I just wanted to know if it's a line like, "it's not you" where it really means something else.
'I've fallen out of love with you' is significantly worse than 'I think I can find someone better', but you can't see that because your wounded ego is trying to process your pain with jealousy instead of forgiveness.

I wonder if he still thinks about me.
Every once in a while, during masturbation.

Why does it hurt so much to find out that a recent ex-boyfriend is sleeping with a new woman? We're not together anymore ... so why does this kill more than the breakup did?
That's what happens when stale jealousy mixes with fresh envy. It's a brutal combo, and it's also a big red flag that you're not over him yet.

I've heard that the time it takes to get over a break up is half the time you were together. How long can I wallow before getting it together?

Quit watching *Sex and the City* reruns, go take a long hot shower, and then call up a couple of friends and make them drag your pathetic ass out into public.

On getting unstuck

I'm 41 and still stuck in a depression from a relationship that ended badly twenty years ago. I rarely get involved with people, and don't even remember the last time I had sex. I feel stuck. Do you have any advice to unstick me?

Twenty years? Are you kidding me? Come on, now. Andy Dufresne didn't spend that much time in Shawshank.

Whatever prison you think you're trapped in doesn't actually exist. That's the good news. The bad news is you might still have to crawl through a river of shit before coming out clean on the other side.

You suffer from depression. Fine. Whatever. That doesn't give you license to pin it on the twenty-year-old version of yourself. Just because you're fixated on some bullshit that happened in the early nineties, that doesn't mean it's the ultimate cause of any present-day chemical imbalance.

If you're clinically depressed, deal with it. Find a shrink and get some meds. Do the fucking work. Heal. On the other hand, if you're just bummed out and full of excuses, then get over it already.

Either way, get your shit together. You're capable of it.

On letting it go

Do you believe in the saying, "If you love something, let it go. If it comes back to you, its yours forever. If it doesn't, then it was never meant to be"?

Fuck no. That's just some simple bullshit people who believe in romantic destiny say when they're going through the bargaining stage after getting dumped.

Nothing about your love life is 'meant to be', nothing is 'yours forever', and it's silly to pretend you had any choice in the matter. You didn't 'let it go'. That shit got up and went.

On sob stories

hi, there. this is going to be a little hard for me to write out, but here goes. i was with this guy for about a year, and out of the blue, he breaks up for me. sure, i was broken hearted, but that i could learn to get over. about a month or so later, i had to abort the child my doctor told me i was likely to miscarry. i hold on to feelings of my ex, but i think it's only because the thought of losing child always brings me back to him, to happier times. i talk to him on occasion, and he is friendly enough, because he knows. but i'm still in love with him. what should i do?

Oh, please. This is a carefully crafted story designed to suck sympathy out of everyone who hears it. I can spot drama queens like you a mile away, and I'm calling bullshit on your pity party.

You got knocked up. Your boyfriend broke up with you. You got an abortion. That's the chain of events.

Of course, with girls like you nothing's ever your fault. You're never accountable for your own decisions and everything comes from out of the blue, so naturally this is all some romantic tribulation.

You want to know what to do? Well for starters, quit characterizing your abortion as an extrinsic manifestation of your failed relationship. That's an incredibly unhealthy way to process the psychological trauma of terminating a pregnancy.

Next, quit romanticizing the past. It prevents an honest evaluation of what went wrong and cripples your ability to move on.

Finally, accept some responsibility for the choices you make and do everything in your power to fight off a victim mentality.

On the edges of relationships

A guy, a friend, who I've had a peripheral crush on for a year and a half is breaking up with his long-term girlfriend. What is the most respectful way to mention "hey, remember that time we joked around about how I would totally hit that if you weren't in a loving, committed relationship? So for real now."

Chill the fuck out. Seriously, take a deep breath and contain your glee at the prospect of jumping on this guy's dick while it's still warm from the ex-girlfriend's dismount.

Think about the consequences. Unless you're prepared to lose a friend in a flurry of awkward rebound sex, don't offer yourself up as his break-up gift bag. Even if you don't mind the potential mess, try and play it cool. Keep it simple. No strings, no bullshit.

You may just want a little sex, but anyone fresh out of a relationship can be a raw nerve. Don't let your peripheral crush add to his drama.

If I am unhappy in my relationship, why do I feel more miserable over the prospect of ending it?
Because you mistakenly think that ending it is failure.

How can I deal with rejection better?
Never take it personally.

How do I let go of the only guy I've ever loved?
Quit using the words only and ever.

How does one act graceful right after being dumped?
Avoid contact. Rebound in public. Cry in private.

Why do men leave when things get tough?
Things? No, no. They leave when *you* get tough.

Can you fall out of love?
Just as hard.

How can i crush a man's ego, rip it to shreds?
Be better than him without needing him.

When my boyfriend broke up with me, he said our relationship "filled him with existential dread." What the fuck does that even mean? I know what existential dread is, but what does that have to do with our dearly departed relationship?
The relationship had your boyfriend contemplating the idea of forever, and it freaked him out. It was a polite (if pretentious) way of saying that the mere thought of spending the rest of his life with you terrified him.

*I can't break up with him because it'll hurt him so much.
I've never purposefully and knowingly caused someone
that much pain.*

You are not responsible for his emotional state. One more time for
the cheap seats: *you are not responsible for his emotional state.* You are
being held hostage by your boyfriend's fragility. That's disgusting.
If you want out of the relationship, get the fuck out. Don't make
his weakness yours.

On brutal fucking truth

*How do you get over a guy you never wanted to be
broken up from? We had been together for five years.
I know our relationship needed to change. There were
communication issues and some lack of compassion
near the end. But I always wanted to fight for us,
whereas he doesn't want to be in a relationship at all.
At times I have clarity and know I can't be with him,
not because of his refusal, but because I need more for
myself than what our relationship was. But most of the
time, I hope that we'll end up with each other. We've
been through a shit load, including an abortion which
was a mutual decision, but left us both with the want to
eventually have a family together. I've never done this
before and I feel like I'm trapped inside of myself.*

Ugh. I know your type. You've been annoying the shit out of
your friends with this emotional autopsy for weeks now, and you've
gotten to the point where you've distilled your shitty relationship
down to a bunch of sad, tired, self-deluding clichés. This is going to
seem cruel, but somebody needs to slap you upside the head with
some brutal fucking truth.

I'm sorry, but your relationship didn't 'need to change'. That
shit needed to end. He was fucking miserable, and you just didn't

know any better. Sure, it was great in the beginning, but that was half a damn decade ago. Neither of you are the same person any more, and if you're honest with yourself you'll start to acknowledge that your relationship probably ran its natural course in the first two years.

After that, he checked out emotionally, and you stubbornly refused to let it go. You wanna know what 'I always wanted to fight for us' really means? It means he was trying to break up with you for years, but you were so relentless that he couldn't figure out how.

Oh, and I promise, he never wanted to have a family with you. Ever. Not even a little bit. That was just a bunch of bullshit he thought you needed to hear while he was holding his breath through your abortion. Yep. It's terrible, but that's what guys do.

You want some clarity? Let me be crystal fucking clear: he doesn't love you any more. You two are never going to end up together. It's time for you to accept that it's over. Pull your head out of your ass and move the fuck on.

Yes, it hurts. No, it's not fair. Tough shit. The sooner you get some emotional distance from this relationship, the sooner you'll realize that there's nothing particularly special about this guy other than the fact that you happened to fall in love with him.

Now, take a deep breath. Exhale. This was harsh, but it needed to be. The good news is you will get over him. The time you spent together wasn't wasted. You will learn from this, and you will fall in love again, probably more than once. In the meantime, quit romanticizing the past. It's time to start letting go.

On total fucking indifference

Hi, first of all I love you, don't care who you are I'm just happy this exists. You've helped me stop being a doormat. But can you teach me how to ruin my ex's life with my own self respect? We are part of the same group of friends and if I go off and start my own life I will be losing some of my friends, I think. I want to be around him but I want to be fair to myself and make him wish he didn't fuck around.

I can teach you how to ruin your ex's life, or I can teach you how to have self-respect. Those are mutually exclusive lessons, babe.

I highly recommend you choose self-respect. To whatever degree that allows you to be in the same room with him, that's entirely up to you. I don't know the circumstances of his particular fuckery, but odds are, he didn't get wildly creative in his betrayal, just some garden variety episode of cheating.

In other words, he's nothing special. Act accordingly.

Hit him with total fucking indifference. Mean it. Show him neither love nor hate. Let him neither charm nor annoy you. As difficult as it may seem, give him only the common courtesy afforded to strangers.

The trick here is for it not to be an act. It's not that you're trying to insult him by not laughing at his jokes. It's that you simply don't care. He doesn't even get an eye roll out of you. Do you see what I'm getting at?

You're not doing this for any desired effect on him, by the way. This is for you. Sure, it will drive him crazy in a way that you will enjoy, but try not to enjoy it. Be indifferent to that too. Well and truly give not one ounce of fuck about anything he says or does, and I promise, you will be content with the way things turn out.

Your friends will think you're a badass, too.

PART III

On Friends

Do you think girls and guys can be friends?
Of course they can, and the underlying premise of this all-too-common question and the infantile assumptions it makes about gender, interpersonal relationships and human sexuality well and truly break my fucking heart.

How do you deal with an atrociously competitive best friend?
Refuse to compete.

How do you protect your dignity and not be an uptight bitch?
I surround myself with good people. Problem solved.

I can't have kids. Hell, I don't even like kids. So why did I burst into tears after my pregnant best friend told me I wouldn't be able to handle it anyway?
Because not being able to have kids makes you feel broken, and your best friend basically just told you that you're better off that way, which is super fucking insensitive of her.

Do you get better at choosing people as you go on? This year's been full of getting burned by people I trusted.
You only get better at it if you actually change how you choose them.

Why do I absolutely hate the fact that my best friend
stays friends with all of her exes? It makes my blood boil
and I don't know why.

If I had to guess, it's probably a manifestation of your resentment
over having to put up with her bullshit during the breakups.

Why do I hate it when my (privileged) college friends call
my dad 'blue collar' and 'salt of the earth'?

Because those phrases are code for poor and unsophisticated.

On jealousy

There is this girl I grew up with who is what society
would deem "perfect". She is smart, beautiful, and
talented. She has an equally smart, beautiful, and
talented boyfriend. She has a family that is so fucking
put together, supportive, kind, and radically different
from my own it makes me want to explode.

We have similar enough interests that it feels like
anything I do, she can do infinitely better. She was born
into better, and just simply was granted better genes. With
this, a horrible jealousy emerges. I guess my question is,
how do you deal with these seemingly perfect people?

I usually have sex with them.

That is to say, I enjoy them. Smart, beautiful and talented
people are fucking awesome. Why be jealous? Besides, I guarantee
your girl is just as fucked up as everybody else.

Listen, you weren't born the Princess of Monaco, nor were you
born in a refugee camp in Darfur. You're in the fucking middle.
We all are. On any given day, there are millions of people who've
got one up on you, and there are millions of people who'd trade
places with you in an instant.

Same goes for little miss perfect, by the way. You think she shits frozen yogurt and has a pet unicorn, but look at her with some distance and she's just another middle-of-the-road, middle-class girl from Middle America.

Perfection is bullshit, especially with our half-retarded species. If she's a cool chick, just be her friend and leave jealousy for the bitter kids to play with.

On not being a doormat

Are there any tips you can give a girl on how to be less of a doormat? I let people walk all the fuck over me, and I have pretty much my whole life. I know the response I'm going to get is probably something like "Well cut it out, tell people to fuck off." I know it should just be as simple as that but it's really just never been that easy for me. And if that's really the only way, then cool, but I thought I would ask anyway.

Telling people to fuck off is easy. That's not your problem.

Your problem is you're terrified that they actually might go and fuck off.

Your fear of abandonment outweighs your need for a little respect, and so all the assholes that worm their way into your life tend to stay there because you'll put up with their shit when other folks won't.

Deal with your abandonment issues. Overcome your fear of losing people and replace it with the realization that your life would actually be better if all the assholes were out of it.

You have to be willing to lose people before telling them to fuck off has any weight behind it. Otherwise, an asshole will call your bluff every time.

This isn't about being a hard-ass. It's about having self-respect. No one else will ever respect you if you don't first.

If someone doesn't show you respect, let them know. Allow them to apologize. Do not turn the other cheek. If they fuck with you again, simply cut them out of your life.

Pretty soon, you'll no longer need to tell people to fuck off, because you'll be surrounded by good people who don't treat you like a doormat.

Is it normal for a person to keep a detailed record of every single person they ever hooked up with? With. pictures and attractiveness ratings.
No. No, no, no. Nooo.

I'm happy with my life and with myself, but there are people who get me down. They tell me that I'm "not doing something for social change," that my open enjoyment of sex is a sign of low self-esteem and being dependent on men, and that I'm not doing something with my life. What do I do?
If you're genuinely happy, then cut those people out of your life. If you can't get rid of them altogether, then tell them to take their social and sexual politics, and stick 'em where the sun don't shine.

How can I get friends that like me and that I like?
Like yourself first.

How do you make girl friends? Middle of college, my boyfriend and his friends are awesome, but I feel my social life is lacking.
Join something – a team, a group or a club. Pick one with other girls in it, and participate without your boyfriend.

*I am constantly able to hear my neighbors having sex …
what should I do?!*

Record them, mix in some fresh beats, and drop a CD off on their
doorstep.

On an asshole

*I'm lonely. I'm in my mid-twenties and I'm surrounded
by very positive feedback. I've earned it, since I'm a
workaholic, I seek perfection in every aspect of my life,
from diet and exercise to my wardrobe. I'm working on
a novel and two screenplays, and I have three jobs.*

*I know I have the tendency to be a control freak, but
I'm a very supportive person, and people always lean
on me for advice or positive reinforcement. I'm tired
of always being the one to initiate social situations,
however. I ask people to do things all the time, but half
the time they're busy, or else I just wind up alone on
weekends.*

*I don't want to compromise my goals and dreams,
but why do I feel so alone? I was popular in college –
what happened?*

This may be tough to swallow, but your real problem isn't that
you're lonely. It's that you simply haven't realized yet that you're
an asshole.

Yes, that's right. You are a magnificent asshole. You self-identify
as a 'workaholic' – *asshole*. You say things like 'I'm surrounded by
very positive feedback' and 'I seek perfection in every aspect of my
life' without the slightest trace of irony – *asshole*. You brag about
how many jobs you're holding down and the number of projects
you're currently writing – *asshole, asshole, asshole*. I mean, come on.
That was just your opening paragraph.

Don't worry. Being an asshole is fairly common for people your age, especially overachievers who enjoyed popularity in college. The good news is that you don't have to keep being an asshole.

All you have to do is chill the fuck out. Learn to be a serious person without taking yourself so damned seriously. Start recognizing when you're coming off as persnickety, and stop being a control freak.

Nobody is asking you to compromise your goals and dreams. In fact, you should start reminding yourself that nobody gives a fuck about your goals and dreams. Most of the time, people don't even give a fuck about what you say. All they really care about is how you make them feel.

So, how do you make the people in your life feel? The truth is, even though they know you're a good person, you kind of annoy them. That's why they only want to deal with you in small doses.

If you relax, pull the stick out of your ass, and quit treating life like it's one big job interview, you'll soon find that people will enjoy being around you more.

On another asshole

I fucking hate my roommate. I fucked her twice. She was annoying before I fucked her. But now, she is the epoch of annoying. Shes younger (21), not particularly mature, attention-seeking, and trashy as a tractor tire. When she speaks my skin crawls. This is a whole other universe of confronting 'the real'. I'm not exclusive in this assessment either, our other roommate agrees. Shes unbearable. Now, however, because of some weak ass lease shit, we can't kick her out. My strategy of headphones and attention denial isn't helping me deal. I'm an asshole, and okay with it; it's my fucking identity. I need a new strategy to get through the next few months.

Slow down there, charm school. Maybe your identity as a self-proclaimed asshole isn't the way to go. Sure, you hate yourself for a lot of reasons, but how about acting like a compassionate human being for once?

I get it. You stuck your dick in an unbearable tractor tire. Twice. It's actually a pretty transparent move, dude. Once you fucked her, you started projecting all of your self-hatred onto this poor girl. She's your cum dumpster and emotional scapegoat all in one.

Listen, she's not the one making your skin crawl. You are. It's time for you to stop feeling so much hate, and a strategy of headphones will never help you deal. It'll only distract you from the consequences of your shitty decisions.

Your new strategy should be to recognize that your own self-loathing is the root cause of your situation. Your new strategy should be to treat yourself and others with some fucking respect. Your new strategy should be to realize that there's nothing else to this life but the time we spend loving other people.

Go ahead, spend the next few months being kind, thoughtful and generous. See if your whole world doesn't change.

On yet another asshole

I am a kind, considerate, and generous person who is never appreciated for what I do for others. Here is a recent example: I shelled out more than 50 bucks in cab fare, bus fare, and groceries for a friend's visit only to have him decide at the last minute to stay with our mutual friend, who happens to be his ex, instead of me, wasting the time and money I put into picking him up from the airport and feeding him. I don't expect anything in return for my thoughtfulness and I don't want to stop being considerate and generous, but I am really tired of being unappreciated and taken advantage

*of. How do I make my family and friends recognize this
without becoming selfish? Moreover, am I an asshole
for demanding that my friends and family recognize
this? Do I just need to get over myself and stop expecting
others to behave in a certain way, or is my annoyance
in the previously mentioned example justified? Is it
even worth mentioning to the friends in the previous
example?*

Fuck you.

No, really. Fuck you. You are not a kind, considerate and generous person who is never appreciated. What you are is a selfish twit
who isn't any good at being emotionally manipulative.

If you feel like someone owes you appreciation for a kindness, then it wasn't a kindness. It was merely a service rendered in
expectation of that appreciation.

That's not generosity. That's *quid pro quo*, and not recognizing
the difference is what makes you yet another asshole.

On not an asshole

*I've helped my friends deal with some heavy shit in
the past and never expected any praise or recognition
in return; really and truly. After a few series of events
where I have needed a friend to help me out they all
came up with an excuse to avoid me every time I needed
a hand.*

*I've been a genuinely good friend to them so am I an
asshole for feeling pissed that no one came through, or is
it time to surround myself with new people?*

You are not an asshole. Friendship is a two-way street. It's time
to surround yourself with new people.

What's the best way to handle someone who is
exhaustingly self-pitying?
Don't put up with their behavior. Call them out. Be kind if you can,
but tell them to shut the fuck up if necessary. Remember, it's perfectly okay to enforce your own mental and emotional well-being.
(Also, if someone drains you to the point of exhaustion, consider
whether they need to be in your life at all.)

I find your advice "to cut people out of your life" to be
overkill. It is great advice if you want to be alone and
disliked. Dumb people take that shit seriously.
It's not supposed to be a hobby, asshole. It's an extreme measure
for people in toxic situations with emotional vampires.

How do you recognize toxic people who feed off drama
before they become a part of your life?
Recognizing them is easy. It's just that most people find it difficult
to not be fascinated by their bullshit.

My roommate expects me to treat her like a sick child
while she's hungover. She wants me to make her food,
bring her juice, rub her head, etc. I feel like she brought
the hangover on herself, so she should take care of
herself the next day. Am I insensitive? Or is she an
entitled brat?
Bitch can get her own juice.

So, we know where you stand on cheating and being the
other man/woman but what do you think about telling
someone they're being cheated on? Do you think people

have a right to know or should a third party just mind their own business?

There's a lot to be said for minding your own business, but there's also a good case for applying the golden rule – it really just depends on the situation. When you're trying to balance compassion with discretion, let loyalty guide you further than honesty.

What do you do when your closest friend doesn't reach out when she knows you're having a tough time? I'm out of sight, out of mind.

How tough a time could it be if what you're really complaining about is a lack of attention? Quit whining and call your shitty friend. If she's still not there for you, take the fucking hint and adjust who she is to you.

On a fresh drinking problem

My best friend and I are both single after bad relationships; while my boyfriend was emotionally abusive, they broke up when her ex punched her in the face.

We made a joke of being slutty as possible this summer to spite our exes or something else that was logical after a couple drinks.

Unfortunately, I think she's taking it too far.

She's proceeded to morph into a drunken mess; she'll get wasted and throw herself at anything with a penis. She'll also be verbally abusive to our closest friends, and there's been several nights where she just breaks down crying over her ex. When she's sobered up, she acts like nothing happened.

She also keeps mocking me for keeping regular fuck buddies instead of sleeping with a new random every weekend like she does.

I'm worried about her, not just because this is self-destructive, but because she's getting a bad reputation amongst our friends. Most have come to me and expressed a growing dislike for her and how if she keeps this up, no one is going to want to hang out with her anymore.

Everyone I've talked to about this has said I have to let her hit rock bottom but I don't want that to happen. So what do I do to knock some sense into her?

Please ignore the idiots telling you to let your best friend hit rock bottom. That's terrible advice. Rock bottom is for hardcore addicts unreachable by any other means, and your best friend isn't an addict. Not yet, anyway.

At the moment, she's just a hot mess with a fresh drinking problem. She's in a tremendous amount of emotional pain, and she has no method of coping other than numbing herself with alcohol.

The whoring around isn't coming from a healthy place either. There's nothing wrong with a wild summer of no-strings sex, but she's trying to fuck the pain away, and that never works for more than a few minutes.

As her best friend, it's time to help her address her underlying pain. She's coming out of an abusive relationship, and she needs to start processing her emotions sober. This isn't about stopping her from drinking, nor is it about slut-shaming. The booze and boys aren't the problem. They're just symptoms.

Knocking some sense into her will require daytime heart-to-heart conversations about her behavior where she doesn't feel cornered or judged. That can be tough. You have to come from a place of love and concern. You have to let her know that it's not what she's doing that's the problem, it's why she's doing it.

She's not drinking to celebrate. She's drinking to annihilate. She's not having sex to explore. She's having sex to escape. If she's ready to start dealing with her emotional pain in a healthier way, she will have to recognize the difference and consciously choose not to numb herself.

This stuff isn't easy. It requires a high degree of emotional maturity on both of your parts. You'll need to bring all of your patience and nonjudgment to the table, and she'll need to bring all of her self-control and self-respect.

I hope she's ready to hear you.

On the real reason he bugs you

After a year and a half, I finally realized why my roommate's boyfriend bugs me: He's boring. He's a perfectly nice, perfectly attractive, perfectly successful functioning adult, but he has nothing terribly interesting to say, or at least not to me. Then, when my roommate is together with her boyfriend, she feeds off his Wonderbread loaf of a personality and ceases to be an exciting person with creativity and dreams.

Am I wrong to think like this? Am I just a jealous single bitch? Am I just as equally boring for hanging out with these boring people?

Yeah, it's all about you, isn't it?

Your roommate's boyfriend isn't boring. You're just bored by your roommate's boyfriend. See the difference? Of course you don't, because you're the center of the whole damn universe.

After a year and a half, what you should have finally realized is that you're an incredibly self-centered girl who gets annoyed when the people in your life stop playing whatever role it is that you've assigned to them.

You don't seem to care how your roommate actually feels. You just care that she continues playing the role of the 'exciting person with creativity and dreams'. Whose dreams are we talking about, anyway? I'm gonna go out on a limb here and guess yours, because it sounds like your roommate is pretty darned happy in her relationship with a perfectly nice, perfectly attractive, perfectly successful functioning adult.

Take a step back and ask yourself: why would a perfectly nice, perfectly attractive, perfectly successful functioning adult have nothing terribly interesting to say to you? Is it because he's boring? Is it because you're boring?

Nope and nope. Shocking as this may seem, he has nothing terribly interesting to say to you because *he doesn't exist to hold your interest.* Sorry, babe. He's not there for your entertainment. Neither is your roommate.

I know your type. You don't feed off of chaos and drama. You're not an evil person, but still, you quietly exist as an emotional singularity around which everyone else in your world revolves.

Unfortunately, your roommate's boyfriend doesn't love you or hate you. He does nothing to piss you off or make you laugh. It's not that he's boring. It's that he's in your world and yet totally indifferent to you.

That's the real reason he bugs you.

What is the proper etiquette when discovering a friend of yours on a sex cam website?
Masturbate quietly to yourself as you shut the fuck up about it.

I feel like I want to break up with him, but I have no other friends.
You will make some.

I'm in love with my best friend. He hasn't accepted that he's honestly bisexual yet. I don't know how to proceed. Help?

Stop sucking his dick.

Is going to a music festival on your own tragic?

Hell no. Rock out. Make new friends.

What's the best way to mentally/emotionally deal with a stupid, little, irrational, yet persistent, crush on your best friend's boyfriend?

Quit it. Recognize that the crush is an unhealthy manifestation of envy.

Do you owe your close friends the duty of telling them that the guy they are dating is a bratty man child? Or do you allow them to make their own choices?

You owe your close friends the duty of not being a cunt. Good luck.

my best friend thinks i've been talking shit, when i love her like a sister, i'm so enraged i just want to give up on this friendship completely

Yeah, that last part about giving up on the friendship? That's you talking shit, which means she's right about you, even if she's wrong. Chill the fuck out, drama queen.

How do you deal with pretentious assholes?

Relentless mind fucking followed by total disregard.

***When are the appropriate times to tell a person to
fuck off?***

During eye contact.

On shaming an aggressive drunk

*it turns out a friend of some of my friends won't take
any form of no as an answer from women when he's
blackout drunk besides literal punches to the face.
he hasn't raped anybody that i know of, but he does
extended following, aggressive cornering, unwanted
touching, turning rejection into flirting, and he forced my
friend to make out with him until she could get away.
how do i negotiate talking to him about his behavior and
continuing to operate within a group of friends that he's
nonnegotiably part of?*

Normally I prefer not to respond to submissions this sloppy, but
your underlying question is too important to ignore. What you're
asking is how to deal with a person in your sphere of friends who
becomes inappropriately sexual and physically aggressive when
he's intoxicated.

If I was in your shoes, I'd first build a coalition within the
group. I would speak individually to each friend I knew would
support me, and I'd get them to agree that the guy's behavior is
inappropriate and should no longer be tolerated.

Spread the responsibility for monitoring his behavior around
to as many people in your group of friends as possible. Make sure
they understand that it's a problem that needs correcting, and that
it's okay for them to actually do something to correct it.

As for talking directly to the guy, don't wait until he's drunk and
acting up before you have the discussion with him. Sit him down
when he's sober and let him know that he can't continue to behave

that way. Shoot him straight. Tell him exactly what he's done wrong and why he can't continue behaving that way.

After you've had the talk with him, if he continues acting inappropriately, that's when you call him out in front of the group. Use shame as your tool to alter his behavior when he's drunk.

On the rules of attraction

I just wanted to ask you to speak more on "on a girl code violation." My best friend is a guy (I'm a gal) and he had a fling with another guy. After that ended, the two of us got involved, harmless fucking. It stopped and now the boyfriend is back in the picture and I'm the "other woman." I lost both of them as friends, even the one I considered my best friend, who I fucked, because they agree I hurt the boyfriend, just as the previous girl was saying she was hurt.

I don't see myself as pathetic, they broke up and I wasn't that close to the boyfriend anyway. If he had cheated with me I'd get it, but the relationship was over..move the fuck on. It was the boyfriend who fucked another person immediately after getting out of a longterm relationship. Why I am the "pathetic" one deserving pity? Isn't the boyfriend in both situations the asshole?

The relationship obviously wasn't over. If it was, they wouldn't be back together. A breakup isn't necessarily the same thing as the end of a relationship, and a best friend should know the damn difference.

Besides, what the fuck are you doing hopping in the sack with your best friend right after he comes out of a long-term relationship? You're insane to think that kind of thing is harmless, and you're an idiot if you think it's consequence-free.

Fucking him may not have been cheating, but only by a technicality. It was still a monumentally sketchy move on both your parts, one that you were too stupid or too thoughtless to know was a mistake. Either way, tough shit.

All three of you sound like assholes from a Bret Easton Ellis novel, but if you're wondering why you are the pathetic one deserving pity, it's because you're basically a fag hag who got rebound fucked and then tossed out like garbage.

That sucks, babe, but maybe this will teach you the real meaning of 'fling' and 'harmless fucking'.

On a broken-people magnet

I seem to be a broken-people magnet. They come to me with their problems and because no one else will step up, I try and help them and end up wasting time that I don't even have to waste. How do I walk away from this? Some of these people are suicidal and refuse help, I can't just leave them like that. I need to focus on my own life right now and I can't keep doing this. What do I do?

You are a broken-people magnet because you yourself are broken. You don't recognize your brokenness, of course. You think you are helping, and no doubt you provide a certain kind of support, but it's not healthy, especially for you.

Here's the thing you need to understand: people don't come to you with their problems. That's just your way of framing it, and it removes your agency from the equation. What you must acknowledge is that you allow people to burden you with their problems. You allow it.

You allow people to burden you with their problems because you are an enabler with boundary issues who feeds off of being in overfunctioning/underfunctioning relationships.

It makes you miserable, but it also validates you, and you'd rather be miserable than invalidated. That's the part that cuts to the core of who you are. You're a person who is so desperate to be validated that you let emotional vampires feast on your time and energy just so you can feel needed.

That's where you're broken. That's the part of you that needs to be fixed, and ironically, there's no one out there who can fix you the way you keep trying to fix other people. You have to do it. You have to learn how to establish boundaries. You have to recognize when you're overfunctioning in a relationship. You have to find healthy ways to validate yourself without enabling people.

You say you can't keep doing this and that you need to focus on your own life right now. Okay, then. Stop doing it. It really is that simple. Just stop. Refuse to allow all these broken people to burden you with their problems.

Oh, but wait. That little voice in your head is already crying out, 'But no one else will step up. I can't just leave them like that.' Yes you fucking can. Not only that, you should.

That little desperate voice is the sound of your brokenness, because it's not coming from a place of healthy concern. It's coming from a place of pathological need. It's coming from your emotional void.

This isn't about you becoming heartless. This is about you having enough self-respect, self-worth and internal validation that you no longer need these sad broken people in your life.

If you recognize your unhealthy patterns that are filling an unhealthy need, if you find some internal validation, if you have a little self-respect, I promise, the broken-people magnet will shut off automatically, and you'll be free to enjoy the company of unbroken people, because you won't be broken any more yourself.

On Family

My father is dying. I just want someone to tell me it will all be okay.

It will, but your father dying will also permanently alter your meaning of okay. This process is going to change you. Don't be afraid of it, and do your best not to shrink away from the painful and difficult parts.

I told my dad I was gay. He said he loves me but *God willing* I'd be able to turn straight one day. Please help. I don't know what to do right now.

You don't have to do anything. You're fine for now. Eventually, your father will be the one to change. If he is a decent man who loves you, his ignorance will slowly start to wear away into compassion, then understanding, then acceptance. It will take time, so be patient and be strong.

Why is it that every time I think of my dad, I get sad? He's alive and I see him all the time. Is it because I feel like he's sad? Because I love him and never tell him I do?

Yes. Congratulations. You just went through six months of therapy in 41 words. Now go tell your dad that you love him.

Will going back home ever not make me feel like I'm suffocating?

Maybe, but you'll have to make yourself a new home before going back to the old one doesn't suffocate you any more.

On cutting her out of your life

For years me and my brother have been living with abuse from my mother. She's had a rough life riddled with the most terrible shit and mental illness to go with it.

Recently, we've come to the end of our ropes with her. The abuse has affected both of us in our adult lives – manifesting in social anxiety and fear of confrontation.

I want to cut her out of my life, but I don't know if I should just stop speaking to her forever or write a letter detailing the harm done and why I can no longer have her in my life.

To make the whole thing more difficult, and honestly the reason why we're still in contact with her at all, she threatens to kill herself whenever anyone confronts her about this behaviour. A part of me is afraid of pushing her over the edge, because we're all she has left. But, I guess another part of me is wanting to call her bluff.

Is my thinking clear? Am I completely fucked up on the matter? I feel altogether ill-equipped for this situation. While I want to choose inaction, she's been forcing my hand by harassing me with messages.

Thank you for listening if you have the time. I hope you're keeping hydrated.

Write the letter, but write it for yourself knowing that you're not going to send it to your mother. Be brutally honest, don't edit yourself, and put it all down on paper. It will be a useful exercise in expressing exactly what you wish you could say to her.

Once you've written it, set it aside for a while. Come back to it whenever you need to add more thoughts. Feel free to start new drafts. Let it become a living document, a reference for all the negative shit you feel. Give it a while for the message to solidify and become strong.

In the meantime, try not to interact with your mother unless it's on your terms. Establish firm boundaries and practice enforcing them. Eventually, your goal will be to only have contact when and if you want it. Cutting her out of your life will be a process, so don't stop speaking to her all at once. Like you said, you aren't equipped for that yet.

She may be your mother, but you're the one who makes the rules now. She doesn't get to force your hand. Don't give her that power, and don't let her manipulate you with threats of self-harm.

Remember, you can't choose inaction. All of this will be a deliberate, active choice, so let it be a conscious decision that comes from a place of strength.

On the evil stepmother

My dad left my mother for a difficult woman when I was 21. At first, I tried to make nice with the lady, which proved complicated, seeing as she repeatedly put down my father in front of me and the rest of his family. He allowed it and I decided that however painful it was to watch him shrink like that, it was his business, not mine.

One night, she got a bit drunk and began to attack my then-boyfriend at dinner, mocking him in a language he did not speak. I stood up for him. She then turned on me. I stood up for myself. She proceeded to shout that I was a spoiled brat (I was 25), that my father didn't need me in his life, and that she wanted me out of it. When I turned to my dad in disbelief, he cowered and sided with her. That was in 2005.

My dad and I resumed a relationship a year later, but he was not there for my wedding in 2010, arguing that his new wife had not been invited and that she was expecting an apology from me. He said he wanted me to have a relationship with her, and I said I gladly would, but that he shouldn't expect me to roll over if she becomes aggressive with me. He said he didn't want any conflict, and so he'd rather we left it at that. I love my dad, so it still hurts. It's taken me the better part of the decade to accept that my father has no courage.

Here's my issue: I want my future children to have a granddad. While he's made huge efforts to mend the relationship, things with his wife are the same. My husband and I sometimes fantasize about showing up at their doorstep and acting like nothing happened, actively ignoring their bullshit and enjoying my father full-time again. Is that a bad idea? If so, what else can I do?

It takes a certain kind of soul-stained bitch to seek out married men as potential husbands, especially married men with children. People like that don't change, and even though it's been a decade, your stepmother still sees you as a potential threat to her marriage.

You will always be the strong-willed stepdaughter that she can't control, and therefore, you will always be an enemy, just as she considered your mother to be an enemy ten years ago when she was pulling her textbook homewrecking maneuver on your family.

It's an ugly way to go through life, one that I doubt she would even admit to herself, but one that nonetheless is affecting your family dynamic to this very day. You need to start acknowledging this. I'm not suggesting you take her on as your enemy. That's a waste of negative emotion. Instead, you should simply recognize that she considers you to be her enemy, and wherever possible, use it to your advantage.

You will always be your father's daughter. Nothing will ever change that. On the other hand, your stepmother might lose her edge one day or your dad might grow some balls, and suddenly she could be out of the picture for good. That is the source of your power. Never forget it.

Of course, your instincts are correct. You're the one with the power, but the best use of your power is in not having to wield it at all. Simply ignore her. Show up at their door and act like nothing ever happened. Let your stepmother be of no consequence to you whatsoever.

Remember, if you don't let her under your skin, she can't interfere with your relationship with your father.

On unburdening yourself

A family friend used to molest me for years. I never said anything to my mom as I was afraid she wouldn't believe me. Three of my friends who didn't know one another had reported he had touched them, at three completely different times. My mom called all three of them liars, and would still ship me over to Uncle Perv's house for unsupervised sleepovers for the weekend. It makes me sick to my stomach even typing this now, as it's the first time I've even admitted to myself that this happened.

I'm in my late 20s now and have grown very distant from my family. Other than the obligatory phone call on birthdays and holidays, I avoid them at all costs.

My question is, do I tell my mom now? She is still close with this "uncle" figure. And, frankly, I don't see how telling her will be a benefit. She can't change the past and all it will do is make her potentially hate herself. I feel I am a well-adjusted adult, but I just want to completely cut all ties with my family so I never have to think about it again.

You may be a well-adjusted adult, but that doesn't mean you're emotionally healthy. Your abuse is still very much an unresolved issue, and while you may have found methods of coping, you haven't found any peace.

An emotionally healthy person wouldn't want to cut all ties with her family to avoid processing her childhood sexual trauma. I'm sure you've got plenty of other reasons for avoiding your mom, but Uncle Perv shouldn't have to be one of them.

It's pretty clear your mother has a powerful mechanism for denial, and I think you're afraid of it. I get the feeling that on some fundamental level, you very much want to tell your mother what happened, but you're worried that her denial will allow her to somehow keep this man in her life.

In other words, you're afraid that if you tell her, she'll pick him over you.

Well, you've got to look past that. You can't change what happened, but you can't deny it either, and you're not going to find any peace until you tell your mom the whole truth. She probably won't handle it well, but that's not what's important. What's important is that you unburden yourself. This is for you, not her. You deserve to move past this.

My dad left when I was five. Twenty years later and today I finally got The Apology Letter. Why don't I feel better?

Because fuck him, that's why. An apology letter doesn't mean shit. At best, it's a souvenir of his absence. At worst, it's a self-serving attempt at emotional manipulation. Set the letter aside and let his actions speak instead.

My dad isn't willing to change his abusive and manipulative behaviors, so why does it scare me so much that he could die when we aren't on speaking terms?

Because you still think your father's behavior is a matter of will.

Why can't my mom just be happy for me?

Because there's nothing in it for her.

Caught him fucking my sister. Him, I can dump. What do I do about her?

Be rightfully pissed as long as you need to be. Eventually forgive her, and then never trust her around your man again.

On forgiveness

I'm 27 and have been estranged from my father for nearly a decade. When he left us, he took off with the woman he was cheating on my mother with.

Life with him before he left us was hell. He was, and presumably still is, an abusive alcoholic. I vividly remember him picking me up by the back of my shirt when I was about 7 and throwing me down the hall. He would mercilessly beat the only dog I ever owned until I literally threw myself on the dog to make him stop.

I remember him getting hammered on more than one occasion and tearing apart furniture, then throwing the pieces at me and telling me I "ruined his fucking life." When I was 16, I had my first boyfriend, and when I came home half an hour late after going to a movie with him my father screamed at me in the middle of the street, calling me a filthy slut, among other colorful things.

This is only the tip of the iceberg, but it gives you a general idea of what kind of person he is.

Anyway, a few weeks ago I got a call from a police officer saying my father had gone in to put out a missing persons report on me. The officer explained that my father told him that what he really wanted was to reconnect with his family. No missing person report was made (because, as the officer explained, estrangement does not equal "missing"), but the officer did ensure my father he would contact me and pass along a phone number where my father could be reached, which he did.

I still have the number and am debating calling. The only reason why I'm on the fence is because recently my aunt mentioned she heard something about him possibly having pancreatic cancer.

While that's a pretty awful hand to be dealt, I don't really feel any sympathy for him after the way he treated me and my family. But for some reason I'm feeling guilty; like I should call him at least once before he dies. However, the more logical part of me is saying, "No, he doesn't just potentially have cancer, he IS cancer and screw it if he's your biological father. You never asked to be related to this jerk and you don't owe him anything."

Am I wrong for wanting to go back to pretending he doesn't exist or should I call him one last time?

Like it or not, your father does exist. You don't owe him anything, but it might be a good idea to say goodbye. If he does have pancreatic cancer, he's not gonna be around for very long. If he dies without you getting some sort of closure, it's gonna mess with your head for the rest of your life.

Consider making your peace with him. That doesn't mean you have to let him back into your life. In fact, you probably shouldn't.

Still, you need to forgive him. It doesn't matter whether your father deserves it. The forgiveness is for your sake, not his.

Find a way. Take the time before you call. Dig deep, and truly forgive him. Let go of all that anger and resentment. That stuff is more toxic than he is.

Feel free to keep your distance from your father, but communicate with him to whatever extent you need to get the emotional poison out of your system. I promise, you'll feel better. It's a powerful thing to forgive.

On things you can trust

I think my dad is cheating on my mum.

I know this kind of thing happens all the time, but it's pretty gutting nevertheless.

I found out when I borrowed my dad's laptop. He forgot to delete his history and log out of some swingers website. His phone constantly beeps with new messages. So, nosy bitch that I am, I had a look through his "profile" and messages on this website. Well, ignorance is indeed bliss.

What I need help on is, what do I do? I'm very close to my mum, but she's coming out of a very rough year of mental health problems which boiled down to low self-esteem and suppressed emotions from a previous bad relationship. The family as a whole is going through a tough time as it is because my younger brother is in Afghanistan. I feel that if I was to share any information with her, it would bring her right back down at a time where she needs to stay positive.

I don't know whom to talk to about this. If a girl can't trust her daddy, whom can she trust?

Before you earn yourself a lifetime subscription to a pile of useless daddy issues, I highly recommend you talk to a therapist about this.

It sounds like your mom already has a shrink or two on speed-dial, so have her set you up an appointment as soon as possible. Don't tell her why. In fact, don't confront either of your parents about this until you've started sorting it out in your own head with the help of a professional.

Just tell your folks that you want to talk with someone about things at school and your brother being in Afghanistan. Hell, you're a teenager. You don't need much more of an excuse than that.

Once you're in a therapeutic environment, take your time with this. You are not obligated to do anything, and whatever else happens, don't feel like suddenly having this information is somehow forcing you to make a choice between your mother and your father.

This isn't your burden. It's not your job to referee your parents' marriage, and the point here isn't to address the infidelity. The point here is to make sure that you get through this in as healthy a way as possible.

This is about you, not them. You're at the tail end of your adolescence, and you're neck-deep in the phase when you start recognizing how flawed your parents really are. How you process this stuff plays a huge role in how you will eventually form relationships as an adult.

You're having to come to terms with the reality that your parents' marriage is a complicated and messy thing. That's tough even in the shiniest of sitcom families. It will be an exercise in patience and forgiveness, but you can get through it.

Just remember, sweetheart, you can still trust. You can trust that regardless of their flaws, your parents want the best for you. You can trust that no matter what, both your mom and your dad will always love you very much.

On Christmas spirit

This holiday season is killing me.

For some reason, this year the Christmas lights and the shoppers and the music are bothering me more than they ever have.

I told my mom I didn't like Christmas anymore and she just started crying, so I can't realistically renounce the holiday...

Do I just need to get over myself and go with it?

Apologize to your mother. Tell her you were in a bad mood, and you didn't know what you were saying, because you didn't.

Feel free to remain disgusted with the tacky decorations and crass commercialism and cheesy music, because that shit is awful. It always was and always will be. That's not Christmas. Well, it is, but that's not what you're going to define as Christmas, okay?

Your mom could give two shits about the shopping and the lights. She wasn't crying because you aren't excited about going to the mall. She was crying because the holidays are an emotionally overwhelming time for everyone, and she can see your teen angst coming a mile away.

She took it personally when you said you didn't like Christmas any more, because in her mind, Christmas is about family. You were rejecting her with that statement, even though you didn't mean to. Trust me, all she wants is some quality time and a little tradition. She's worried that she's losing you, and she's about had it with your shitty attitude.

Redefine Christmas in your head. Only keep the good stuff. Separate out all the tacky bullshit. Seriously, kid. Do you blame the band for the annoying crowds and horrible traffic after a concert? Fuck no. You can bitch about it, but it has nothing to do with the show. Same rules apply here.

Renounce the crowds. Renounce the music. Hell, renounce Christ if you want, but don't go around renouncing the importance of the holidays. Family tradition is more important than you're capable of understanding at your age. There's no way to say that without sounding condescending, so fuck it. Would it kill you to plaster on a smile and make your mom happy?

I didn't think so.

I haven't come out to my parents mainly because I vividly remember my mom telling me that she "likes gays, just not in our family." Is it awful of me to put off telling them until after they pay for college?

If your parents would cut you off for coming out of the closet, then you should probably hold out for some therapy money too.

I walked downstairs to find my dad rushing away from the computer and pulling up his pants the other night. How do I act around him now?

Loudly, especially as you walk down the stairs.

Today is the 7th anniversary of my brother's death. I know heaven doesn't exist and that he isn't watching over me. Does it make me stupid and/or a hypocrite to still "talk" to my brother when I miss him?

Talk to your brother all you'd like. There is no heaven, and he's not watching over you, but that doesn't mean he's not still very much a part of you.

I'm thinking of coming out to my extended family over Thanksgiving dinner. Should I do it before or after dessert, and with or without graphic details of why I am getting a sex change?

Don't make Thanksgiving dinner all about your giblets. That's tacky. Let everyone finish their pie before telling them about the sex change.

On your mom

I just found nude pictures of my mom, addressed to a woman who was at her wedding. She has suggested in the past that this woman and her husband are swingers, but she said she's "not into that".
   What the fuck do I do?

Put the pictures back where you found them. Make a mental note to never, ever look at them again. Take a deep breath, meditate for a moment on the fact that you owe your existence to your mom getting laid, and then laugh hysterically at the whole situation.

On understanding suicide

Three years ago my brother tried to commit suicide. He was fifteen then, which is how old I am now. A month ago he tried to kill himself again. He came home from the hospital a week ago, and I'm ecstatic to have him back again, but I'm also extremely angry at him. He didn't see my mom just about die or my dad break down, or my sister fly halfway across the country to come home for him. My family almost fell apart over this, and it kills me to know that, and I know that if he knew that it would hurt him too.   For three years I've been trying to figure out why he tried to kill himself, and I still can't grasp it. I understand depression and I deal with SAD myself, but I just can't see why he hates his life so, so much. We live a lovely life, he's a smart kid, and extremely popular. People adore him. And more importantly, we love him. So I just don't understand why my brother hates his life so much. Am I being selfish or ignorant? How can I understand my brother better? I'd really like to.

You say you want to understand your brother, but I get the feeling that you'd rather your brother just understand you.

You're angry, and you want him to see the world as you see it. You want him to acknowledge his lovely life, his popularity, and how much he is adored.

In your mind, you think those external conditions are enough to keep him from wanting to kill himself. You're the type who says, 'If only he knew how much we loved him, he wouldn't want to kill himself.'

You couldn't be more wrong. This isn't about you.

Once again, this isn't about you. You have to know that. It has to be your guiding principle when talking with your brother about this.

Don't assume that he hates his life. Those are your words. Did you ask him why he attempted suicide? Don't assume that he feels popular or adored just because you see him that way. Do you know how your brother feels about himself?

Ask him.

Start a conversation with him. Don't challenge him. Don't try and help him. Don't even come from a place where you assume he needs help. Just come from a place of unconditional love.

If you want to understand your brother, talk to him about life and death rather than his suicide attempts. Talk to him about love and relationships rather than his popularity. Talk to him about his purpose and his future rather than his depression.

We're all going to die one day. The fact that your brother tried to speed up the process probably isn't the most interesting thing about him. Find out what is.

On living in sin

How do I break it to my religious, highly conservative parents that I'm moving in with my boyfriend? Just to provide some context: they got me a "purity ring" for Christmas when I was fourteen, and they likely still maintain delusions of my virginity. I don't want to hurt them, and I really don't want to irreparably damage my relationship with them, but I need to move on with my life and I feel like it's time that I stop living according to their values and not my own. Every time my mom hears about someone moving in with their significant other before marriage, she snarks about "living in sin." Is there a way to manage this situation respectfully and relatively calmly?

I don't know your age, but I'm guessing early twenties. Based on your grammar and punctuation, I'm also guessing college-educated. In other words, you're an adult – young, but nonetheless fully capable of making life decisions according to your own set of moral standards.

It's good that you want to remain respectful, but you need to start making a distinction between showing respect for your parents and showing respect for their belief system. They aren't the same thing.

Showing respect for your parents means being honest and straightforward with them about your decision to move in with your boyfriend. It also means being patient as they come to terms with the fact that you're an adult who makes her own decisions. Beyond that, though, you don't have to put up with their conservative religious bullshit.

No doubt their ideology is deeply intertwined with their identity, so don't be surprised when your parents take an open rejection of their values personally. You'll also find them rather impervious to rational discussion, which means you're going to have to accept a certain measure of disapproval as an inevitability.

Get comfortable with the fact that you'll never change their minds, know that they love you, and don't ever expect their approval. I'll say it again, because it's the most important thing you can possible learn from this: *know that your parents love you, but don't ever expect their approval.*

Moving in with your boyfriend might be a huge mistake. Then again, it might be the best decision you'll ever make. It's imposs- ible to know, and that's not the point. What matters is that you give these decisions careful consideration and start making the best possible choices for yourself that you can make according to your own set of moral standards.

It's okay that your value system is different, and if 'living in sin' damages your relationship with your parents, so be it. Just remem- ber, you won't be the one doing the damage. They will.

On pressure to have kids

My husband and I have been together 10 years, married for 3 of them. Even before we were married, but especially after, there has been a lot of pressure for us to have kids. Coquette, we just don't wanna.

We like our lives just as they are. We get to take nice trips and drive nice cars. We just don't have that urge to be parents.

I do flip flop on this decision every now and then, usually when a close friend has a baby or sometimes when my parents put the "you are robbing us of grand parenthood" pressure on extra thick. I turned 35 yesterday so the point of no return is looming ever closer.

Are we making a huge mistake?

Maybe. Maybe not. Either way, it's you and your husband's decision to make. No one else's.

I'm sure your parents are lovely people, but fuck what they think. Fuck the pressure they put on you to make major life decisions for their sake, and fuck their selfish desire to become grandparents at your expense.

This is the world our parents made. The American Dream is a smoldering pile of shit. We're stuck cleaning up their mess, and yet somehow we're robbing them of grand-parenthood? Fuck them. That's what they get for robbing an entire generation of the economic security it takes to responsibly become parents.

Fuck every last Baby Boomer who feels entitled to give any of us shit for our choices. They're so used to having all their dreams come true, they don't even know how insulting that shit sounds.

On Work

On being an artist

What's the difference between an artist and a craftsman? I've always wanted to be an artist but my dad is adamant that artists are born, not made, and the most I'd ever be is a crafts person, which is better left as a hobby. I'm 27, is it too late?

Your dad is a dream-killing asshole. He's also wrong about artists being born. There's nothing magical about being an artist. Artists make themselves, so if you have art in you, go make it. That's not to say it will ever become your career, but who gives a shit? Just because you keep your day job, that doesn't mean you're not an artist.

(Oh, and since you asked, an artist masters a medium for the sake of the artist's expression. A craftsman masters a medium for the sake of the mastery of the craft itself. It's a subtle distinction with quite a bit of overlap.)

On being an expert

I just graduated and got an 'important' government job. I can't handle people regarding me as an expert. It's frightening for me, and it should be frightening for the world.

Oh, please. None of us know what we're doing. We're all faking it. Every last one of us, especially the experts. Our species has consistently been wrong about almost everything we've ever thought or believed.

So, as a freshly minted expert, work hard, do your best not to fuck things up, and don't take your important government job so damned seriously, because human civilization is just a thin topcoat of sheer dumb luck, and it could all collapse at any moment.

On finishing what you start

I have one semester of college left, and I just found out I got a job in Los Angeles working at a non-profit. So this white girl from a decently well off family is about to move across the country to make just under $1,200 a month. My parents are begging me not to, and promised no financial support. I'm not too worried because I've been working two jobs since I was a sophomore and have a couple thousand of my own to get me started along with a true streak of Irish stubbornness. Any advice? (also just to make it super obvious I have no interest in tv/movies/etc except to watch so I'm not trying to catch a break)

Get your fucking degree, you idiot. You've come this far. Finish what you start.

It's not like you're ducking out of your last semester because you found venture capital for your tech startup. You're just in a stupid hurry to earn slave wages. Don't waste three-and-a-half years of educational investment for a false start at a shitty non-profit gig.

Chill the fuck out. Los Angeles will still be here in a couple months. So will any number of entry-level jobs in the non-profit sector with low pay, no benefits, and absolutely zero possibility for advancement.

Working two jobs as a college student doesn't mean shit, either. You have no clue what's about to be expected of you as a full-time employee. Those fuckers are gonna work your punk ass like a rented mule, and in six months to a year, after your dreams have been crushed and you're both physically and spiritually exhausted, you'll wish you had a bachelors degree on your résumé.

Don't fuck up here. Be smart. Take a deep breath, knock out your last semester, and save up some more money. There will be plenty of time to make poor life decisions once you get to Los Angeles.

I worked at a shitty job for 8 months, they made my life hell just so they could get me to leave. My unemployment is almost done, why do I keep obsessing over their social media accounts and why can't I move on?
Because you're young and entitled and you're not used to having your ass kicked.

I'm a high end escort. Is it wrong to sleep with men I know are married and/or cheating, even though I'm getting paid?
Willfully participating in infidelity is pretty much the only ethical gray area of your job, but in terms of moral high ground, that still puts you above the average lawyer.

Can you help me articulate why I feel blinding anger when, after doing something unprofessional and shitty, my boss apologizes and says, "Are we cool?" and if I don't say "Yes," he pouts? What is the exact phrase for the manipulative bullshit he is pulling?
He's not apologizing. He's trying to excuse himself, and he's demanding your complicity. Real apologies don't come with emotional strings attached.

*Which is more obnoxious: for me to accept nepotism
to get a job I may end up loving, or to refuse nepotism
because "I don't want to get a job that way"?*

Don't be an asshole. If you can get a dream job through family
connections, fucking take it. Just be worthy of it. Pay your dues.
Work your ass off.

*A man that I met while traveling in Europe is launching
a Bitcoin exchange, and wants to launch a social
networking site in tandem with it. I am a community
manager between gigs. He recently offered to buy a plane
ticket and pay my salary for the next two months before
I start my Masters in the fall. This doesn't seem like a
real thing.*

Yeah, unless your dad is Liam Neeson, you might wanna consider
a little extra due diligence before accepting this gig.

On the boss's wife

*I recently got written up at work for calling the boss's
wife, "the boss's wife" the first time I met her. We have
the same title and position at work and I'm a pretty light-
hearted and sarcastic guy at times. Who was wrong? Me
for jokingly referring to her that way or her for shoving
that stick up her ass far enough to complain to HR?*

Fuck who was wrong. This ain't about that. You need to quickly
wrap your head around how badly you fucked up.

Congratulations, dumbass. You've officially made an enemy
at work who can get you fired. Not only is she the boss's wife, but
she's clearly demonstrated that she knows how to use the system to
her advantage. There's paperwork involved, and guess what? On
paper, you're the bad guy.

Is she a hypersensitive cunt for having you reprimanded? Maybe. Do you come off as more of an asshole than you think you do? Probably. Still, all of that is beside the point. What matters is that she doesn't like you, and you need to recognize that this was a warning shot from a master manipulator who made you her bitch on the very first day she met you.

Don't think of this in terms of who was right or wrong. This is a power game. It's about who wins or loses, and despite you two having the same job description, she's already asserted her dominance.

Good luck keeping that title and position.

On why everyone at work hates you

I accidentally let it slip that I think of people that liked the movie Gravity as the ones that fucked "the dumb girl." I feel the movie pays lip service to science. So my issue is this; everyone at work hates me. Is there some weird trick for blending in with the herd without feeling oppressed? I've had this problem before in religious environments.

Yeah, I haven't seen *Gravity*, but I have had a similar history of frustration when it comes to Sandra Bullock movies.

Still, I just blog about my opinions. I don't go around acting like an arrogant jerk to people's faces over something as trivial as a popcorn flick. There's a time and a place to be a cunt, and it ain't during water cooler talk at the office.

People hate you because you're a dick. You refer to your co-workers as 'the herd', and you believe you're special just because you have a different worldview. Well, guess what? You work there too, numbnuts.

You wanna know the weird trick for blending in? Simple. It's called being kind to people. You could instantly and dramatically improve the quality of your life if you would stop walking around with a chip on your shoulder.

You're not oppressed. You're just an asshole. Get used to the world being full of people with different opinions.

On running a business

What would be your rules, regardless of what kind of business you were going to start, on running that business?

Never give up controlling interest.

Never take on a partner who doesn't have skin in the game.

Always be the one who signs the checks.

Always be the one who maintains the key business relationships.

Always draw a hard line between business and personal relationships.

Always use contracts, and document everything.

Never give the government a reason to look at you.

Always be prepared for either a lawsuit or an audit.

Always know your numbers. No one should ever be more familiar with the general ledger than you.

Never forget why you are in business.

I'm afraid that when I quit my job I'll realize that it wasn't the reason I am so unhappy.

The irony is that you're unhappy because you're afraid.

Can you ever be friends with your boss?

Sure you can, but never forget that in his role as your boss he is not your friend.

I got fired for missing a staff meeting today. (I've been working at a coffee place for 2 months). I forgot about the meeting. How can I get my job back?

You didn't get fired for missing the staff meeting. You got fired for being the kind of person who misses staff meetings. There's a difference, and that's the lesson you need to take away from this.

I'm finishing college, and I'm trying to come to terms with the idea that college has been the most anticlimactic experience I've ever had.

Good. Maybe now you'll think twice before believing in our society's institutionalized bullshit. Enjoy your twenties.

Do you believe if you work hard enough, you'll get where you need to be?

Of course not. Work hard, sure, but there are no guarantees in this life. Wherever you end up, it's definitely not going to be what you expect.

Does being lazy make me a bad person?

No. It makes you a bad employee.

On a soon-to-be working mom

I am 18 weeks pregnant with my first child. I am currently employed, but am experiencing some serious job malaise. Now, I TOLD myself not to do this, but in a moment of weakness I checked a job site, and saw that an amazing job I'd be perfect for was just posted two days ago. So my question is: how crazy is it to apply for a job when noticeably pregnant? Obviously I wouldn't get hired unless they have some crazy-flexible hiring schedule, but I can't help thinking, what if? Help me put my mind to rest.

Help you do what now? You've got a half-baked bun in the oven, and you want to play bird-in-the-hand bullshit games with your employment status in this economy? Are you fucking nuts?

I think you're in a little bit of denial here, babe. It's fine if you wanna juggle motherhood and a career, but I don't think you're grasping the magnitude of how much your life is gonna change in twenty more weeks.

The last thing you want to do right now is give your current employer an excuse to replace you, and even if you got the other job, you'd still be the most recently hired, most expendable person in the room who also happens to be a first-time mom going through the most stressful year of her young life. Fuck that shit.

Come on, girl. The only amazing job you'd better be perfect for is coming up in April. Knock it the fuck out. You'll get a full night's sleep again sometime in 2013, and by then, the economy will have picked back up.

I know it seems like forever, but don't worry. Life is long. You'll get to do all the cool shit you want to do.

On quitting

I just got my dream job, I like it, but I think I suck at it. Should I stay right where I am or consider finding something that I can do without getting fired?

What kind of punk-ass question is this? It's your dream job. Bust your fucking hump until you reach ninja status or until they have to shovel your emaciated carcass out the door.

Don't you dare fucking quit.

On mediocrity

How do I stop others' success from making me feel inadequate..? I want to be a doctor but I did horribly my first year of college. My friends are the ideal pre-med students. I feel like there's no point in trying to compete against them.

You may very well prove to be inadequate, but the success of your friends will have nothing to do with your failure.

Can you do the work or not? That's all that matters. Make an honest assessment of your abilities, and don't get distracted by the kids at the head of the class.

So what if you're average? Every Salieri has his Mozart, or in your case, his Doogie Howser. Get comfortable with your mediocrity or it will destroy you.

Meet the requirements, and don't be a whiny little bitch. After all, you know what they call the guy who graduates dead last in his class at medical school?

Doctor.

On entry-level ethics

I work at a bank and recently found myself in the middle of my boss stealing 20 bucks from a customer (ie a liquor store employee who brought in too much cash for his deposits – he was over by at least $200) My manager gave me half of what she stole, even though I said I didn't want it and openly tried to give it all back to the liquor store employee. I wanted to take more immediate action, but I felt uneasy because this manager is very friendly with me, has invited me to her wedding, ect. I'm a fairly new employee and just a student trying to pay

for school. My instinct is to go to my boss and report it,
but I fear the repercussions from this manager. Other
than this event, she has appeared to be a great leader and
manages people well. I called the "ethics hotline" I found
on my company site, but they said all they could do was
file a report. Not knowing what exactly would happen to
the report made me apprehensive to file one. It was only
20 bucks, but I feel dirty having that 10 dollar bill in my
purse and I know it was wrong.

Never allow someone to make you complicit in a crime.

I'll say it again – *never allow someone to make you complicit in a crime.*
Not for ten dollars. Not for ten thousand. Either have the strength
of will to refuse, or the strength of character to fully accept your
role as an accomplice.

You realize what she's done, right? That shady bitch bought
you. Cheap. This wasn't about the money. Now she owns your ass
like the mob owns a dirty cop.

You've only got one move here. Take the ten dollar bill out of
your purse, and give it back to her in full view of other employees.
'You gave this to me the other day, and I don't want it.' That's all
you have to say, and then just walk away.

Don't bother with ethics hotlines. That kind of human resources
bullshit is worthless. It's corporate liability window dressing.

Don't bother reporting it to your boss either. No one likes a
snitch, and he doesn't want to deal with a shit-ton of hassle over
twenty bucks.

Besides, once you hand back the ten dollar bill, the balance
of power shifts back to you. If you were a bit more savvy and had
a fucking backbone, you might be able to subtly use that to your
advantage.

Good luck doing the right thing.

Why do I always go to the bathroom during work to masturbate?

Because you'd get fired if you did it at your workstation.

I'm 30 years old, in grad school, and I realized I'm just not that smart. What do I do?

Relax. Just do your best, try not to let people find out, and don't use it as an excuse to quit.

I'm trying to get a great internship. Do you have any suggestions on how to stand out with either my cover letter or résumé? Or both?

Those are just pieces of paper. Find other ways to stand out than pieces of paper.

How do I find my calling?

Look for purpose in what makes you happy.

What is your advice to a girl heading off to her first year of college?

Sleep more than you study. Study more than you party. Party as much as you possibly can.

Any advice for a young female entreprenuer?

Learn how to spell entrepreneur.

On fucking your way to the middle

How do you know when to call it quits with a fuckbuddy?

A few issues: He's my boss. He's practically engaged (he's shown me the $20k ring, which I find outrageous), and has said that he "loves everything about me and would totally date me if it weren't for his girlfriend".

I don't want to date him and I know that things will eventually change (or so he says, once he actually proposes) and that's fine, but I'll admit that I enjoy having control and I would like it to stay that way.

So, if your boss followed the three months' salary rule, he's pulling down 80 grand a year. If he's corporate, that puts him at the non-professional junior executive level, probably early thirties, and clearly a world-class douchebag for cheating on his soon-to-be fiancée with a subordinate at work.

Unless his dad owns the company, this guy probably doesn't have the power to single-handedly promote you, but he can make a recommendation.

If you enjoy having control, I suggest you exert some.

The balance of power shifts dramatically in your favor the day he proposes. On that day, congratulate him and then make a formal request for a promotion with a raise. Do it all with a smile, and don't even hint at anything shady. Trust me, he'll get the message.

It will immediately end the fuckbuddy status of your relationship because he'll be terrified of you, and yet everything stays friendly. Plus, he'll do everything in his power to get you all the perks you ask for.

On making a difference

Is it possible to make a difference without coming off as a left wing activist nutjob?

I am a graphic designer and I want to use my abilities to help change the world for the better. I believe in sustainable food production and reversing climate change.

I know I can create compelling work, but how can I help my audience actually PAY ATTENTION?

Fuck all the insufferably trendy beliefs that you wear like fashion accessories for your identity. Fuck your untested self-esteem and the assumption that any of your work is the least bit compelling. Fuck whatever social media follower count you've confused with an actual audience.

Do you have any idea how much of a naïve asshole you sound like when you say you want to change the world with your graphic design abilities? You will never 'make a difference', whatever that bullshit phrase means. Hell, you aren't even interesting enough to come off as a left-wing activist nutjob. At least those people have something to say.

Nope, you're just another insufferable twat with a popular pair of pet causes and a vague sense of self-importance who thinks that just because you breathe air and have an opinion, you deserve everyone's undivided fucking attention.

Sorry, kid. You don't deserve shit. You came knocking at the wrong fucking door if you wanted someone to blow smoke up your ass and slather your ego with Astroglide and affirmations.

No one gives a fuck about your hopes and dreams, and you don't get credit for good intentions. Compelling work speaks for itself, so please, by all means, feel free to go off into the world and prove me wrong. Then again, you should also feel free to go fuck yourself.

Either way, somebody needed to tell you.

Am I supposed to be having fun in college?
You're supposed to be having fun in life, my dear.

What's your advice for a starving artist?
Eat something and don't refer to yourself as an artist.

I've been working my ass off for years trying to get where I want to be in life. It's not working, and it's starting to seem like it never will start working. When do I throw in the towel and settle for mediocrity?
Mediocrity isn't a measure of your title or your tax bracket, fucko. It's a measure of your state of mind. Never settle for mediocrity.

why is it so hard to find a job?
Because the global economy is slowly collapsing as it runs out of oil. No biggie.

With this economy, what job positions do you recommend, then?
Geriatrics. Taking care of old people is all our generation will have left.

Should i quit my job?
Go find another one first.

How do I get into acting?
Come out to LA and treat your life like a lottery ticket.

On achieving your stupid fantasies

Will I achieve my dreams of becoming what I'm passionate about which is being a Singer/Model/Dancer/ Actor even tho I'm completely unsupported by my parents both morally and financially, because their totally against it should i give up is it worth carrying on and pursuing this dream or should i just give up.

You are never going to be a professional singer/model/dancer/ actor. That's not even a thing. In fact, you will never achieve your dreams if all they are is ridiculous fantasies.

You are not passionate about singing, modeling, dancing and acting. You're just a silly child who's fascinated by the idea of fame, and your parents are right not to provide moral or financial support for your self-absorbed fantasy of becoming a singer/model/ dancer/actor.

I'm sure your parents are intimately aware of what was obvious to me after reading what you consider to be just one sentence: you're an idiot. They're not going to tell you you're an idiot because they love you, but to their credit, they're also not going to encourage your idiocy.

Let me tell you a secret I've learned from all my years in Los Angeles. People who use slashes in their self-bestowed titles are losers. Always. Every time, with no exceptions. The more slashes, the bigger the loser. The most common form is model/actress, and they're bad enough, but when you start adding singer/dancer/ whatever into the mix, shit starts getting insufferable.

Do not become one of these sad, pathetic losers.

If you have a dream (not a fantasy) of becoming a performer of some kind, and that dream is backed up with a shit-ton of talent and a burning passion to dedicate your life to perfecting your craft, and you're willing to spend years broke and hungry while paying your dues, grinding your way through mountains of bullshit, avoiding all the pitfalls and predators, getting your ass kicked repeatedly to maybe one day have enough blind fucking luck to get a shot at earning a meager living doing what you love, then there's an outside chance that it might be possible for you to become a singer. Or maybe an actor. Probably not a dancer, and definitely not a model.

Point is, you can pick one. Just one. Get rid of the slashes. No one will ever take you seriously until you do, and even then, whatever stupid fame-whore dream you have is almost definitely not going to come true, even if you devote your life to it.

Oh, and if any of this seems harsh, it only further proves my point that you're a silly child who doesn't know the difference between a dream and a fantasy.

I'd tell you good luck, but I really don't think it's gonna matter.

On a monumental mistake

This spring I'll be graduating college. It's taken 5 years, three degree changes and tens of thousands of dollars in loans before I found something I'm passionate about.

I'm slowly realizing I'm not passionate about it, though. I took it because it was easy and just thought-provoking enough to let me fool myself into thinking it was challenging. I feel like I've made a monumental mistake and am officially at a loss for what to do with my life. Thoughts?

Yep, you've made a monumental mistake. You've wasted five years and tens of thousands of dollars chasing what you thought was passion to earn a college degree that (if you're lucky) will buy you a shitty entry-level job where you can work your ass off for another five years trying to pay down those tens of thousands of dollars before one day in your late twenties it finally dawns on you that never, not once in your life, have you ever really been passionate about anything.

Of course, that part isn't the monumental mistake. The monumental mistake is continuing to buy into the system. It's believing you have to be passionate about some stupid college major, or that you feel like a failure because you haven't mapped out exactly what you want to do with your entire life at an age when you're barely qualified to answer phones and fetch coffee.

Fuck that shit. It's perfectly okay to be clueless and terrified. The only wrong way to handle it is to freeze up and do nothing. The good news is that it doesn't matter what you do with your life, and it sure as hell doesn't matter what you studied in college. Just get the fuck out there and do something.

PART IV

On the Mental

On expanding your mind

Aside from drugs and sex what activities would you recommend for someone in their twenties with an interest in mind-expansion?

Get a passport. Use it as often as possible. Read (books, that is: ones without pictures). Surround yourself with brilliant and fascinating people. Say yes whenever you can, except to religion and authority. Create things. Fall in and out of love. Never forget that you will die one day.

I'm more content than I have been in a long time. Why does that fill me with a vague sense of dread?

I like to refer to that as cosmic background anxiety. It's a sort of low-level existential angst that's always there, and you only feel it when all the other noise and static is gone.

How can I stop being bitter when the world is full of such shitty things?

You don't have to fill yourself with the shitty things.

I'm terrified of taking medication for depression because I'm afraid that I won't ever be able to do without it. Is that a thing that can happen? I can't ask a doctor, I really don't think they'd be honest with me.

Okay, but you *can* ask a doctor. You should, actually. If possible, ask more than one, and don't be afraid to ask direct questions. They're not gonna lie to you. (I appreciate that you trust me, but don't let your anxiety prevent you from getting the treatment that you need.)

How do you find the courage to ask for therapy? I know I need it but I hate the idea of someone else knowing that.
I understand how vulnerable it makes you feel to ask, but please know that everyone needs therapy. *Everyone*. It doesn't make you weak, sick or broken in any way. Go ahead. Take the next step. You can do this.

What will make me feel less lonely when I get home? The drugs aren't working.
Connect with other humans. That's the only thing that will work.

The days when I do want to live, I don't know where to start. What do I do?
Start by making your bed.

On making your bed

Is it strange that your advice to start by making your bed brought tears to my eyes? Being suicidal is basically the most difficult thing I've had to live with (pun slightly intended) and the simplicity of that first step… it just hit home. Thank you.

It may seem simple, but making your bed is quietly one of the most important daily rituals a person can have. I promise, it will change your life. I know that sounds like hyperbole, but it's not. Those of you who already do it know exactly what I mean.

First and foremost, making your bed forces you to get out of it. That's not necessarily a small feat, especially if you're suffering from depression. Not only are you out of bed, but you can't get back in. It's a line of demarcation that officially starts your day.

More than that, though, it's a ceremonial act of respect for oneself. It's a deliberate measure of control that you can always take, even when the rest of your life is complete and utter chaos.

Do it. Every damn morning. It only takes a minute, but it will have a cascading effect that subtly improves everything else about the rest of your day, right up to the moment when you get to crawl back in to a well-made bed at night.

When I think of all the truly successful people I've known in my life, the ones who really have their shit together, all of them – *every last one* – routinely make their beds every single morning. This is not a coincidence.

On wanting to live

Please, say something that will make me want to live. If anyone can do it, it's you.

You can only feel relief from your pain if you're alive.

On bedtime death panic

I've just recently come to the realization of my own mortality. In the time before I fall asleep, it absolutely terrifies me thinking not about how it will end, but that it ends, period. I know you've given this sort of advice before, but I can't even get past this fear to the part where you realize, "This is it, enjoy it while it lasts." I feel trapped by the inevitable, and I've been trying so hard to channel you, Coquette, so I just have to ask, will the fear subside? Will I eventually be able to fall asleep without having a near panic attack over my mortality?

When your head hits the pillow, your mind begins the process of winding down after a long day of nonstop thinking. It's dark. It's quiet. The day is over, and suddenly it doesn't have anything left to grind and chew.

Of course, your mind is built to grind and chew, and it isn't ready to stop processing thoughts for the day, so what does it do? It reaches back into the dark and sticky parts of your brain to pull out whatever low-level anxiety it can find.

Your mind doesn't know any better. It just wants to think, so you go ahead and let it gnaw away on your basic fears. That's when your spine turns to glass and your ears become refrigerator coils and your guts squeeze dry and you're filled with the warm oily horror that one day, yes, in fact, *you are going to die.*

We've all been there. It's terrifying.

You allowed your mind to trigger what is essentially a fight-or-flight survival response when there isn't any actual danger. It just wanted to play a game of chess, but instead, your mind started playing a game of global thermonuclear war.

If you don't have a Xanax prescription handy, the best way to handle this kind of situation is to give your mind something to do while the rest of your sympathetic nervous system ratchets back down from DEFCON 1.

Read a book. Turn on the television. Find an activity, and do a little deep breathing. Don't worry, it doesn't take much to distract your mind.

Once you're done freaking out and you've relaxed enough to fall back asleep, stay aware of your mind's tendency to grab on and chew inappropriate anxieties. Stay apart from it, and don't let it keep chewing.

The trick is in separating yourself from your own mind. Allow yourself to stop thinking, and you'll fall asleep peacefully every time.

Any insight as to why high school absolutely wrecks some people for the rest of their lives?

It's not high school. It's adolescence. The transition from childhood to adulthood is a brutal fucking experience. That's just the nature of the human condition, and some folks just don't make it.

I've got the house, the wife and the money, so why am I not happy?

Yeah well, I've got cheddar cheese, a pumpkin and some carrots, so why am I not the color orange? (And for those of you in New Jersey, I'm not suggesting that self-tanner is the key to happiness.)

I'm very lost. I'm very sad. I'm very confused. I'm very sober.

Stay off Hollywood Boulevard, because you're just how Scientology likes 'em.

When a guy refers to a girl as intimidating, what he really means is???

That he believes her to be either sexually or intellectually more experienced than he is, and he finds her at least somewhat attractive.

On grief

Dear Coquette,

Eight months ago today, my husband killed himself. Last weekend, I finally held his memorial. I'd been planning it since the day he died. It was a big party, with food and drink and fireworks and friends and so many memories. Lots of family, too—including my in-laws, whom I met for the first time (he'd been estranged

from his family). It was both very good and very
painful, which I expected. I didn't expect the emotional
aftermath. I'm spacey, exhausted, irritable, fragile,
unstable. Can't eat. Can't sleep. Can't read. Can't listen
to music. I feel like I did in the first weeks and months
after he died. Before the party, I was feeling ok. Not
great, but better than I had in a long while. Now, the
grief is raw and fresh again. I've learned that grieving
isn't a tidy, linear process, but I'm desperate to make
some sense of it. If I could parse it, I think I wouldn't feel
so overwhelmed, but I can't. It just seems chaotic and
terrifying.

Can you explain grief?
Thanks for everything you do, always.

It's never going to make any sense. That's not part of the deal. We don't get answers to those kinds of questions. Never have. Never will. There's no point in trying to parse it. You'll spin yourself dizzy and just wind up confused (or worse, religious).

Instead, sit down next to it and just be. Feel all of that shit. Let it wash over you and through you. Do it again and again, as many times as necessary. Don't be afraid of it.

In a few days, you'll be back to relative normal, but four months from now on the anniversary, be prepared for this to happen again. It won't be quite as intense, but it will still be significant. Let that be okay. (And when the day comes that you finally move on, let that be okay too.)

Your grief is real, and nothing real is tidy or linear. You're doing it right, though. You're supposed to be exhausted, irritable, fragile and unstable – but you're also resilient. One day food will bring flavor again. Sleep will bring rest. Books and music will bring joy.

That's how this works. It's not the same thing as any of it making sense, but it's all we've ever had, and on most days, it's enough.

On hate and unavailable jerks

How the hell can you NOT hate someone who abused you for 18 years?

If you can't imagine yourself *not* hating someone, that means you've allowed that hate to become a part of your identity. You believe the hate you feel is an integral and inseparable part of you, but I promise, it's not. You think it defines who you are, but all it does is corrode your soul.

It really is as simple as letting go of the hate. It may take some time to process all of your emotions, but that's perfectly okay. The moment you realize that you don't have to hold onto all that anger and resentment, you're on a path to forgiveness.

And yes, forgiveness is your eventual goal. Not for your abuser's sake – for yours. Forgiveness is not the same thing as absolution. It doesn't mean your abuser is free from the consequences of his or her behavior just because you've let go of your anger and resentment. All it means is that *you* are free from the consequences of *their* behavior.

Remember, as long as you hate someone, that person still has the power to bring chaos into your life, but by letting go of the hate, you take away that power forever.

On self-worth and acceptance

All my life I've been told I'm gorgeous and talented. Modeling contracts, Ivy League college, NYC, Paris, Milan, LA. Now I'm 40 and have no self love and a string of failed relationships. I've tried everything: therapy, drugs, sobriety, vision quests, psychics, celibacy, meditation, reading all the books, whatever. I'm no closer to accepting that soon, "pretty" will run out, and then what will I have going for me? Point me in the right direction, please.

Your relationships didn't fail. They simply ran their course, and the part of you that believes you were a failure in love is the same part of you that believes your value as a human being is directly tied to an arbitrary beauty standard you happened to meet in your youth.

I can't point you in the right direction. There is no direction. There's nothing out there that you can smoke, seek, fuck, find or read that will suddenly give you the self-love and acceptance you're so desperate to discover.

You wanna know why? Because all those things you tried were just different flavors of the same old broken-souled search for external validation. All that bullshit, and it still never occurred to you that the only thing you ever had to do was forgive yourself.

Just fucking forgive yourself. Let go. That shit was never yours. It didn't belong to you. The beauty and the talent and the hubris and the superiority – they were all someone else's idea of you, and they felt so good for so long, you made them a part of your identity. It was all a fucking fiction, and you can just let it all go. It's okay, really. Have a good cry, shake it off, and then forgive yourself.

Keep forgiving yourself, and keep rejecting every instinct you have to seek external validation until one day you wake up and realize that you are worthy.

You're worthy of love. You're worthy of acceptance. You're just plain inherently worthy. Trust me, you don't even know the meaning of real freedom until you finally discover what internally validated self-worth feels like.

All you gotta do is let go.

What's the next step after realizing you're a narcissist?
Stop behaving like one.

Why do I feel lonely all of the time?
Because you are disconnected from the people in your life.

Why do I feel like I don't deserve to be happy?
Because you hold false beliefs about the nature of happiness.

*How do I quit torturing myself over things I've said/
whether I've offended anyone after every night out? It's
fucking with my zen mode big time.*
Oh, fuck off. You don't have a zen mode, and you torture yourself
because you like the way it feels. You'd rather labor under the false
impression that you might have offended someone than accept the
fact that nobody gives a shit.

*I'm insecure. Super fucking insecure. Need people to like
me insecure. I recognize the problem. I want to change.
How?*
It's not that you need people to like you. It's that you need people
to approve of you, and you don't know the difference. Stop seeking
approval.

On the grind

*Everything makes me angry. People I used to like are
insufferable, I hate the girl I called my best friend, the
job I felt important doing is a soul sucking mess, and my
6 year relationship feels tired and boring.*
   *What the fuck happened to me? Why isn't life fun
anymore?*

If your six-year relationship is tired and boring, then do something about it. Spice that shit up, or move the fuck on.

If you hate your best friend, then confront the source of that negativity. Either fix your friendship, or cut her out of your life.

If the job you once felt was important is a soul-sucking mess, then rediscover what's important to you. Quit if you want. Stick it out if you have to. Whatever. Just find a new way to do your best.

Nothing fucking happened to you. Maybe you're depressed. Maybe you're bipolar. Maybe you're just an irritable cunt, but no matter what, never forget that life is a grind. It's hard sometimes, and the only way to improve shit is by doing the fucking work it takes to change.

Quit whining about fun and go do something.

On vague existential threats

Every once and a while I feel this intense fear knowing the state of our environment and the imminent carbon fueled suffocation of the human race. I feel this intense sense of foreboding when I think about the future. We're all driving our Co2 spouting automobiles headfirst in to the apocalyptic hell-scape of global warming. There's no denying it, and even though I do my daily part to be greener, the fact remains that the sheer amount of people choosing ignorance and denial far outweigh the active. I was just thinking about how pointless all my prom photos are in the face of it all. I stress about finals while the world around me melts. Everything is pointless and I will die but how do I reconcile my fear? Not of death, but at never getting a fair shot at life?

Ugh. I know your type. You've decided to take your first-world free-floating anxiety and make it all about some vague yet trendy existential threat. In your case, it's global warming. Please. Get some real problems, bitch. Either that or take a Xanax and shut the fuck up.

First of all, you have no sense of scale and you don't know shit about climate science. Sure, global warming is a big fucking deal, and go drive a fucking Prius if it makes you feel better, but don't act like doing your daily part to be greener makes you special in any way whatsoever.

I mean, come on. You wanna talk ignorance and denial? You're the one who's blatantly projecting your fear of mortality onto the fucking weather. Quit it. Life may be pointless, and you're definitely gonna die, but in the meantime you still have to show up and be a part of this ridiculous experiment.

Put down your stupid fucking prom photos, get your shit together, and go study for your finals. Remember, there's no such thing as a 'fair shot at life'. Only a child thinks life is supposed to be fair.

On special snowflake disease

How do I deal with the realization that I have no special talents, nor am I as intelligent as I thought to be? I feel like I am not going to be able to accomplish anything I wanted to do in my life.

You'll be fine. You're just going through the withdrawal phase of a self-esteem addiction. It's a natural part of your recovery from Special Snowflake Disease.

Let me guess: you're young, white and a product of the American suburbs. From preschool through senior year, you were fed a constant diet of self-esteem-boosting, feel-good encouragement. You were told you could be anything and do anything, and that everyone was a special snowflake.

Sure, you grew up as one of the good kids. You took an AP class or two, your report card usually had a couple of As in it, and you weren't bad at whatever sport you played. You even got accepted to a decent college, but when you showed up for freshman year, you promptly had your ass handed to you by the brutal reality that no one cared any more.

You were suddenly surrounded by people who were smarter than you, and there was no one there to make sure you showed up and did the work. As a result, your grades have been in the toilet lately, and you find yourself struggling for what used to come so easily.

No, I'm not psychic. This is simply what's happening to most of your generation, especially from your little slice of the socio-economic pie. All of you special snowflakes are coming to terms with your own raging mediocrity. Yes, that's right. You will not cure cancer. You will not win the lottery. Worst of all, you will not have your own reality show.

Don't worry, though. You're gonna be OK. Sacrificing your dreams at the altar of reality is a rite of passage for everyone but a handful of rock stars and ballerinas. You can't ever let it get to you, or else you'll end up leading one of those lives of quiet desperation. In fact, it's good that you caught this early. The sooner you face the harsh truths of the real world, the better off you'll be.

The first step is taking comfort in the knowledge that you're like most people. You're not the best. You're not the worst. You're just average. The next step is getting cozy with the notion that no one cares. Right now, that kind of bums you out. You're still a bit of an encouragement junkie. Soon though, you'll mellow out and realize that there's a certain kind of freedom in no one giving a crap. You'll start taking strength in your own independence, and you'll learn to validate your existence through internal rather than external criteria. In other words, you'll stop caring what other people think of your accomplishments.

Not to skip ahead a few lessons, but maybe one day you'll even discover that it doesn't matter what you accomplish with your life. None of it matters, but that's okay too, because at the end of the day, if you're able to surround yourself with good people and find a few things that make you happy, you'll have lived a good life.

On a sociopath

I read in one of your responses to a question that if you feel guilt when you cheat, steal or lie that it's good news because you are not a sociopath. I do not feel any remorse or guilt when I do these things. Actually I quite enjoy doing these things and the feeling that comes after knowing that I've gotten away with it. Does this mean that I'm a sociopath? I'm 21 years old and am doing well enough to easily retire at 40. I'm extremely successful in life and happy with where I am. Even if I am a sociopath, does it matter?

Of course it matters, asshole. It matters to the people you hurt and betray. That's the essence of what makes you dangerous, the fact that you inherently don't get why it matters.

How do I stop romanticizing my personality flaws? How do I stop secretly loving being "broken"?
Grow the fuck up.

Why the fuck do I hate myself so much?
You don't hate yourself. You hate an identity that you associate with yourself, and you can't tell the difference.

Why am I still determining my self-worth though men's sexual interest?
Because you don't believe you bring anything to the table other than the ass you put in the chair.

Why does everyone piss me off so much?
You're just angry at yourself, and you're projecting that anger onto others.

How can someone have low self-esteem and an enormous ego at the same time?
It's easy. You don't have to like yourself to think you're the center of the world.

On a girl with real problems

I've had a really unstable and dramatic life. Raped twice, molested by several family friends, beat by my parents and ex boyfriends, and much much more. I also am extremely bi polar (I've been diagnosed several different times by different psychiatrists since I was 6 years old). I've tried to get over my issues and just live life, be happy, and leave the bullshit behind. But I can't help but let these things creep in. It ruined a long-term relationship, every relationship I've had since, and every friendship I have. My family hates me because of it and treat me like a monster. I'm afraid to get on medication for it, because I've done so much to overcome my past and make something of myself and I know if I get on medication my family will claim that I'm a quitter and take away all credit I've earned for what I have accomplished. But it's really getting out of hand. I see a therapist, I know all the steps, I've tried to get over it, around it, through it, under it, and it's just not working. I can't continue to live my life a victim to my illness and my past and continuing to have suicide in the back of my mind every day of my life. My therapist recommends medication, and after struggling with self-harm and

attempting suicide earlier this week I think she might
be right. But I can't help but feel guilty and like I'm
admitting defeat if I get on medication for this.

You've already admitted defeat in the way you talk. You've
given your disease the power to ruin your relationships, and you've
given your family's backward way of thinking the power to influence your mental health. Fuck all that.

Are people with brain tumors admitting defeat when they go
on chemotherapy? Of course not. They are simply admitting that
they have a disease. You are no different.

In your own mind, there should be no distinction between the
neurophysiological disease of a brain tumor and the neurochemical disease of bipolar disorder. They are both measurably real.
They are both beyond your control, and neither can simply be
willed away.

Therapy is vital. No doubt the work you've done has helped
manage the symptoms, but still, all the psychological tools in the
world won't fix your underlying brain chemistry.

Go on the medication, and don't let anyone judge you for it.
Fuck what your family thinks. You have no reason to feel guilty for
taking control of your disease. At the same time, don't let it define
you. Your disease may affect your mood and behavior, but it is not
you. Don't give it the power to ruin your relationships.

You're not a monster. You're just a girl who's been dealt a shitty
hand, and you're doing the best with what you've got.

Good luck with the meds. I hope that shit works for you.

On loneliness

i'm going through a lot of shit right now, and i just
need to tell someone who is a complete third party who
doesn't know me who isn't my dad just trying to give

advice or my friends who don't actually give a shit.
but i'm trying not to make any definitive statements,
because that's a serious flaw i have.

anyway, i'm not happy, basically. the cure seems
pretty fucking simple. be happy in the present moment,
don't take anything for granted, be grateful for your
lucky ass life (i mean, i really am lucky to have
everything i have. it's not like i'm poor on the streets), be
kind and blah blah.

but i'm going through a serious dilemma of having
friends. one of my tumblr friends just said, "fuck 'em.
if people wanna be your friend they will be, you just
have to be content living with yourself." which i agree
with but i don't know. i don't HAVE to be completely
alone just because. it seems when i do make efforts to
hang out with the people i've met (i'm in college away
from home, by the way. third year) they seem to have an
excuse. i don't think i'm trying hard enough but if they
make an excuse but never ask me back to hang out later,
shouldn't i take the hint?

You need to separate the idea of loneliness from the idea of
being alone.

Loneliness is the negative emotion you feel when you are disconnected from others. Being alone is merely not being in the
physical presence of others.

You can be lonely in a room full of people you call friends. You
can also feel connected to every other living soul while still being
completely by yourself.

Once you separate loneliness from being alone, you can better
analyze the true nature of your underlying emotions. Are you reacting to genuine loneliness, or are you reacting to the social stigma
attached to the experience of being alone? They are two totally
different problems.

Once you understand the difference, instead of trying to

remedy loneliness by not being alone, you'll start to remedy loneliness by connecting with others.

The difference may seem subtle, but it's everything.

Outside of getting a therapist and/or a puppy, is there any basic advice you can suggest for a person on their quest to become emotionally healthy?

Don't waste your life in the company of assholes.

I don't want to live anymore.

No, you don't want to suffer any more. There's a big difference.

How do I find happiness in the present moment?

Smile. No, really. Smile.

I'm going through an existential crisis. Any tips on making it through?

Keep existing.

I just made it through my first pregnancy scare. The test turned out negative, so why am I upset?

Because it crystallizes how you're all grown up without really being an adult. That shit is upsetting.

On how

I just started reading your blog, and I've noticed a pattern: people write to you with a seemingly one-dimensional question, and you answer by pointing out more underlying issues. You say things like "deal with your intimacy issues", or "stop being so afraid", but my question is HOW?

Are there some sort of exercises one is supposed to do to no longer seek attention in the wrong places? Should we tell ourselves nice things in the mirror everyday to know that we deserve to be loved? How does someone get past codependency when every relationship they've ever had or seen is codependent?

Is the answer therapy? It seems therapy can tell you that you have daddy issues, but not how to stop chasing every alcoholic older man that gives you a little attention. I am aware of my issues, just not how to deal with them.

Just because your issues have a name it doesn't mean you're aware of them. Say nice things into the mirror all you like, but looking at yourself isn't the same as seeing yourself.

Self-awareness takes work, and dealing with underlying issues is always a unique and intensely personal struggle. Sure, I'm good at parsing people's issues out of a few hundred words of bullshit, but that's just a parlor trick. Telling you what's broken isn't the same skill set as being able to fix it.

Short of following you around all day and sticking a little red flag into every behavior that's a negative manifestation of an underlying issue, there's not much else I can do.

I deliberately stop short of telling you how, because I can't. I know better, and I'm not one of those assholes like Dr Phil or Dr Laura who deal in cheap platitudes and feel-good McTherapy.

Nobody can tell you how. Not really. Over time, a good therapist may be able to give you the tools for you to come up with your own solution, but that's not the same as saying therapy is the answer.

That's why this shit is hard. You gotta do the work yourself, one shovel full of crazy at a time.

Hell, you're already off to a good start. It sounds like you've made enough bad decisions to realize that dating in your daddy's drunken shadow makes for a pretty miserable love life.

Good for you. Now fucking quit it, and no, I can't tell you how.

On your inner child

Sometimes, in the midst of a brand-new relationship, I'm plagued by the sound of my mother's voice, coupled with my screaming ovaries and the emotional stability of a 13-year old inner child, I get confused. I forget what's important. I forget myself. And what/who could be enchanting/enchanted for the next 5-10-50 years. So can you help me quiet the anxious voices? Just long enough to be enchanting?

First of all, your inner child is the most emotionally stable part about you. Your inner child is that little girl who can still find utter joy in the present moment. She's the always-smiling kid who isn't worried about yesterday's bullshit or what might happen tomorrow.

Your inner child is not that confused, angst-ridden thirteen year old you have in your head. That version of yourself is just a projection of your anxiety. So is the voice of your mother. So are your screaming ovaries. None of them are real. They are just manifestations of negativity, complete figments of your imagination.

But your inner child is very real. Find her. Listen to her. I promise, if it's enchantment you seek, she will show it to you wherever you are. If you want to be enchanting, she's the one that will make you glow from the inside out, and all will notice.

When you find yourself plagued by confusion and anxiety, take a step back in your mind and invite your inner child out to play instead.

Take a deep breath, and let her make fun of you for a quick second for being worried about something as ridiculous as the next 50 years or something as useless as your mother's nagging voice.

Shake it off, and then let her play or laugh or sing or dance. Hell, let her do whatever spontaneous happy thing she wants, because I guarantee, the kid knows how to have fun no matter where she is.

On what comes next

After a lifetime of feeling bummed out, I recently started taking antidepressants for some real-er reasons than that. A side effect of the medication is I never want to do coke anymore. I read about it before starting the meds and didn't believe it was going to be true. Now I never want it and when I'm around it, the thought of doing it bores me. So, I don't. Also, because I'm not supposed to be drinking alcohol at all, but do anyway I get drunker faster which translates to sicker quicker. Smoking pot seems to work out just fine, but then I also want to go to sleep. So, here I am, faced with the startling reality of interacting with my world with the most sober mind I've had in maybe 2 years or more.

I've been traveling this velocity for so long, moving with a familiar momentum. It's always been weekend to weekend, party and bullshit (×9). Ebb and flow. So now I feel like WHO THE FUCK AM I NOW!??!! I almost always learned new things during hightimes that I could bring into the rest of my life and that always felt really good. I think about the life I lived between the lines and key bumps, between the joints and gin and I'm unsure which bits to retain in my sober-er life. Maybe my personality dripped out with the bloody noses or whatever. I just can't pull my brain together about my new, 80% less hedonistic social life. Like, am I supposed to find a boyfriend or something? Put money in a savings account? Wear underwear everyday? Get places on time? What do real people do? Do these questions make me sound like research for a serial killer or what?

So, you might be thinking "Why the hell is this girl asking me about being sober?" Well, first, most people would use their judginess to congratulate me on not doing cocaine and pat themselves on the back cause their horse is so friggin high. That aint you. Also, I don't know every thing about you or anyone else and maybe you've had a sober stretch and can share something insightful. In any case, my crazy brain says you're the one to ask. I'm not asking you to tell me who I am. I'm just interested in your thoughts on this matter.

I'm freaked out by possible impending stability! What if I turn into whatever the opposite of a degenerate is?

I hate to break it to you, but you are real people. Also, don't get ahead of yourself, stability is not impending just yet. Life has a way of making sure you earn something like that. Besides, you're not freaked out by the impending stability. You're freaked out by the impending boredom.

Boredom has been your deepest fear this whole goddamn time, and now that you're checking your mirrors on all the crazy trails you blazed, you've come to the terrifying realization that you're too smart to bottom out like they do on TV. Sure, you've got a few respectable scars, but you've still got all your fingers and toes. Worse than that, you've got your fucking brain, all of it, and that motherfucker is sharp when it pulls focus.

I know. It's an uncomfortable sensation when you realize that your neurochemistry is finally done letting you try to annihilate it. You feed it the same old shit, and all it gives you back is static and sand.

So now what? Well, you'll be happy to know this raw nerve phase passes into a mellow acceptance of your own imminent survival. The world becomes a place where neither underwear nor savings accounts seem ridiculous. Don't worry, you'll still show up late for shit, because that's just naturally the kind of asshole you are.

Eventually, you'll learn to do what the rest of us do to keep from pulling a front page nutty. You'll partake in an exercise of duality. You'll make stability your bitch. You'll build a white picket fence around a house with whatever freaky shit you like to keep locked up in the basement. You'll figure a way to pay the rent and keep your teeth sharp. Oh, and yes, you'll realize that the freaky shit is a lot more fun with a partner in crime.

Again, don't worry. Have no fear. The ebb and flow of party and bullshit doesn't automatically get traded in for anniversaries and mortgage payments. You get to pick your own standard units of measurement. That's what you've earned for coming out the other side on your own terms. You can do whatever you want, because you know how to get away with it.

This whole time you thought you were broken, and it turns out you were unbreakable. You're not a degenerate. You never were. You were just faking it, and now you don't have any more excuses. Now go live a life less ordinary.

Oh, and if you need a kick start, I suggest you try volunteering a couple days a week. Pick a local cause that produces tangible results and go sign up to do some good. Altruism is a squeegee for the soul, that and a little yoga, and I think you'll have enough fresh perspective to start enjoying the possibility of whatever comes next.

Welcome to the first days of your adulthood.

On the point

*I think I visit your page so often and read through
all of the posts because I want to have some magical
revelation that'll grow me up through your words.
It'll make the world all fluffy and nice again, and my
problems will go away.*

*But that's not the point, is it? The point is, the world
ISN'T all fluffy and nice, and if I can get used to that,
and even take solace in it, then I'll be alright, even when
everything's fucked three ways from Sunday. That's
what you're trying to say, isn't it?*

Yes.

On the Physical

On changing your hair

You're blond, right? I don't know why I think that, maybe you put a photo or something once, but it's relevant... OK, so here it is. Do you think there is an age where a woman should stop dyeing her hair blonde? Or she should slowly do a darker hue? I'm in my mid 30s and have been a (well done) bottle blonde since my late teens. My mother is in her 60s and still going blonde, and I think it looks tacky and graceless. When should I change mine? Should I go brown or just a darker blond?

Sorry for the stupid question, but this is the internet.

I will neither confirm nor deny my status as a blonde, but I will tell you that this is not a stupid question. It may seem superficial, but there's a lot going on here, so strap the fuck in, because we're gonna go pretty deep.

First, a word about my grandmother. She was a wily old lady who loved to gossip, and perhaps my favorite of her many quirks was to comment loudly whenever someone she knew changed their hair.

'A woman's hair is her crown,' she would say. 'If she's doing something different with her hair, that means she's doing something different with her life.' My grandmother was right, of course. It could be big or small, internal or external, but a change in your hair always reflects a change in your life.

That brings me to you and your mother, two bottle-blondes from two generations, both dealing with two of life's major transitional phases. There's a reason marketing demographics break down into ages 18–34 and 35–55, and it's no coincidence that you've been blonde from your late teens up to now when you're in your mid-thirties.

You are passing from young adulthood to middle adulthood. It is a significant transition into a completely different stage of psychosocial development, and of course, it's the reason you're asking this question about your hair color.

Your mother is also passing from middle adulthood to late adulthood. It's just as significant a transition, one she might not be prepared for yet. Her resistance to that change is reflected in her refusal to be anything but blonde, which is why you think her choice to keep the same color is tacky and graceless.

For each of you, your blonde hair represents a part of your identity. You seem ready to acknowledge the changes in your life. Your mom, not so much. That's fine. You should both do whatever the fuck you want to do with your hair, but since I can tell how these things are gonna play out, let me go ahead and predict your future.

After reading this, you are going to go significantly darker with your hair. You won't go all the way brown, but you won't be blonde any more either. Your friends will say it makes you look younger. Your mom will say it makes you look older. (For the record, you'll look pretty much the same.)

After a few months of minor adjustments where you go a bit darker, you'll settle into the new color. Eventually, you'll catch yourself looking at pictures when you were blonde and you'll wonder what in the hell you were thinking.

At some point, your mom will turn up with brunette hair. She will credit you as her inspiration for going non-blonde. This will be true, but not for the reason you think. She will refer to her new look as her 'natural' color, which is kind of ridiculous, but you'll let her get away with it, because that's what daughters do.

On tattoo ideas

What's a good tattoo idea?

Get a pretty little butterfly tattooed onto your lower back.

That way, all the boys will know you're an unoriginal whore, and it will give them a place to aim while fucking you from behind so as to avoid eye contact during orgasm.

Or maybe, you could reflect on the important themes and meaningful events in your life and imagine a visual representation of your innermost passions that you would like to permanently embed into the living canvas of your skin.

Or get a star next to your cooter.

On what LA does to women

I achieved my dream job, but with barely enough pay to get through my rent and bills. I moved from Brooklyn to L.A., so I really don't have a support system. Not that being skinny isn't awesome, but I've shrank about 45 lbs, leaving me at about 97 lbs (I'm only 5'0, still, that's pretty close to being an emaciated carcass.)I usually eat a couple of bananas in a day, and take a shit ton of supplements so I don't die. They're roughly 12 cents each, unless someone I know comes around, which is rare, and I fake it by making some pasta and sauce, (a relatively cheap meal.) The amount of work I put in from home is unpaid and though it's really time consuming, I enjoy it, but it leaves me pretty much no time for a second job.

There's talk of me moving up in the workplace, and calling home with my tail between my legs and asking for cash which isn't something I'm willing to do unless dire straits really come about.

This is my career, and I'm on fucking fire, but I need to eat. What do I do? I don't qualify for welfare or food stamps.

Who's looking over your shoulder as you write this? My guess is a concerned boyfriend or sibling who's been out of town for a while and come back to find you looking like you need to be sponsored by Save the Children.

You're a model/actress/whatever who's been making excuses all morning why you can't afford to eat and why you're too busy poring over breakdowns or trying to get bookings to get a second job to pay for food, but things are great, and your career is about to take off.

Bitch, please. I can see right through you. Literally. There are entire apartment buildings in West Hollywood filled with your flavor of crazy.

Poverty is no excuse. No one with internet access and an LA dream job gets to act like this shit is Malawi. Proper nutrition is available for a few bucks a day, and no one in heels loses a third of her body weight without willful intent.

Since the only thing you're filled with at the moment is denial, I'm gonna put this as plainly as possible: you have an eating disorder. Let me repeat that one more time for anybody else who's there with you: *she has an eating disorder, a massive one.*

It sounds like you've been averaging less than four hundred calories a day, and to have dropped 45 pounds, it's been at least three, possibly six months that you've been living like this.

At this point, your thyroid looks like the baby from *Trainspotting*, you haven't taken an honest shit since bikini season, and you walk around shivering like Paris Hilton's dog after a line of blow. You are not healthy, kid.

I know there's no getting through to you, but maybe, just maybe, the boyfriend or sibling who's all up in your shit right now will see this and decide to take action.

Get some treatment. Immediately.

Don't worry, sweetheart. This isn't about putting weight back on. This isn't going to threaten your career. This isn't going to get in the way of your dreams.

This is about getting healthy. You're doing an incredible amount of damage to your body living like this. Deep down, on some level, even you know that.

Most folks will tell you it's not worth it. Fuck that. I'm here to tell you it doesn't have to be worth it. You can be healthy and have your dream job, but first you have to take a little time and get your mind right.

Best of luck. I really hope you beat this shit.

One of my worst fears is getting fat, and I hate myself for it.
You've got that backwards. You hate yourself, and therefore one of your worst fears is getting fat.

I'm not gorgeous, nor beautiful, nor even quite pretty. I'm honestly rather average. I know his flaws, both physical and personality-wise, and he knows mine, but my question is purely vain/physical: why, when he can and has dated model-material, would a man like that settle for someone like me?
Because you're better than them.

Can someone change leagues through exercising, diet, promotions in their field of work, surgery, reading more books and improving their intellect?
Sure, you can change leagues, but try not to lose sight of what game you're playing.

*Will you please comment on the recent media interest in
and admiration of the dad bod?*
The 'dad bod' media trend is just the highly processed residue left
behind after the deeper trend of body positivism was sanitized for
mainstream white male consumption.

*As a man, am I allowed to have any preference for what
my girlfriend does with her pubic hair? I'm worried that
expressing or having a preference of any kind would be
very un-feminist of me.*
It's fine to have a preference, and it's fine to express a preference
if she asks, but expressing an unsolicited preference isn't cool, and
expecting your preference to take precedence over hers would be
very un-feminist indeed.

*Is it hypocritical of a person who advocates natural
beauty to get a nose job?*
Sure it is, but natural beauty is an inherently hypocritical concept.
(Besides, just because you advocate it doesn't mean you have any.)

Would people be nicer to me if I were thin and pretty?
Yep.

On stupid teenage shit

*I'm 16 years old. And I really want to get a tattoo, but my
parents won't let me. It isn't even something prominent!
Just a word on my finger. But no. They're acting all
parent-y and lecturing me about it. I understand that
they don't want me to get something I would regret*

later, but I'm really sure about this. How do I convince them? :|

Jesus fuck, will whiny little cunts like you never learn? I'm not on your side.

You're sixteen. I know you don't look it, and I know you don't feel it, but you're still a fucking child. There is no convincing your parents. They're right. You're wrong. End of story.

If you want respect from people like me, you have got to quit the whining. That means either one of two things. Shut the fuck up and obey your parents, or engage in legitimate teenage rebellion.

I'd prefer it if you'd listen to your folks on this one, but maybe your balls are brass, so fair warning. If you get the tattoo without parental consent you will suffer consequences. Be prepared, and take it like an adult.

Also fair warning. Whatever this word is you want forever emblazoned on your finger at sixteen, I promise, you will eventually regret it, because the whole idea is stupid and juvenile.

On body issues

How the fuck can I feel sexy with stretch marks on my tits? I shouldn't even have them in the first place; I'm only an A-cup. My previous boyfriends never said anything about them, but I still feel damaged and undesirable. There's no permanent removal method that I know of, so how do I reconcile these scars?

We all have something we hate about our bodies. All of us. Everyone.

Get over it, or start saving up for surgery.

On penis size

From the very beginning you've made yourself out to be a straight-shooter with an awesome sense of humor. So, I pose this question: How MUCH does size matter?

Ever met a donkey-cock that flopped in the sack? A tiny guy with the hands (or tongue) of a god? While a guy's size certainly helps, would you be willing to make an exception if he had other merits?

Gentlemen, please stop assuming that the dimensions of your genitalia are in any way a direct measure of your sexual prowess. Of course size matters, but not nearly as much as porn and late-night infomercials would have you believe.

This is a bell curve situation. There is an 80/20 rule at play here, with 10 percent at either end representing the *really* big and the *really* small.

If you're wondering whether you fall into either extreme, *you don't.* Trust me, fellas. You would already know. Your cock is not the biggest. Your cock is not the smallest. Give or take an inch or two in width and girth, most of you are essentially sporting the same equipment.

Do you get what that means?

Let me spell it out for you: if your cock is neither freakishly big nor freakishly little, by the time we're in a position to size you up, the proportions of your penis are quite low on the list of things upon which we judge you.

Now, if you happen to fall into the 10 percent on either end of the spectrum, the same rules still apply. The bitter insecurity of a little-dicked guy is far more likely to ruin the mood than the actual size of his penis, just as the supreme confidence of a big-dicked guy is far more likely to impress than the extra meat he's packing in his shorts.

And yes, we know how easy it is to manipulate you with this shit. You could be swinging eight thick inches of pipe, and we could still crush your ego with three little words, 'I've had bigger.' Why? Because you know there are a few guys out there with nine inches. It's fucking ridiculous.

This shit drives me crazy. Really. I can't wait for the human condition to reach a new stage of evolution where penis size is no longer a dominant cultural motif. Ugh. It's right up there with world peace and no religion.

You may say that I'm a dreamer, but I'm not the only one.

Does Barbie really create negative body images in young girls or is that argument as invalid as I think it is?

It's not Barbie *per se*. Impossible beauty standards are what create negative body images in young girls, and Barbie just happens to be the unofficial mascot of impossible beauty standards.

Rate your own level of hotness between one and ten.

To answer with a number is to commodify myself and compete with my entire gender. Fuck that. No one should have to accept the premise of this question.

Why am I so jealous of better looking people?

You're not jealous. You're envious, and it's because you want what they have.

What's the difference between curvy and fat?

Advertising.

I'm a 29 year old woman — am I way too old for a nose piercing?
No, but you are way too old to be asking anyone's permission to stick things into your stupid face.

Is it possible to be a feminist and still wear high heels and makeup? I just can't seem to merge the two.
That's because you don't understand feminism, and you aren't comfortable in your own skin.

On settling your own debate

Can please you settle a debate for us? My boyfriend says that repeated "pounding," as he so eloquently calls it, will stretch out a woman's vagina to the point where it's "blown out." I say this is such BS – the skin's elasticity retains shape. Sure, after kids it might stretch a bit, but do porn stars or those who are frequently "banged" need to worry about "blown out pussy holes?" thanks.

No. I will not settle the debate.

If you don't have the courage of your convictions in the face of such monumental stupidity regarding your own gender's anatomy, then you don't deserve to win the argument.

This is tough love. Be strong. Go make the world a better place by learning something on your own and then teaching it to your ignorant boyfriend so he shuts the fuck up.

On the tyranny of self-hate

My girlfriend hates her body intensely, seeing it as grotesque and flabby and too tall and too square and too boyish. It's none of those things. She hates it if I compliment it or tell her she's not any of those things, because she has a "right to feel this way." What can I do?

Yes, I suppose self-hate and body issues are a natural-born right to girls across this great nation, but so is it your duty as a good boyfriend – nay, a good American – to stand up for your own First Amendment rights and shout to the fucking rafters that she is not only beautiful in your eyes, but beautiful in every way a woman can be.

Stand up to the tyranny of self-hate. Tell that girl she's gorgeous.

On guys having no idea

One of my friends is a very pretty girl, but she has one fatal flaw—lady has a beard. Not just some peach fuzz, that's one thing. She actually has a full on, blonde, lady beard. More than half my well-natured male friends could manage. How do I tell her, gently, that she would be absolutely perfect looking—minus the beard? I don't just want to give her a can of shaving cream and a gilette razor.

Yeah, no. She's well aware of her facial hair, and she knows better than to start shaving it, so unless you've got a couple grand lying around to pay for her electrolysis, I suggest you shut the fuck up.

On bucking the fuck up

Do you ever actually put yourself in other people's shoes? You tell people to, but the thing is, you're self described as smart, well-off, hot, and cool, and desirable as hell. Most of the rest of us aren't. How are we seriously supposed to be able to behave and act the same way you do, and carry ourselves with your crazy confidence, and live our lives with so much dignity and confidence that you do, when most of us are barely one of those things? Get off your high horse sometimes and realize that most of us don't possess the qualities you have, and it's not because we haven't tried hard enough or we're spending too much self pitying. It's because that's the way it fucking is.

Get off my high horse? Fuck you.

Quit whining and do something fabulous with your life. You have an internet connection and a firm grasp of the English language. That's already more than most.

I'm sorry that you didn't win the genetic lottery, but tough shit. Most people are ugly, and none of us are as pretty as the freaks on TV. Get over it.

Buck up and have some fucking character. Chisel the chip off your shoulder and develop a little personal style.

Be interesting. Be positive. Be your own person.

Remember, dignity and confidence doesn't flow from beauty. Beauty flows from dignity and confidence.

That's the way it fucking is.

Why does being thin mean you have good genes? Can I not have awesomely curvy, Christina Hendricks-like genes? Bitch.

Sure, you can have awesomely curvy genes. You can also have inappropriately personal reactions to things that have nothing to do with you. Get the chip off your shoulder. Bitch.

Should I be ashamed at showing my breasts for free drugs?
The drugs weren't free, sweetie. You paid for them. Whether it was with your dignity is entirely up to you.

How does a woman masturbate? Its a question I've wanted the answer to for a long time, and I don't know anyone I trust enough to give me an honest serious answer.
A woman masturbates with her vagina. Now go finish your homework.

am i pretty?
Not when you're asking needy questions.

Am I a bad feminist because I used to be anorexic?
Absolutely not. You're a bad feminist for hating women. Well, one woman actually. Yourself. Quit it. You haven't done anything wrong, girl. You are never your disease. Ever. Stop beating yourself up. Love yourself instead.

Is it true that I have cold feet because my vagina lets out all the heat?
Yes, and if you tape your vagina shut, your shoes won't fit any more.

On painting over rust

I spent my high school years being a bitter introvert and wasting my time hating girls who had boyfriends, because nobody was attracted to me. But now in my first year of college I'm trying to start my life over. I have a new haircut and wardrobe, I lost 12 pounds, I smile at people, I joined clubs… and it isn't working.

I don't know, maybe there's something I'm still doing really wrong. I thought the skirts and thinner frame and sunnier personality would make me more attractive, but of the handful of guys I've met here, I've still got no takers. It's hard not to ask myself "Why?" and fixate on stuff like my teeth or scalp problem. Those old feelings of being ugly, smelly and undesirable are coming back, and I'm beyond done. I'm sick of being the girl who sits in the corner and really wants to say hi to the good-looking classmate, but won't because she's too afraid of looking awkward and being rejected. I'm tired of thinking that Man A or B is too gorgeous to get stuck with a double bagger like me, and resigning myself and giving up.

I figured if there was anybody to ask how to get some confidence and self-worth, you'd be the woman for the job.

A haircut and a diet is how you start bikini season – not a complete life change. You're trying to mask an inner core of bitter anxiety and self-hatred with cosmetic changes. That never works.

All I'm hearing from you is teeth, scalp and skirts. It's all spray paint and a thin coat at that. Come on, kiddo. Everyone knows you can't paint over rust. You're fooling yourself if you think this stuff makes you sunnier. Quite the opposite. You're still very bitter.

Do you even realize how negative you sound? No one wants to put up with that kind of attitude. You can't fake sunny. Positive energy radiates from your core. I appreciate that you're trying to smile at people, but I bet that's just a coat of paint too.

You can't smile with bitterness in your heart. Not really. Sure, your face will make the right shape, but people can tell that it's not real. A smile is a projection of an emotional state of love, and if your conscious mind is fixated on negativity, it's gonna come off looking awkward, or worse, fake.

You want confidence? Okay. Give this 'whole new you' process one more try, but this time, start from the inside and work your way to the surface.

Those old feelings of being ugly and undesirable have been there the whole time, and you need to sandblast them off of your soul. There is no easy way to do it. You've got to use all your inner strength, and it has to be tougher than all that gunk to get the job done.

You have to be more sick of all this negativity than you are sick of sitting in the corner. Your desire to be friendly has to outweigh your fear of an awkward moment of rejection. I can't tell you how to stop hating yourself, but that's what you gotta do.

Never again referring to yourself as a 'double bagger' is a good place to start.

On not being pretty

I'm not pretty. It's cool. Not everyone can be pretty. However, I don't date a lot because well... I'm not pretty and I live in a college town where there are a lot of pretty girls. One of my guy friends keeps insisting I tell him why I don't date (he has a girlfriend, he's not trying to date me). How do I explain without sounding like I have super low self-esteem?

I don't accept your implied premise that being pretty is a prerequisite for dating, nor do I accept your excuse that you don't date a lot because you're not pretty. Come on, bitch. You're in college. Surely you know that correlation does not imply causation.

It doesn't matter if you're uglier than mormon sex, if you really wanted to be on a date right now, you could make that shit happen. This isn't about your looks or your self-esteem. It's about your priorities, and to some degree, it's about your standards.

That's not criticism, by the way. I've got no doubt that your priorities and standards are well adjusted. I'm just saying if you want to explain it to your guy friend, frame it in those terms.

In other words, you can tell him that you've got high standards, and dating just isn't that high a priority for you right now. That's the high self-esteem excuse you're looking for.

Also, who the fuck is this guy that you owe him answers to personal questions in the first place? Friend or not, that shit isn't any of his goddamned business, and you should feel free to tell him so.

Oh, and one more thing. You may not be a carbon copy of the local beauty standards, but that doesn't mean you're not pretty. You don't know it, but I guarantee, every day you're surrounded by people who think you're hot.

Are you afraid of getting old?
No. I'm afraid of looking old.

How do I find the beauty to become confident if I hate everything about myself?
You did not hate yourself as a child. Somewhere along the way, you learned how. Retrace your steps and unlearn. Forgive yourself, and get rid of the negativity.

How can I let go of the belief that beauty matters?
Beauty does matter. Just quit letting other people tell you what's beautiful.

On the Spiritual

On a good person

Do you think you're a good person?

Sure, but that's not the right question.

I'm human. I'm capable of both good and evil, to the extent that those concepts even have meaning beyond our limited moral comprehension of the universe. I do what I can to alleviate suffering and add some measure of benefit to this bizarre little experiment we call a world, but it's all ultimately insignificant.

It doesn't matter whether I think I'm a good person. It only matters whether I am good to other people.

On critically examining your beliefs

I have been following you since before 2009, and I enjoy the cut-throat advice and wisdom you provide, and the aid you have given me indirectly through this blog.

But, I have a question/comment for you. In some of your posts you speak very negatively of religion. You've touched on the close mindedness of Christians.

My question for you is this, isn't kind of close minded to lump and entire group of people like that? I am a Christian, but I don't think less of people based on their own religious beliefs or who they go to bed with at night.

I'm not trying to show you that every Christian has an open mind. You and I both know that a majority of people in the Christian faith are what you assume them to be. Heck, I even assume them to be close minded.

What I am getting at is that there are Christians out there who are open-minded. Not all of us are alike.

Sure. Not all of you are alike, but what every practicing Christian has in common is enough for me to lump you all together and think less of you.

I don't have to respect your beliefs. Respect is earned, sweetie.

That's not closed-minded of me, by the way. I'm educated in comparative religion. I have the Bible, the Qur'an, the Bhagavad Gita and the Tao Te Ching all next to one another on one of my bookshelves. Can you say that?

I doubt you've even taken the time to critically examine your own religion's sacred texts beyond whatever Sunday school fantasy-adventure ride you were strapped down for as a child. Even if you have, you still identify as a believer, and all that tells me is that you aren't enough of a rational thinker to separate myth from reality.

Listen, I get that you're asking me for a Christian hall pass. You want me to wink and nod and tell you that you're one of the good ones because you don't think less of me for my lifestyle. Well, no. It doesn't work like that.

You're not doing me any favors by not condemning me. That sentiment isn't an expression of open-mindedness. It's an expression of tolerance, and you know what? Fuck your tolerance. I don't need it.

You have a holier-than-thou attitude. Literally. Do you understand how condescending it is to be tolerated by someone like you? I don't owe you respect just because you smile and pretend to show me some.

Part of the problem here is that you're missing the point about what it means to be open-minded. As a Christian, you've co-opted a set of canned answers to life's greatest mysteries. It's bullshit.

You don't know any more about the nature of the universe than I do. All you've done is surrendered your rational thought to an ancient cult in exchange for peace of mind. That is inherently closed-minded.

Right now, all you've got is the *potential* for an open mind. Start asking questions. Examine your religion with a critical mind. Stop fearing the unknowable. Open yourself up to all possibilities and *never surrender your rational thought.*

Hopefully, you'll stop being afraid of the insignificance of your life and the inevitability of your death, and you won't need an imaginary friend in the sky to tell you everything will be all right.

On religion in general

We know your view of the Abrahamic faiths, but I'm curious to know if it extends to the other religions of the world, such as religious Buddhism, Hinduism, Bahá'í, persisting indigenous faiths, the various branches of modern paganism, etc.?

I'm opposed to any organized belief system with fundamental tenets based on revealed knowledge from a supernatural entity, and I am radically opposed to any closely held belief that allows for a supernatural entity (deity or otherwise) to be used as the proximate cause or justification for human behavior.

That said, I am not opposed to maintaining certain religious traditions as an important part of cultural heritage, except (as is often the case) when those traditions are used as the proximate cause or justification for human suffering.

I will pray that one day you come down from your throne and realize how little you know about life and start believing in God before you are on your death bed. I would hate to see anyone end up in hell.

I'm pretty sure that passive-aggressive threats about my eternal damnation don't count as prayers, but hey, who knows?

It takes as much faith to believe there is no God as it takes to believe in one.
No it doesn't. You're the one asserting god's existence without any evidence. Dismissing an assertion made without evidence isn't an act of faith. It's an act of reason.

Why don't you capitalize the g when you write "god"?
To me, god is a conceptual term, not a proper name like Jehovah or Allah or Zeus. It may not be the accepted capitalization, but I choose my words carefully for a reason.

I'm a 20-year-old atheist who wants to be more spiritual. What do I do?
Study philosophy, psychology and comparative religion. Don't get involved with any organization that relies on its own spiritual jargon.

On ego death and spirituality

You're the first person I've heard explain ego death as a constant gradual process (re: is your ego really dead?) rather than some kind of singular, life-changing event an ex-frat boy experienced after sucking on three tabs of acid. Would you care to elaborate?

The constant, gradual process of ego death. Yes. You've just tapped into the core of what spirituality is to me.

I'm not religious, and I don't hold any supernatural beliefs, but I am still very spiritual. I believe that spirituality can be a rational and valid practice of philosophical exploration, and that exploration most often comes in the form of some kind of ritualized exercise in killing one's ego.

The human condition comes with a built-in capacity for mystical states of transcendence, ecstasy and bliss. Unfortunately, for most people that capacity either goes largely untapped or it ends up warped by religious flimflammery.

Nevertheless, those transcendent states can be discovered, studied and developed like any other human experience, and if you devote yourself, those states can be sustained for longer and longer periods of time. (And yeah, there are those who say a transcendent state can be sustained permanently, but I find those claims are almost always adjacent to religiosity and charlatanism.)

As a general rule, anyone who claims that ego death is a singular life-changing event is either missing the point or selling something. I don't mind the ex-frat boy who sucks on three tabs of acid and then gets smacked in the head with a little taste of transcendence. Good for him. That kind of thing can certainly be life-changing, but he is woefully mistaken if he thinks that experiencing ego death means that he's actually killed his ego. (This is especially true for those whose first and only ecstatic experience is chemically induced.)

I guess part of the problem is in the phrasing itself. 'Ego death' and 'killing your ego' are useful as conceptual shorthand, but they imply a certain finality. Perhaps 'annihilation' is a better term. Then again, perhaps 'self' or 'mind' might be more useful as terms than 'ego'. Regardless, it can all sound like a bunch of eye-roll-worthy mumbo jumbo to someone who's never personally experienced it, and even for those who have, it's still intensely personal and nearly impossible to describe.

On disrespecting god

*I am a beautiful, intelligent, confident, and capable
18 year old girl (or woman… fuck if I know). I have
beautiful eyes and lips but my huge-as-fuck nose throws
it all off. It isn't RIDICULOUSLY huge, but having a
straight and petite nose would lead me to resemble
the spawn of Brangelina. I'm risking sounding like a
vain douchebag so you know that I'm not a whiny and
insecure bimbo looking to feel better about herself. I
know I'm beautiful. I've been raised to believe that
getting plastic surgery would be disrespectful to God.
The act of getting a nose job would basically tell God,
"You didn't do a good job". I'm on the fence between
respecting God and flipping him off while on the
surgeon's table. I'm considering alternative ideologies
and ways of thinking apart from the ubiquitous
mythology of creation/hero/deity/whatever, that is the
Bible. You are enlightened in areas that my mid-western,
"aw shucks" self is not. My question is, nose job or not?
Would it be worth it?*

Sweetheart, there is no god. Get a fucking nose job if you
want one.

I know you're just a kid, but I really can't abide the kind of
thick-skulled arrogance it takes to believe that the creator of the
universe would give a flying fuck whether you snip off the tip of
your nose, especially considering this is the same sadistic creator
from the insane mythology where all the men are required to snip
off the tips of their dicks.

Normally I'd give you a bucket of shit for all your self-indulgent
god talk, but I get the sense that you're about to start exercising
your rational mind in the face of your irrational belief system for
the very first time in your life, so I say again, *there is no god*.

That's right. There is no invisible man in the sky with a moral objection to your vanity, which means you can't fail to show respect for what doesn't exist.

Don't worry. It's really no big deal. Right is still right. Wrong is still wrong. You still know the difference, which is why it's perfectly acceptable – and yes, a little bit vain – to get a nose job.

Now go be a good person, and try not to be so fucking superficial.

How do I begin to practice self-reflection and understanding myself? I have no religion and little experience with spirituality. Where do I start?
It's called philosophy. Take a class.

Why, if I don't believe in Christianity, do I still fear that there may be a chance that hell exists, and that I might go there when I die?
You're just using a mythological framework that you learned during childhood to process some existential terror. Your fear isn't really of hell. It's of death.

Do you have an opinion about transcendental meditation?
If meditation is like spiritual exercise, then transcendental meditation is like spiritual CrossFit. It's basically the same thing, but it costs a lot more, it's slightly cultish, and people who do it talk about it constantly.

On magical jesus baby souls

I am pro-choice. But when those pro-lifers start banging on about abortion being murder and "your choice? what

about the child's choice?"- I hesitate… maybe due to years of religious brainwashing.
   Help me be smarter about this?

When religious wingnuts chant on about how 'life begins at conception', what they're really expressing is their ridiculous belief that White Jesus up in Sunny Heaven reaches down into every woman's uterus the very instant that a sperm fertilizes an egg and magically imbues the resulting single-celled zygote with a fully formed human soul.

They really truly believe this, and you will never convince them otherwise, and that's why this is a dumb-fuck religious issue instead of a pragmatic scientific one.

Here's the thing, though. *There is no Jesus. There is no magic. There is no soul. THERE IS NO CHILD.*

More to the point, a zygote isn't a child. It's just a clump of cells. Same goes for an embryo, as it's just a slightly bigger clump. Hell, a mid-term fetus still isn't a child, even though it kind of looks like a squishy one. Only when we start talking about later-term fetuses that are viable outside the womb can anyone start making a rational argument that it's a child, but post-viability abortions aren't even an option unless the mother's health is at risk.

So, why is any of this still controversial? Because babies are cute and make people emotional and America is full of halfwits who believe in magical Jesus baby souls.

That's why you hesitate, because there's enough irrational static out there to make you feel like somehow an innocent child is involved, but there isn't, because *THERE IS NO CHILD.*

On settling for a religion

I was agnostic for a period of 10 years or so. I have been dating a Christian for the past two years. He did not

force his religion upon me at all or passive aggressively
try and make me adopt it. I chose to explore it on my
own to see what he believes. But because I have been
exposed to it, I am starting to believe in God again and
I am attracted to what Christians believe. Am I being
brainwashed? Why do I feel manipulated into believing
something? Should I hold myself back from further
exploring it?

You're not exploring. You're settling. You've found a convenient belief system by way of a boyfriend, and you can't be bothered to do any critical thinking because it's all so easy.

You're taking on Christianity like other women take on country music or college football. It's just another thing you accept as part of your life because of the guy you're currently fucking. You might even convince yourself you kind of like it, right up until the relationship ends. That's when you come to your senses and wonder what in the hell you were thinking.

Admit to yourself that you're not attracted to what Christians believe as much as you're attracted to what your boyfriend believes. While you're at it, stop being so spiritually lazy. If you want to call yourself an explorer, do some fucking exploring. Curiosity is an active pursuit, especially where fundamental belief systems are concerned.

Don't just passively go to church. Use your rational mind and challenge your newfound religion. Learn all about its history, rituals, traditions and beliefs. Study it. Hell, study all religion.

Put some fucking effort into your life choices.

Any advice for a shit out of luck, confused, almost
21-year-old girl who is still trying to figure out her own
beliefs, ideologies, and life in general?
Don't let anybody fuck you – spiritually, mentally, emotionally or physically. Whether it's religion, ideology, shame or a penis, don't

let anyone put anything inside you without thinking about it first
and then making up your own mind.

How do I reconcile my atheism with my spirituality?
You don't need a supernatural god to hold the mysteries of the
universe sacred.

**People who believe in heaven: why are they sad when
anyone dies?**
Because death is real and heaven isn't.

On spiritual paralysis

*Due to the fact that everything is meaningless, I have no
motivation whatsoever to do anything in particular with
my life. I keep myself busy by fulfilling my basic human
needs of water, food, sleep, internet and weed. Outside of
that, fuck all happens.*

*This has been made worse by learning vipassana
meditation techniques. Now even my obsession with
a cute stoner boy has dissolved and I am fucking
bedridden with boredom. I'm not even miserable, I'm
irritatingly equanimous. How can I stimulate some
sort of desire to make a positive contribution to society
and how do I figure out what type of contribution to
make? Its really hard to make decisions when you see
everything as equal measures of dark and light. I am
literally just sitting here in a hotel with too much money,
no responsibilities, and I am debilitatingly free. Are you
looking for an assistant or know anyone that needs a
blank slate to train as their slave?*

By the way, I know I'm in a pretty fucking enviable situation right now, I'm not complaining. Just looking for direction.

You don't need direction. Direction is just a path. You need purpose. Purpose is the engine that propels you down that path, and without it, you are adrift.

Of course, finding purpose is easier said than done, especially for those of us who've embraced the meaninglessness of existence. The trick is to never forget that meaninglessness is not the same thing as emptiness, and right now, you are confusing the two.

You are paralyzed. Not physically, but spiritually. You are consumed with emptiness and self-negation because you are only fulfilling your basic needs. Water, food, sleep, internet and weed are just the bottom rung of Maslow's Hierarchy, and not for nothin', but the internet and weed aren't necessarily helping your situation.

You're missing out on a whole bunch of higher level stuff like love, belonging, esteem and self-actualization. That's why Vipassana is wasted on you right now. That's why financial independence is wasted on you right now. Pretty much everything is wasted on you right now, because you are clinically depressed.

Yes, that's right. You can call it irritatingly equanimous or debilitatingly free, but just because you've got some money and little Buddhism, that doesn't mean you're immune from your own neurochemistry.

I know you insist that you aren't miserable, but that's kind of the problem. Misery would at least be an emotion, and you're totally fucking numb. One solution is to go see a shrink and let 'em smack you upside the head with some psychopharmaceuticals. Feel free to try that. It might very well work, but you also need to get out there and find some purpose.

Here, I'll make it easy for you:

1. Spend half an hour a day exercising. (Break a sweat.)

2. Spend half an hour a day grooming. (Take a shower.)

3. Spend a few hours a day volunteering. (Alleviate the suffering of others in some small way.)

That's it. That's all you have to do for now. Making a positive contribution to society doesn't have to be a daunting task. Don't worry about doing anything with your life, and don't worry about any of it meaning anything.

Just do something with your day, and the rest will work itself out in time.

On ghosts

My philosophy teacher said if you don't believe in god but you believe in ghosts, you're contradicting yourself. I'm pretty sure I've had a ghostly encounter but I don't believe in god. Am I just crazy?

There is no inherent contradiction in believing in ghosts but not god, just like there's no inherent contradiction in believing in angels but not unicorns. Belief in one supernatural phenomenon doesn't require belief in all supernatural phenomena, and an afterlife doesn't necessitate a supreme being any more than a supreme being necessitates an afterlife.

So yeah, your philosophy teacher got it wrong. Of course, just because there's no inherent contradiction, that doesn't mean you're not an idiot for thinking you had a ghostly encounter. For the record, there are no such things as ghosts. Your experience wasn't supernatural, and there is a rational explanation for whatever happened to you.

Don't be a schmuck. If you're ever again in a position where you think the laws of nature are being suspended just for you, trust me, they're not.

On purity rings

I wear a ring to be faithful to god, and not have sex till marriage. im 18, and i've been in situations where its hard NOT to want to fuck the guy. Would it be wrong to have sex, and just say im still a virgin?

Silly little girl, there is no god. No one cares about your virginity except for your parents and whatever boy is currently trying to fuck you.

Your moral dilemma is a fabrication. It doesn't exist. There is no divine inspiration behind biblical laws of virginity. It's all just a primitive form of institutional slavery designed to protect your value as a piece of property.

If you had half a brain, you'd pawn that ridiculous piece of jewelry and use the money to buy condoms.

PART V

On the Individual

On greatness and killing your ego

How do I accept that I won't ever be great or outstanding? I always thought I had talent, and maybe I'm not bad, but a great many people are far better. I can't stop thinking this and it's causing me great anxiety.

Kill your ego, because nothing you do will ever matter. That's okay, though. It's not just you. It's all of us. It's taken 100,000 years for our species to hump and grunt its way into momentary dominance on this pale blue dot, but nothing we've accomplished is all that outstanding when you consider that a Mall of America-sized asteroid is all it would take to turn humanity into the next thin layer of fossil fuels.

Greatness is nothing but the surface tension on the spit bubble of human endeavor. On a geological timescale, our measurable effect on the planet is a greasy burp. We are 7 billion tiny flecks of talking meat stuck to an unremarkable mud ball hurtling through space in an unimaginably vast universe for no particular reason. There is no difference between kings and cripples, my friend. We're all the same hodgepodge of primordial goo, and the pursuit of greatness is a fool's errand.

Pursue happiness instead. Find peace in your insignificance, and just let your anxiety go. Learn to savor the likely truth that the sum total of human achievement won't even register in the grand scheme, so you might as well just enjoy whatever talents you have. Use them to make yourself and others happy, and set aside any desire to be great or outstanding.

That's not to say you shouldn't do your best. You should. If you're talented, by all means, exploit that talent to the fullest extent possible. Just don't do it for the sake of greatness. Do it for the sake of happiness. If the distinction is a little hazy, that's because your ego is doing its best to get in the way. Your ego wants to put you on a pedestal at the center of the universe. It wants to convince you of silly things like jealous gods and life after death. Your ego would never allow you to believe that you are anything other than a special snowflake, which is why you have to kill it.

Annihilating your ego is the quickest way to happiness. Embracing your insignificance will make your anxiety suddenly seem ridiculous. You'll recognize petty emotions like schadenfreude and envy for the childish tantrums that they are. You'll stop comparing your talents to others', and you'll be able to enjoy being good at something without the need to be great.

I keep thinking there has to be more to life than this, but I don't know what it is or how to find it.
Nah, there isn't more to life than this. Stop looking for something that doesn't exist and go do something you enjoy with the time that you have.

Why is it that having a stable relationship in my 20s, not partying or hooking up with other guys all the time, makes me feel like I'm wasting my life?
Take a step back and realize that you're the type who'd feel like you were missing out either way.

I keep doing the same stupid shit over and over again. It makes me feel terrible but I can't figure out how to stop. Any advice?
The behavior won't change until you do. 'You' aren't going to stop, but you can become the person who will.

Coquette, I'm scared I'm not doing what I want, and I'm only doing what I 'should' be doing. How do I tell the difference?

Figure out what you want, kid. If you don't know that, then trying to tell the difference is kinda pointless. In the meantime, just do your best to avoid falling into a day-to-day routine that feels like a mind-numbing hellscape of compromise and drudgery.

Life is much harder than I ever expected.

You're confusing your life with your circumstances.

On not going places

Hi, Coquette. Honestly, I'm not sure what I'm doing. I'll be 26 in 2 months, I've dropped out of school hmmm... 4 times now? I'm in massive amounts of debt. I currently don't have enough to make rent next month so I'm taking a bus from my dream city back to my hometown. I just got fired from the best job (on paper, at least) that I've ever had. The only serious relationship I've had was emotionally and physically abusive (that ended about 2 years ago). And I still don't know what I want to do with my life, or how to dig myself out. I read a lot new age-y self-help stuff about staying positive and shit because I've dealt with depression on and off and it seems to help. But honestly, I just want someone to give it to me straight – is there any way out of this? I wasn't always this way – I was a star student and the girl that was "going places", and I just want to be productive and happy and driven again.

What the fuck? Fired from the only decent job you've ever had? Dropped out of school four times? New age self-help books? Ugh. You're a fucking disaster.

You were never going places. You were never productive and driven. Get that public high school pep-talk bullshit out of your head, because you're remembering yourself as happy during a time when all you were was innocent.

Stop romanticizing the past, because the brutal truth is that you were weak and unprepared. You couldn't cut it in college. You can't hold down a job, and now you've got a one-way bus ticket back to what I'm guessing is one of your family members' guest rooms.

Yeah, your life fucking sucks right now. You're getting your ass thoroughly kicked by the real world, and you're not even bothering to give me a list of excuses – probably because you know I'd call you out on them.

Please, do yourself a favor. Take all your stupid self-help books down to the local thrift store and trade them in for one decent Tina Turner album. I swear to everything holy that you'll get more useful inspiration out of one of her B-sides than you will from an entire wall full of positive-thinking books.

I'm serious. Self-help books are for fucking losers, and staying positive for people like you means living in a constant state of denial. Stop blowing sunshine up your own ass. Your life is a steaming pile of shambles, and a bunch of smiley-faced wish-thinking won't make it any better.

The only way out of your situation is through slow and steady progress. It will not be easy. It will not be fun. You need to come to terms with the inevitability that you are going to have to work a shitty job, and since you're a flighty mess, you're going to have to summon all your willpower just to hold that job down.

You don't get to sulk. You don't get to whine. You have to be thankful and grateful and show up every day with a good attitude. (There's your positive fucking thinking for you.) You will do this week-in and week-out for the rest of your life. Maybe you'll meet a guy who doesn't treat you like shit, and maybe you'll squeeze out a rugrat or two, but odds are good that you're never leaving your hometown again.

And you know what? You'll be just fine.

You'll make your way. You'll have your set of friends. You'll do some cute local Etsy shit on the side to occupy your spare time, and then one day you'll wake up and realize that this is all there is to American adulthood. It's all there ever was.

The whole time you thought you were 'digging yourself out', that was actually your life, and sure, it could've been easier, and it would've been nice to have had more money, but really, on the whole, it wasn't all that bad.

On advice for the ages

What single piece of advice would you give to a 5 year old? 10 year old? 15 year old? and so on. It's vague but I'm curious on what you'd find important for someone to know at various stages in their life.

Age 5: Never stop asking questions.

Age 10: Never stop questioning the answers.

Age 15: Don't take anything personally.

Age 20: Let go of your childhood.

Age 25: Surround yourself with good people.

Age 30: Hustle.

Age 35: Let go of your bullshit.

Age 40: Change while you still can.

Age 45: Delegate your hustle.

Age 50: Let go of your youth.

Age 55: Go do that thing you've always wanted to do.

Age 60: Get the fuck out of the way.

Age 65: Let go of your legacy.

Age 70: Give away everything that you can.

Age 75: Stay connected with the world.

Age 80: Let go of everything.

On living forever

It's interesting that you seem so nonchalant about death, but I was wondering, if you had the opportunity to live forever, would you take it? I keep asking myself the same question, but I can't decide if things would become boring or lonely or numbing after a time. All the same though, the lack of existing horrifies me. Even if I know it's my ego making me feel this way, that knowledge doesn't exterminate my fear. So, would you live forever if you could?

Please. Our brains aren't even capable of contemplating forever, much less living it. Immortality is such a ridiculous notion to anyone with the slightest sense of scale.

Sure, if science allowed for it, I'd be down to live a few hundred, maybe even a few thousand years in good health, but you can't really go beyond one or two orders of magnitude from a natural life span before shit starts getting sticky.

I mean, what are we talking about here? Is this thought experiment one in which you're a living, breathing immortal, magically destined to walk the earth forever as a biological curiosity? What happens when the rest of the species starts to evolve? Or worse, what happens when another mass extinction event wipes out every living organism except for you? (I can hear you wanting to bring up spaceships. Cool your jets, Gene Roddenberry. That line of thinking creates more problems for you than it solves.)

Then again, maybe we're talking about some artificially reproduced form of consciousness where you exist indefinitely, snowglobed in a Matrix-like world. I suppose that could work too, but then suddenly we've wandered off the philosophical deep end.

Besides, what's so horrifying about not existing? It's really not that big of a deal. You did it for billions of years before you were born, and that doesn't make you the least bit queasy. Why, then, are you so worried about the billions of years that you won't exist after you die?

I don't know what I want to do with my life and it's really fucking scary.
Enjoy that fear. You're lucky to have it.

Why do I have it in my head that if I'm not famous, recognized as an expert, or popular in my peer group, I haven't lived an important life?
Because you're a product of consumer capitalism steeped in celebrity culture.

Is it normal to be nervous about life?
Yes. (The trick isn't to not be nervous. The trick is to not be normal.)

Is this it? Being social, having friends, making small talk, it just doesn't appeal to me anymore. Not that it ever really did, but I never thought I'd be so bored with everything at 25.
Go DO something, asshole.

I just turned 22 and I hate feeling so old.
You don't feel old. You just resent having to act like an adult. Toughen up, buttercup. It gets a helluva lot worse.

Why am I so bored of getting out of bed, taking showers, brushing my teeth, eating, socializing, music, television, internet and basically everything? Ugh.

Because that's your list of basically everything.

On your best interest

My parents are miserable people with no substance. They see my "best interest" as financial security rather than actual happiness. I go to college next year, and they refuse to pay for me unless I major in business, because it's "stable". What do I do? I know what I love, and I have passion, but I don't have the money to defy my parents and pursue it.

Shut the fuck up and enjoy your complimentary college education, you disrespectful, shortsighted little twat. Major in business, minor or double major in whatever else you want, and then go spend the rest of your ungrateful existence following your bullshit passions until you realize how big of an asshole you were for putting quotation marks around the word stable.

On breaking it down

To others, I look like a success. I know what a screw up I really am. I never really live up to my potential, have bad habits that don't amount to addiction but aren't healthy, etc.

I've gone farther in life than anyone would have expected from my beginnings. I don't care about being rich or famous. I could make real contributions to the world, but I can't motivate myself to work hard.

What the hell is my problem? Why can't I make a reasonable effort in life? The easy answer is that I'm just smart enough to get away with it. I sort of want your existential answer mixed in with a bit of ass-kicking, please.

No problem. Let me break this one down for you line by line:

To others, I look like a success.
Actually, no one cares. Appearing successful is merely part of the identity you're trying to project.

I know what a screw up I really am.
This is self-loathing or false modesty. Either way, shove it up your ass. We're all screw ups, and no one's ever gonna throw you a pity party.

I never really live up to my potential, have bad habits that don't amount to addiction but aren't healthy, etc.
Yeah, this is called 'being human'.

I've gone farther in life than anyone would have expected from my beginnings.
What do you want, a cookie? Tell you what. If you put down that yardstick you're using to measure how far you've gone in life, I'll give you a cookie.

I don't care about being rich or famous.
Liar.

I could make real contributions to the world, but I can't motivate myself to work hard.
Sure, sure. You'd be Tony Stark if you could just put that bong in the closet.

What the hell is my problem?

Nothing. You don't have a problem. You're perfectly normal. Totally average. That's what really scares the hell out of you.

Why can't I make a reasonable effort in life?

Reasonable to whom? Your parents? It's a bit too late to be bargaining with the cosmos for their approval, isn't it?

The easy answer is that I'm just smart enough to get away with it.

No, that's the bullshit answer. The easy answer is that you're lazy.

I sort of want your existential answer mixed in with a bit of ass-kicking, please.

My answer is that you are nothing special, and that's perfectly okay. Don't be so afraid of your mediocrity. Find freedom in it, and just enjoy your life.

On being a grown-up

I'm in my mid-20s, but sometimes I fall into the habit of acting far less mature than my age when I'm around other people. It's something I find myself regretting later on when I'm finally by myself. I feel childish just asking this question, but is this really what it's like to be a grown-up? Wasn't I supposed to get married or something?

Yep. This is it.

Welcome to 21st-century adulthood.

You've been out of college a few years now, and you know what it's like to put in some of that entry-level grind. Maybe you're waiting tables. Maybe you're in grad school. Maybe you're bucking for some junior-level corporate gig. Whatever. Point is, you're not the new girl any more, but you aren't management yet either.

Take a good look around at the view, because for better or worse, this is all you can expect out of being a grown-up. Sure, you might squeeze out a child of your own in a few years, but other than that, the American experience isn't gonna come along and saddle you with any life-changing, pillbox hat-wearing, polyester-blend responsibility that would otherwise clearly indicate you're not still one yourself.

Sorry, kiddo – it doesn't work like that any more.

Your state of emotional maturity might seem stunted by previous generations' standards, but we Millennials have been blessed and cursed with an unusually extended adolescence filled with social networks, smoking bans and selective serotonin reuptake inhibitors.

The befuddled Boomers and bitter Gen Xers before us are quick to talk all kinds of smack about our relative immaturity, but do your best to ignore the negativity, because quite frankly, this is how they raised us. Besides, it's their turn to be old and in the way, and they should shut up and be thankful that we're willing to pick up the tab on their ballooning Social Security and Medicare. But I digress. How tacky.

Speaking of attention deficit disorder, our generation's extended adolescence is part and parcel of a much grander sociological cycle that also includes the crumbling of the institution of marriage and the death of the American Dream. Good times. I'm not suggesting that you owe your individual immaturity to such abstract generalizations, but it's food for thought next time you find yourself with nothing but a throbbing hangover and morning-after regret.

Marriage was once the threshold to adulthood. It wasn't just something you wanted to do in a happily-ever-after sort of way, it was also something you needed to do to survive, but shifting gender roles and skyrocketing divorce rates came along and turned an

294 [the best of] Dear Coquette

economic necessity into a lifestyle option, and in so doing, unblazed the trail to official grown-up status.

Things are different now. There is no clear demarcation line, but you know what? It's better this way. Such things were always arbitrary. Forty years ago, a housewife in her mid-20s was no more a grown-up than you are today. She just thought she was, and ultimately her confusion resulted in things like daytime television, ennui and the aforementioned skyrocketing divorce rates.

You're just as confused, but don't worry – that's what your twenties are all about.

I feel like my life has no story yet.
It does. You just don't know how to tell it.

If nothing matters why do I have to live by the rules?
Why should I do anything I don't want to do?
Because your actions have consequences. You don't have to live by the rules. You don't have to do anything at all, but your life will become a miserable shit-storm if you don't learn how to play along.

I don't want to get old. Please make it stop.
Growing old is a privilege reserved for the lucky and the strong, so quit your fucking whining and accept the fact that the human condition is a death march of futility and decay.

If "the human condition is a death march of futility and decay," which I agree with, is there any good reason for a person to have kids?
Most people tend to find purpose in their children, and there's something to be said for perpetuating the species.

*Can I integrate my fragmented, dislodged, self-reflexive
post-modern self into a whole person? If yes, do you
happen to know how?*
Stop being so full of shit.

On normal happy people

*Do normal people exist? I don't mean heteronormative
people—just people who are emotionally stable, have
no underlying neuroses, and aren't secretly in a world
of pain/self-doubt. Are those people real or are they a
universally accepted fiction?*

You're not asking if normal people exist. You're asking if happy
people exist. The answer is yes, of course they do, but people aren't
static. Neither are pain and self-doubt.

Happiness (or normality or stability – whatever you want to
call it) isn't a permanent gift granted to a select and steady few. It
may be found more easily for some than others, but it's all still just
a transitory phase.

Every emotional state, stable or otherwise, is impermanent.
It's all a shifting, flowing, ever-changing hot mess of pleasure and
pain, neuroses and normative behavior. Happiness is fleeting, but
then again, so is suffering.

Yes, there are plenty of people out there today who are emotionally stable with no underlying neuroses who aren't secretly in a
world of pain or self-doubt, but they weren't all that way yesterday,
and it won't all be the same people tomorrow.

Your path to being among them is in recognizing that it's not
some country club that you get to join by virtue of any birthright
or accomplishment. Happiness isn't something you achieve. It's
something you discover, and it's a discovery that can be stumbled

upon again and again, depending largely on your ability to be mindful in the present moment.

I keep retreating into inactivity and mindlessly surfing the web. I've been asleep for at least ten years now. How can I wake up?

There is no grand answer to that question, nor does there need to be. The point is that you keep asking yourself every day.

I try to stay active, eat right, volunteer, but I am so unhappy. Are some people just sad for life?

Quit looking for an excuse to keep your head up your ass, and stop looking for happiness on the back of your box of granola.

Give me some reassurance that my life isn't pointless.

No. Go get it yourself.

How do you forgive someone?

Let go of all your anger and resentment for them.

I'm scared that no one will come to my funeral.

That means you're either lonely or an asshole. It'll be too late to do anything at your funeral, so I suggest you start dealing with your problems now.

On panicking

I am 25 years old, and I live a very "day-to-day" life style. I have absolutely nothing planned for life. I have no savings, no long term goals, no specific dreams of

any sort (other than the vague "contentment with life").
When asked what my dreams in life were, I couldn't
even think of a single legitimate answer. I know the
future isn't guaranteed to me, so there is that. I realize
I am still relatively young, but is there a certain time
when I should start panicking?

Panicking about what? You could die tomorrow or in fifty years. Either way, your dreams don't mean shit. They never did, except to the extent that they keep you chasing after that vague sense of contentment, however distant and out of focus it always seems to remain.

Make a plan. Don't. It doesn't matter. Sure, it couldn't hurt to start saving a little money. Lord knows when you'll need it for a college fund or a Disney cruise or a halfway decent DUI attorney.

This is the part where you're supposed to keep your head down and work. Be productive. Be a good little consumer. Earn. Save. Spend. Have your well-regulated units of fun on the weekend, but nothing too crazy.

You'll blink and ten years will have slipped away. You'll still consider yourself relatively young, but the teenagers will already have started to confuse you. You'll realize that you've accidentally fallen into full-on adulthood. Marriage. Mortgage. Kids. Where the fuck did they come from?

Blink again, and you'll be fifty years old, just as lost and clueless as you are today. You'll catch that first real glimpse of your own mortality. Still, no reason to panic. The blood tests came back negative. It's only a minor procedure. You're going to be just fine.

One more blink and it's all over, a day-to-day lifestyle stretched out to its inevitable conclusion, and if you're very lucky, your last day will include good drugs and a comfortable mattress. That's it. That's the most you can ever hope for, because even in that final moment, you still won't have a single legitimate answer. You never will.

So go ahead, make a plan for your life if you think it will help. Have a specific dream if it makes you feel better. Just be sure to work hard. Stay out of trouble. Fill your free time with yoga and book clubs and fantasy football leagues and cable news. Do whatever you can to avoid gazing inward into that gaping void, because the simplest answer to your question is yes.

Yes, there is a certain time when you should start panicking. Yes, that time is right now. Yes, every fucking second of your waking consciousness should be filled with existential terror at your utter insignificance and inevitable annihilation. Yes, the entire human experiment is nothing more than a sick and futile joke.

So yes, go ahead and start panicking. It still won't do you any good.

Is it reasonable for a woman to want kids, but not to go through the scream-pee-poop phase by adopting a 5 year old?

It's not a puppy, you fucking twit.

What if nothing makes you happy. Then what should you do?

Stop relying on external sources for your happiness.

Why can't I stop feeling like I'm nothing but wasted potential?

Because you're living your life like it's a preamble to some eventual state of accomplishment.

"...living your life like it's a preamble to some eventual state of accomplishment" — Oh my God, that's me!

So, if we're not working toward some eventual state of accomplishment, then what?
Live in the present moment. Duh.

Why do people get stuck in adolescence? It's shit.
Yeah, but it's shit without any accountability.

I wear plaid shirts, and have been ever since I learned to dress myself. Does this make me an asshole?
It's not the shirts.

What do you do when you realize you have become what you fear most?
Either embrace what you've become or change.

I'm a 28-year-old woman. Are my late twenties supposed to be this crappy?
There is no such thing as 'supposed to be'.

Why is it that I know everything that's wrong with me, and my life, and how to fix it, but I can't seem to want to change it enough to actually do it. Why?
Self-awareness is not the same thing as self-control.

On overusing apologies

How many chances do you give someone you're dating who occasionally says awful things? My benchmark for 'awful' is pretty low in most people's eyes, I'm a self-confessed strident intersectional feminist. I think

I'm letting myself down by not kicking him to the curb straight away, even if I do really like him. He's never made the same shitty comment twice and always apologises and seems to learn… So is this a dumb move, a time for patience or a case of me being a controlling bitch trying to force someone to change? Sorry for rambling.

The quality of your life will improve a thousandfold if you stop using apologies as emotional currency.

You demand them from others as a means of control. You offer them unsolicited as a sign of deference. Hell, you even try and sneak them into your language by saying things like 'self-confessed' instead of 'self-proclaimed'.

Apologies are built into the source code of your interpersonal communication skills, and even though you're a perfect stranger, I can tell it's one of the most annoying things about you.

This is one of those traits you learned from your mother. Trust me, you will do well to unlearn it. Apologies are not for everyday use. They are meant to be rare. They are worthless if demanded, and they are useless as a substitute for respect.

As for your boyfriend, chill the fuck out. I've yet to meet a dude who doesn't occasionally say awful things. If you can call a guy out on his shit and he never makes the same mistake twice, then that's really the best you can ever expect.

On various states of ruin

Over the past four years, I've been laid off twice and ultimately spent 16 months unemployed. My self-esteem, marriage, finances and career are in various states of ruin. Presently, I'm underemployed and bitter. I don't know where to begin. How do I engage the second act of my life?

I fought hard to carve out a career in an industry that I always dreamed about working in. While I treasure that achievement, I have no idea where to begin anew. I feel the weight of supporting a family in my thoughts of career change.

On top of that, after 14 years of marriage and two small children, our relationship has crumbled. I feel a tremendous burden of guilt at the thought of putting my children through our divorce. I know what it did to me as a child.

I've been in therapy for over a year now and I'm making some progress. I don't know that I can get her into couples therapy, but I do know it is the only thing that might save us.

I understand that the shitstorm is going on all around us. I've just run out of juice to fight it off. What the hell do I do next?

Take care of your kids, man. That's it. That's all.

As for your career, there is no difference between the achievement you treasure and the bitterness you feel. They are the same thing. Let that mess go.

While you're at it, take your self-esteem and shove it up your ass. It doesn't deserve a spot on your list of things in ruin. Get your ego out of the equation, because it's in the way of things that actually matter.

As for your marriage, quit whining and take action. Get your wife into couples therapy. Turn 'for worse' into 'for better'. Do it for your kids, and if you can't pull it off, keep the divorce amicable.

This is your life, dude. It's not a shitstorm. You're just in a transitional phase. It's not your first, it won't be your last, and you don't get to run out of juice. Suck it up and keep going. You may not have it easy, but you've got it a hell of a lot better than most. Never forget that.

Oh, and did I mention? Take care of your kids, man. That's it. That's all.

How can I stop defining myself by who I'm dating and instead find self worth through my career?

You're wrong twice, babe.

What do YOU think happens when we die?

Our consciousness ceases to exist, and then we rot in the ground for a hot minute. That's it, dude. Don't worry. It's no big deal. You didn't exist for the first 14 billion years, and you won't exist for the next 14 billion either.

What gets your furthest in life: Good looks, social skills, or intelligence?

Showing up.

How do I know if everything I am learning is wrong or not?

Factually wrong? Check your sources. Ethically wrong? Check your conscience. Epistemologically wrong? Check your reasoning.

Tell me what to do.

Think for yourself.

I've just come out of what has hands down been the worst experience of my life. I will never complain about depression again. Over the past few months I've done some solid reckoning with the abyss, and I'm proud to say I see what you fucking mean. It is good just to be alive.

Fuck yeah, it is.

On what's wrong with you

Dear Coquette,
*   I'm in my second year of university and for the past while I've been feeling drained. I'm doing well in school and I make time to go out for drinks once in a while — I should be having a better time than I am now, shouldn't I? What's wrong with me?*
Nothing.

I'm 25. I have a full-time job with health insurance, a secretary, an office and a paid-for parking spot in the city. Why am I unhappy? Why do I want to give it up and go back to school? I'm trying to be happy with what everyone wants but I can't. What's wrong with me?
Nothing.

I just worked my ass off on a project at work. Lots of people are congratulating me ... but when I hear it, it just falls dead. What's wrong with me?
Nothing.

I don't know what to do with my life, and I have absolutely no motivation to find out. What's wrong with me?
Nothing.

Sex is just so complicated and I always get so nervous and psych myself out that I let it ruin the experience. What's wrong with me?
Nothing.

I can only come in one position. One position. It's universal — every man I've been with, I can only have orgasms in one damn position! What's wrong with me?
Nothing.

I'm 21 years old and I've never been out on a date. I've got plenty of friends and I don't think I'm boring, so what's wrong with me?
Nothing.

When boys like me, I get weird. I will like them and flirt with them, but as soon as they want to hang out, I freak out and try to come up with excuses not to. What's wrong with me?
Nothing.

I really really like this guy. But sometimes when we're together I get really worried. I worry about when we'll stop liking each other. Why can't I just be happy? What's wrong with me?
Nothing.

I've never been in love although I've dated plenty of guys. What's wrong with me?
Nothing.

I always think I'll be happier someplace else. What's wrong with me?
Nothing.

On the Greater Good

On our extinction

Do you look forward to the extinction of humankind? I sure do, I feel like the most beautiful thing that humans could achieve would be to finally die off and let the good earth try to heal itself. When I say this to close family members they never agree and sometimes are angry at me, calling me morbid. There isn't anything more morbid than our species smothering and poisoning every other one on the planet. I'm not worried about being judged, just worried about those who are reproducing and those who want to cure major human diseases.

The good earth? You fucking idiot. The earth is an ethically inert mud ball hurtling around an amoral little star in an infinitely vast universe that is neither good nor evil. On a geological timescale, the measurable effect of our species on the planet is an insignificant burp.

It takes the human condition to color the world with value judgments, and yours are self-hating and silly. Besides, we're not going to make it anyway. Not at our current stage of evolution, and certainly not if we stick around this corner of the solar system. Ninety-nine point nine per cent of all species that have ever existed on earth are now extinct, and one day we will be too. We aren't that fucking special.

Does that mean we should wish for our annihilation? Fuck no. Only arrogant malcontents think like that. All you're doing is projecting your own self-loathing onto a species-centric worldview, one that's no different from the ignorant fucks who think we were put on the planet to rule over the animals.

Humanity is a fleeting and beautiful experience, the sum total of which probably won't count for shit in the long run. So what? Don't resent your species. It's a wasted emotion based on a primitive way of thinking.

If you really look forward to the extinction of humankind, then do your part and kill yourself. Otherwise, shut the fuck up and enjoy the ride.

On that dollar in your pocket

Why's some motherfucker ask me for a dollar to specifically refill his 42oz big gulp at 7/11 like I just have fucking money to give to him (he said all this yes)? I have to work hard for this money; why does it piss me off so much that someone thinks I'm just there to give it away to them?

It pisses you off because you're a selfish person who thinks the world revolves around you. It doesn't, so stop taking every little thing personally. I'm not suggesting you give a dollar to the guy – you aren't there yet, but at the very least, summon up the few drops of empathy it takes to shake your head no without letting some poor bastard's very existence anger you. If you really want to improve yourself, watch out for that ego-based Republican instinct to announce to the world that you're a hardworking taxpayer who earns things. Resist the urge to make comments like, 'I have to work hard for this money.' Yes, you are paid a wage in exchange for your labor. Congratulations on grasping the basics of capitalist micro-economics, but saying shit like that to help prove a point is a big red flag that you are an enormous gaping asshole.

The problem with your way of thinking is that you fundamentally believe there's a difference between you and that bum trying to refill his Big Gulp. You lack compassion and any sense of economic scale, and it prevents you from recognizing that you two motherfuckers are on the same team – Team 7/11, Team 99% – whatever you wanna call it, man. We're all American peasantry.

I know that makes you uncomfortable. You don't wanna wear the same jersey as the Big Gulp bums, but you really need to start taking a broader view of the socio-economic system that has you conditioned to direct your anger at the underprivileged. Fuck that shit. The guys asking for a dollar outside the 7/11 aren't your enemy. Aim your animosity upward. The guys earning net profit off your labor are the ones taking money out of your pocket. That's your true enemy. That's who should be pissing you off.

On black market economics

I was having a chat with a dear old friend today about the legalisation of drugs. While I am pro-legalisation, he doesn't believe ANY drugs (even cannabis) should be legalised. His reasons are as follows: During the 1920s or whatever when alcohol was made illegal, it was so completely illogical that people (read: dodgy gangsters and shit) immediately set up complex systems to smuggle and create it. When alcohol was again legalised, the framework for organised crime was in place; just not any actual crime- and it was through this that both drug and arm smuggling became a much bigger issue. His point is that, when you then legalise cocaine/ heroin/ meth/ pot, the people that make these drugs or smuggle them into the country aren't going to suddenly turn straight and start being legal drug dealers- they're going to start shit like arms smuggling and people smuggling, which fucks shit up a whole lot worse than a little bit of mind fuckery.

308 [the best of] Dear Coquette

I was just wondering whether you think this is a
legitimate issue with the legalisation of drugs, or just
some shielded conservative bullshit to hide his own
issues?
Thx bby.
xxx

Wow. You actually write with an Australian accent. I can almost hear this guy mansplaining his dumbfuck anti-legalization argument to you over schooners at the pub. I fucking love that.

Unfortunately, the only thing your dear old friend understands less than criminality is basic fucking economics.

First of all, he's wrong about his underlying premise. As black markets shift from gray to white, the organizations involved really do turn straight and go legal. It proved true after America's prohibition experiment, and it's proving true again as we slowly decriminalize marijuana across the Western world. Dodgy gangsters are more than happy to become legitimate businessmen. (As if there's really much of a difference to begin with.)

Secondly, your friend is confusing the criminal underworld's various command hierarchies with its supply-chain logistics. Black markets aren't a zero-sum game, and the 'framework' for organized crime isn't a rigid thing. It's not as though with fewer drugs to smuggle, suddenly there's more room in the cargo hold for guns and Eastern European women. That's just not how it works.

Your friend is also forgetting the other side of the criminal equation: an obscene amount of law enforcement resources are wasted on the drug war. If those same resources were suddenly freed up to deal with illicit arms dealers and human traffickers, the world would be a much better place.

I'm sorry, but your friend is completely full of shit. Please tell him I said so. His only valid point is that prohibition is illogical. Whether it's alcohol or any other kind of drug, prohibition in a supposedly free society is nothing more than a grotesque means of social control, and it's ultimately doomed to fail.

On politics and punishment

Despite my numerous far-left political tendencies (I am a registered Democratic Socialist), I still think public hanging should be reinstated as a method of the death penalty. Does this make me nothing more than a chicken-shit centrist, or am I just overthinking?

A desire to reinstate public hanging doesn't push you towards the political center. It pushes you back around towards the fringes where wingnut ideologies start to blend into a hazy purple of both far-left and far-right lunacy. In other words, you don't sound like a chicken-shit centrist. You sound like a fucking fascist.

Democratic Socialism is all well and good, but not when coupled with a state powerful enough to perform barbaric death rituals as punishment for crimes. Government should exist to regulate, not punish.

As the systemic extension of the will of the people, government's role should be broad, but its power should only extend as far as its benevolence. The death penalty is the institutionalized representation of the most abhorrent and inferior aspects of our human nature.

We are never lower as a people than when we allow the state to take murderous revenge on our behalf.

On people against feminism

What do you think about all the people who don't understand feminism? Especially the women who

supposedly "are against feminism because they don't
hate men"? Should we argue or is it a lost cause?

No, we shouldn't argue. We should teach. We should enlighten. We should in the friendliest of spirits and without the slightest trace of condescension drop so much fucking knowledge on those people that it crushes their flawed and simplistic understanding of gender politics.

We should be patient in the face of ignorance until we know for sure that it is willful. We should give them every opportunity to change their minds, because ultimately, very few people are built around a core of malignant, incurable misogyny. Very few people have a worldview so grotesque that they actually believe women should be subjugated. Very few people will openly admit that equality isn't a noble pursuit – especially women for whom so often their only fault is being misguided about the fundamental concepts.

No one is a lost cause until we find out for sure that their identity is tied to an aggressively misogynistic belief system, and when we come across those broken souls, we don't argue. That's wasted breath. We simply mark them with red flags and keep them at arm's length, because those are the ones who aren't safe to be around.

On feminism and porn

Am I a hypocrite if I believe in feminism and want to be
a respected woman, but I like watching porn?

What kind of porn are we talking about?

Better yet, what kind of feminism are we talking about?

If you're an old-school iron cunt – one of those angry, man-hating second-wave feminists left over from the early seventies – and you secretly get off to bukkake gangbangs, then sure, that's pretty damned hypocritical.

On the other hand, if you're just a garden-variety sex-positive post-feminist with a college degree, a tattoo and a lesbian experience, then there's no hypocrisy whatsoever in watching some hardcore anal action, especially if it's well lit.

When you think about it, the debate between pornography and feminism has a lot in common with the debate between science and religion.

Folks are constantly trying to intersect two institutions that have no business together in the first place, and it's only when you superimpose a closed-minded ideology on the situation that you run into problems of hypocrisy.

I don't know about you, but I'll always be on the side of porn and science. If a narrow-minded belief system is making you feel like a hypocrite, maybe you should leave it at the door.

On giving feminism a bad name

YOU CALLED FEMINISM A 'NARROW-MINDED BELIEF SYSTEM'? Haha.

It's funny that you think you're being 'open-minded' by watching porn. Wow, what a free spirit! Succumbing to the objectification of women, the assigning of gender roles and misogyny!

WELL FUCKING DONE.

You idiot.

Capital letters *and* sarcasm? Wow. I almost didn't notice that you completely misquoted me. I didn't call feminism a narrow-minded belief system, although for your angry brand of the stuff, I might be willing to make an exception.

Do me a favor and don't talk to me about words you don't understand. I know sex workers with more feminism in their clit rings than you've got in your entire gender studies department. Free spirits, indeed.

Here's a thought exercise: if a camera crew filmed me pulling the stick out of your ass, would that be considered porn?

The correct answer: only if you enjoyed it.

(Oh, and you know how you got all offended just now instead of laughing? Yeah. That's why nobody likes you.)

are politics + economics just our egos fighting each other over who is right?

Nope. Politics and economics are just our species fighting over who gets the limited resources.

Do people have an obligation towards the country they were born in?

Fuck no.

Why do so many working class white people in rural areas vote against their best interests?

Because they've been institutionally conditioned to use their vote as a means of justifying their belief system rather than protecting their interests.

Liberation feminism or equality feminism?

In a patriarchal society, there is no difference.

Why can't I help but feel that billionaires are better than me?

Because you think they earned it.

There is a war coming towards us and I am frightened.
That's what they want you to think, and that's what they want you
to feel.

On nationalistic pride

Are you proud to be an American?

No. I have a deep appreciation for the privileges my citizenship affords me, but I am highly suspect of the tribal nature of the
human condition and I consider nationalistic pride to be a particularly ugly and regressive emotion reserved for simpletons and the
charlatans who hope to take advantage of them.

On fucking the police

You keep bringing up the mantra "fuck the police."
I agree that the police can and do abuse their power
and that reform should be an ongoing and continuous
process. I also agree that the police are forced to
enforce unjust laws that have led to an overcrowded
and unsustainable prison system. But don't you agree
that the police do serve the public interest in much of
what they do such as bringing burglars, white collar
criminals, rapists, and murderers to justice?

You're confusing the police with the criminal justice system,
and you're confusing public interest with the establishment.

For the record, the police do not bring people to justice. All
they do is enforce the law. If you don't understand the difference
between justice and the law, then you're fired from America, and
you should drive down to Home Depot and give your citizenship
to someone who deserves it.

Admittedly, the public interest is well served by criminal investigators and emergency first responders, but so fucking what? Those duties aren't inherent to police. Any number of governmental departments and agencies can (and do) serve those functions.

What makes the police special, what makes them internationally fuck-worthy, is that they're granted authority by the state to preserve order through the use of force. That, my friends, is the opposite of liberty.

Whether it's sharia law in Tehran, drug laws in Los Angeles, or public nuisance laws at your local Occupy protest, the police are the ones who can (and do) legally compel obedience through violence. I'm not cool with that.

At best, police power is a necessary evil. At worst, it's a boot on your motherfucking neck. It will never be okay with me. I will never consent to that codicil of the social contract.

I do not recognize the state's right to use force to compel my obedience, and that's what I mean when I say, 'fuck the police'.

On church and state

Why does the government think it is okay to force the church to go against their core belief (right wrong or indifferent)? Their core value of preserving life hasn't changed and anyone who wants it can get FREE birth control at their local health department. The government wants the separation of church and and state and you can't have it both ways. Catholic hospitals are self insured and provide more charity care than all other hospitals combined. We didn't allow the church to stop us from legalizing abortion. How can the government force them to go against their core values? Do you really think this is ok?

1. The Catholic Church's core value isn't preserving life. It's preserving power.

2. Your statement that free birth control is available to anyone who wants it from the local health department isn't even close to being true. That's like saying free housing is available to anyone who wants to live in the projects, or free food is available to anyone who wants to sign up for food stamps. Only the poorest of the poor actually qualify for government safety net programs.

3. You clearly don't understand the concept of separation of church and state. Freedom of religion also includes freedom *from* religion. The church doesn't get a free pass to do whatever it wants to its employees in the name of its own belief system. Religious organizations still have to obey the law.

4. I don't know where you're getting your statistic on Catholic hospital charity care, but even if what you're saying is true, so what? You're just making an irrelevant appeal to authority.

5. On American soil, the authority of the Catholic Church to enforce its core values does not supersede the authority of the US government to enforce its laws. If you can't handle that, by all means, brush up on your Italian and move to Vatican City.

6. Yes, I really think it's okay for healthcare mandates to require church-affiliated hospitals, charities and schools to offer birth control to its employees.

7. All you bible-thumpers might want to shut the fuck up about stuff like this before the rest of us all decide it's finally time to revoke your church's tax-exempt status.

8. None of this is an attack on your religious freedom. Feel free to continue being an ignorant twat who believes in angels, demons and a jealous god.

On basic fucking economics

It's easier to make a lot of money than to make "just enough" money. EVERYONE's trying to make just enough money. There are so few actively trying to make a lot of money that they tend to help one another more. If you make a lot of money and don't want it, you can always give it to worthy causes or people. But why let your state of mind be determined by a boss who decided they want to make a lot of money from your work? Go make it yourself.

Okay, fuckface. Lemme break down your stupidity line by line:

It's easier to make a lot of money than to make "just enough" money.

No it's not. It's damn hard to make 'just enough' money, and it's downright impossible to make a lot of money without access to privilege, influence and a fuck-ton of capital.

EVERYONE's trying to make just enough money.

No shit, Sherlock. Life's a fucking grind. Don't act all superior, like you know some special trick that all the poor working stiffs haven't figured out yet. Social mobility is a fucking myth, and you sound like an airhead talking about money like this.

There are so few actively trying to make a lot of money that they tend to help one another more.

Oh, you mean members of the elite class serve their own self-interest through nepotism, cronyism and favoritism? Yeah, I like how you tried to make unfair advantage sound like a good thing.

If you make a lot of money and don't want it, you can always give it to worthy causes or people.

You sound like a fucking child. Do you even understanding how corporate capitalism works? Obscene wealth hoards itself at centers of power, relentlessly flowing back into its own gaping maw as value is leeched from helpless pools of human and natural resources. There are no worthy causes or people, just public relations and consumers.

But why let your state of mind be determined by a boss who decided they want to make a lot of money from your work?

Ugh. Social stratification is more than just a state of mind, you privileged little shit. The real world is a harsh and unforgiving place. I sincerely hope you discover that when you're shat out the other end of whatever cut-rate business school is stealing your parents' money.

Go make it yourself.

Go fuck yourself.

I first learned about you three years ago and back then I was a hardcore Republican. Now I'm basically a socialist hippie. What have you done to me?

I've sharpened your critical thinking skills while helping you become less selfish.

How do I accept the inevitable?

By realizing that it doesn't matter whether you accept it or not.

I'm empty. What do I fill myself with?

First, hope. Then some strength. After that, motivation. Then finally, purpose.

Isn't having a "purpose" delusional? Life has no purpose other than what it is.

You're confusing purpose with meaning.

People often wonder what the meaning of life is, the point of existence. There is none. So what's wrong with committing suicide? It's just skipping to the inevitable end anyway.

A meaningless existence is almost always preferable to a meaningless annihilation, and inevitability is the absolute worst reason to skip to the end.

Please tell me it gets better.

Sometimes it does. Mostly it just changes.

How do you ethically defend eating meat? I do too, but I'm conflicted about it all the time.

I don't defend eating meat with an ethical argument. The argument against eating meat has the ethical high ground. I defend eating meat simply by saying it's delicious, which it is, and I accept the fact that I am not ethically pure in that regard.

Here's a crazy thought experiment: 1% of the world's population has to be eliminated. How would you do it?

Every year for a millennium, I would send the world's wealthiest .001 percent to the guillotine.

On eating the rich

Can you explain in simple terms why you would choose to send the wealthiest .001% to the guillotine? What if they're giving more than they're getting?

I know it seems a bit Hunger Games-ish, but it's actually a fairly well thought-out edict.

The premise of this outrageously hypothetical thought experiment is that 1 percent of the world's population *has to be* eliminated, and it's up to me to do it. Okay, fine. I can work with that, but at the same time, I want to make the best of a bad situation.

Now, the premise didn't stipulate a time frame, so I'll take a gracious millennium to do it. (There are several reasons for this.) First off, eliminating 1 out of 100 people all at once would be quite messy and traumatize the collective consciousness. However, eliminating 1 out of 100,000 people every year for a 1,000 years would barely be noticed.

More importantly, though, spreading it out over a millennium ensures that the desired effect is permanent. Now, what is the desired effect? To eliminate grotesque wealth inequality, of course.

The first year would be rather shocking. A lot of well-known billionaires would end up with their heads in a basket. Obviously, a handful of them would be deeply missed, but by and large, the world would instantly become a much better place without the world's wealthiest .001 percent.

Now, as the second culling approaches, do you think the remaining super-rich are gonna hold on to their wealth? Fuck no. They're gonna redistribute whatever's necessary to keep from losing their heads. Everyone will.

Entirely new global financial industries would spring up to automatically and inherently correct the world's wealth inequality problem, and after a period of painful adjustment, we'd have 1,000 years of relative equality where the richest person on earth would only have about 10,000 times more wealth than the poorest person on earth, or risk being sacrificed each year. (A 10,000 to 1 ratio may still seem like a lot of inequality, but on a global scale, it really isn't.)

Obviously, there would be plenty among the rich and powerful who'd try to game the system through complicated trusts and schemes, but as empress of this little scenario, I would reserve the right to call shenanigans and send those folks to the guillotine.

Actually, the most interesting thing about this edict would be all the bizarre rituals, institutions and unforeseen consequences that would spring up as a side effect of such a new world order.

It'd make for a fascinating utopian/dystopian novel.

On our ecosystem

I know you believe that buying fair trade is self-righteous and doesn't really make a difference because we're all still buying from the same system and I agree with you. So what is your overall opinion of the damage humans are doing to the earth's ecosystems? What changes, if any, would you make if you had the power?

I never said buying fair trade is self-righteous. It's a consumer preference just like any other. Whether it's a fair trade logo, a recycle symbol or a 'Made in the USA' sticker, you're only self-righteous if you think your consumer identity somehow makes you a better person.

As for your larger question about the planet, people tend to ignore the rather obvious fact that the earth as an ecosystem is self-regulating and self-sustaining. It doesn't give a fuck whether we're here or not, and on a geological timescale, human influence on the earth's ecology is a fucking burp. It's nothing.

When people talk about damage to the earth's ecosystem, what they really mean is damage to the extent that humans aren't able to continue living in it, either comfortably or in such numbers. Sure, we also care about a short list of our favorite species, but ultimately it's all quite self-serving. Of course, that's perfectly fine by me. I'd prefer that we all thrive, because we've got some serious evolving yet to do.

The best way to ensure that our ecosystem stays habitable is to make a dramatic shift in our primary energy source in the coming decades. The world economy is petroleum based. That simply has got to end. It's dangerous, dirty, and quite frankly, it's not like we really have a choice. At our current rate, we're probably gonna run out of oil in our lifetime anyway.

As a species of 7 billion strong and growing, it's inevitable that we'll reach a tipping point where the necessity for clean, renewable energy will outweigh the moneyed entrenchment of petroleum-based energy. I just hope that tipping point doesn't come in the form of World War III or global economic collapse.

If it were up to me, I would have gotten ahead of the curve already. Instead of dumping 3 trillion dollars into the Iraq war, I would have made a concerted, multinational push for the major scientific breakthroughs that are needed in solar power and inertial confinement fusion technologies to revolutionize our global supply chain with clean, renewable energy.

That shit would have made the race to the moon look like fireworks, and honestly, that's what it's gonna take if we want to keep upwards of 10 billion people alive after the oil is gone.

So, on behalf of the earth's ecosystem, what changes would I make if I had the power? Short answer, I'd move humanity into a post-petroleum world as soon as possible and on our own terms by throwing a bazillion-dollar party for solar and fusion technology.

On ethical consumption

You've been known to take a drug or two on occasion, and I feel like you're someone whose behaviours are not lightly criticised by sensible persons. So perhaps you can clear this question up for me.

I wouldn't buy ivory, eat a whale or wear conflict diamonds, so why am I ok with buying cocaine? Ought one apply the same logic of ethical consumption to drugs? Does one have to take the hard road of total abstinence to get the proverbial blood off one's hands?

There is no washing the blood off your hands, you pretentious hippie fuck.

The simple act of paying taxes in any first-world country makes you complicit in an unholy global raping of such magnitude that no amount of dolphin-safe tuna or fair trade coffee could ever restore the cosmic balance.

You're guilty of original sin just for living on the grid, so quit pretending you're ethically superior because you get your politics off a Starbucks cup.

Besides, ivory is tacky, whale blubber tastes like shit, and diamonds are a sucker's bet. Do you have any idea how smug you sound by acting like there's some noble sacrifice in avoiding products that you wouldn't have consumed in the first place?

Go ahead, boycott cocaine on ethical grounds. That'll teach the Sinaloa Cartel a lesson. You idiot.

Ethical consumption is a marketing ploy. It should be ironically transparent, but weak-minded consumers are so desperate to assuage their hippie-flavored white guilt that they're willing to believe a holier-than-thou consumer identity actually has a positive net effect on the world's political and environmental atrocities.

Seriously, don't let them fool you. When they tell you that 'every dollar you spend is a vote for how you want the world to be', it's just because they want your fucking dollar.

You're being programmed to think that your consumer choices are the equivalent of moral acts, but they're not. You're just buying shit like the rest of us.

On balancing the scales

Regarding your "ethical consumption" post—I agree with you, nothing will ever balance the scales. People are terrified of having to feel guilty about anything, and they'll use whatever they can to keep on walking around blind to their negative impact on the world and on others. But are you saying that we shouldn't try to make conscientous decisions about what we buy when we can? If I can buy the laundry detergent bottle made from recycled plastic instead of new, shouldn't I? Not to the point where it makes me struggle finanically, or cripples me in some other way. I know it's just a drop in the oil-tainted ocean, that all corporations see is dollar signs, and that balancing the scales is impossible, but isn't tipping them a little bit back still worth it?

I just want to keep some hope and some sea turtles alive. Even if it's foolish and makes you want to call me a hippie.

Balancing the scales is not impossible. All you need to do is go develop the major scientific breakthrough in the field of photovoltaics or inertial confinement fusion that finally revolutionizes our supply chain of clean, renewable energy.

Somebody's gonna do it. Might as well be you.

If all you want to do is tip the scales back just a little bit, then I suppose you could move to Malawi and start an orphanage or something. You know, devote your entire life to easing the suffering of the third world in some personal way. As you put it, it's just a drop in the oil-tainted ocean, but hey, it's a start.

Short of that, please stop kidding yourself. You're not making a difference.

Feel free to buy whatever laundry detergent you like, but do not for one second let yourself believe that your decision was somehow more conscientious because the bottle was made of recycled plastic. Do you have any idea how mind-bogglingly self-centered that sounds?

I wish common sense included a sense of scale. You and your consumer identity have absolutely no moral mass whatsoever. Nothing you can buy at Walmart will ever count as an ethical unit of measure that has weight on a global scale.

Green products are a marketing strategy. All you're doing is paying a premium for that fleeting moment of self-satisfaction you feel when you buy something labeled as environmentally conscious.

That's fine. There's nothing wrong with having a consumer preference, but please know that it doesn't earn you a single inch of ethical high ground.

I know, you can make arguments for aggregated effects, but those are still just passive market forces tied to a capitalist system built on corporate self-interest. Buying a Prius doesn't mean you're 'doing your part' to conserve oil. It merely means you get better gas mileage.

I'm not a cynic. I really do believe that you can make that drop in the ocean, but doing your part actually requires that you fucking *do* something. You can boycott shrimp all your life, and it's not gonna help a single sea turtle. If you want to keep those little bastards alive, become a marine biologist and go save some fucking turtles.

On the Coquette

Who are you?
Wouldn't you like to know.

Would we know if you had kids?
No. (But I don't.)

Do you want to get married someday?
I don't care whether I get married, but I'd like to find a life partner or two.

Have you ever planted a question so you would have a platform to share your views on a certain topic?
Nope, never. (I get dozens of questions on every topic, so if I feel like ranting, I just pick one.)

Did it take you a long time to get comfortable with the way you look?
I'm not at all comfortable with the way I look. I know I can look hot, but that sure as hell doesn't mean I'm comfortable. Huge difference.

Sometimes I think you're a product and consumer of the system as much as anyone is.
Of course I am. Just because I understand systems theory, that doesn't mean I've transcended the system. I enjoy air conditioning, steak and premium channels way too much to be any kind of counterculture drop-out.

Are you an introvert or an extrovert?

I'm an introvert. (I'm great at parties, but my default setting is pleasurable solitude, and the stuff going on in my head is almost always more interesting than the stuff going on in front of me.)

How do you stay so invincible when it comes to situations that would otherwise cause negative emotions? I feel like I'd be so much more powerful (and happy) if I learned your abilities.

No, no. I'm not invincible. I've just gone through some shit. I've had all the negative emotions, and I've realized that after the first few minutes, they're almost entirely optional.

Why do you answer all these dumb questions from girls who don't have a backbone who should obviously break up with their boyfriends and/or stand up for themselves?

Because they ask, and I'm happy to provide a surrogate backbone long enough for them to feel what it's like to stand up for themselves.

i think i have you all figured out.

I bet you think strippers really like you too.

Would you reveal your identity if offered $1,000,000 for it?

Feel free to make me an offer and find out.

What's your favorite book?

Are we on a shitty first date or something? There is no possible way for me to answer this question.

What kind of girl were you in high school? Slut? Loner? Popular? Nerd? Outcast?
Yes.

Do you think of yourself as a judgmental person?
Not on my better days.

You're getting soft. Are you pregnant?
You're getting presumptuous. Are you the father?

Do you care about your readers?
Of course I do. How the fuck would this be possible if I didn't?

Do your peers know about this successful blog?
Nope. Only a tiny handful of my closest friends.

Have you ever had any sort of cosmetic surgery?
Yes, I had the go fuck yourself procedure done a few years ago.

Why can't more girls be like you?
Oh please, you couldn't handle us if there were.

On guilt and shame

Do you feel guilt? That's not a loaded question, I mean it in regard to your very (very) well developed sense of mature morality. You just seem like such a morally advanced person that you'd sort of be "beyond" guilt.

The only people who are beyond guilt are narcissists and socio-paths. I feel guilty for shit all the time, and I'm glad that I do. Guilt is evidence of a functioning conscience.

If anything, I'd like to be beyond shame. Shame is different than guilt. To be shameless is to not give a fuck what other people think. It requires the moral code and strength of character to know you're in the right even though others believe you're in the wrong.

On profanity

I find it amusing that you contradict your intelligent outlook on life by using stupid swear words all the time – especially when you've said in the past "I'm perfectly capable of expressing my emotional state with actual words." – which really is the height of unintelligence, particularly when expressing yourself. You remind me of some fourteen-year-olds I went to high school with who all thought they were so cool when they started to call each other bitches and sluts, and had extended their vocabulary to include words like fuck. Could you perhaps tell me the point of swearing so often? Do you even know?

I use profanity because I'm profane, you persnickety cunt.

When it comes to creative use of the language, swear words aren't the height of unintelligence. Cliché and closed-mindedness are, and sweetheart, you're a walking closed-minded cliché.

Someone has you convinced that vulgarity and irreverence are synonymous with stupidity when nothing could be further from the truth. Profanity is a weapon for someone like me. It's a linguistic tool with a blunt face and a sharp edge. It's dangerous and essential.

Find it amusing all you want, but you're the smug little bitch going through life with your nose in the air, constantly judging others with a value system you haven't even taken the time to examine.

Now that's what I find amusing.

On grammar

you shouldn't be such a bitch about grammar. only uppity 15 year old 'gifted' girls who reblog harry potter do that. as long as one is intelligible, whatever dude. some of the greatest writers of all time have ignored many facets of grammar. it doesn't make you an idiot. it just means you are more right-brained, and those people are better writers anyways. grammar is the most mathematical and lifeless part of language. essential, yes, but getting on everyone's ass about petty grammatical things just shows what an insecure little bully YOU are. have fun with your harry potter, sweet cheeks

I don't know who's filling the right side of your brain with this lazy bullshit, but starting your sentences with lowercase letters does not make you ee cummings.

Great writers can ignore grammar because they know it in the first place, and a condescending opinion on top of a shitty attitude isn't evidence that you know anything at all.

This isn't about rules. Fuck the rules. This is about fundamental beauty inherent in the system. If you want to deconstruct the language in furtherance of personal expression, by all means, I'll give you a poetic license to kill, but don't piss on me and tell me it's raining.

I can tell the difference between a deliberate and meaningful manipulation of words and the ramblings of some half-retarded teenager who wouldn't know where to stick an apostrophe unless I lubed it up and put it in myself.

This shit isn't petty. I'm not walking around with a red pen and a stick up my ass. People write to me for help with their problems, and if I'm pointing out that they can't string a sentence together, it's for a reason.

Mastery of language is the primary indication of intelligence, education and grace, and the inability to effectively communicate is at the core of pretty much all the mental anguish we inflict on ourselves.

Just being intelligible isn't enough. Style matters. Make all the excuses you want, but whether it's on paper or on the street, if you come at me all sloppy, I'm not gonna respect you.

I've got standards, motherfucker.

Do you think you'll ever be too old to be an L.A. party girl?

Definitely. The mid 2000s were my peak party years. This decade is for slowing down with a very select group of friends. (I don't mind getting older. I'm good at it, and I appreciate the perspective.)

Do you want to have kids someday?

Not nearly as much as I want people to quit asking me this question.

What's your biggest dealbreaker in dating?

Stupid.

Bitch, you're totally a lawyer. It takes a lawyer to know a lawyer.

The lawyers think I'm a lawyer. The shrinks think I'm a shrink. The escorts think I'm an escort. I'm seeing a pattern here.

On the Coquette   331

Why does everyone assume you're white?
I guess I seem pretty white.

How do you know multiple sex workers well since your not in the business?
Do you think that all sex workers live in a magical whorehouse in the sky? They walk among us, my friend. It ain't that big a deal.

how come you don't have an instagram?
Too much potential for me to reveal my identity when I'm fucked up.

Aren't you just as full of shit as anyone else?
Yep.

You're in fashion.
Are you complimenting my popularity or making an assumption about my occupation?

What do you do with your free time? What does the Coquette do with a lazy Sunday?
This.

Do you ever think you might be wrong?
I'm wrong all the damn time.

Why does everyone assume you're a famous person?
Everyone doesn't, but the ones who do tend to think that the only reason a person wouldn't want fame is because they already have it.

Why are you so angry?
I'm not angry. I'm just paying attention.

Are you a bitterly wise older women or just an ordinary gay man?
Are you implying that gay men are ordinarily bitter or that younger women can't be wise?

Would you allow yourself to be described as a socialite?
No, I work for a living. To be called a socialite implies otherwise.

On coming from money

My friend thinks you come from money. I say you've worked and hustled your way up the ranks. Who's right?

I did not come from money, but through a combination of scholarships and just plain faking it, I grew up around people who did. I know what money looks like. I know how it talks. Most importantly, I know how money protects itself and those who have it at the expense of everyone else.

I've worked and hustled since I was a teenager. I moved to LA by myself, and made my own way here. I've been lucky a few times, and I've had my ass kicked a few times. I've been broke as fuck more often than I've been comfortable.

Hopefully I'll always be able to earn a decent living (fingers crossed), but I know that I will never be wealthy. I've deliberately chosen not to marry it, I don't have the capitalist instincts to build it, and I'm not one of the genetic lottery winners who'll get to inherit it. That's fine. I've spent enough time in the presence of wealth to know that I don't need it.

There was a time during my adolescence when all I wanted was to be rich. As an adult, I know better. Hell, I'd probably be dead by now if I had grown up a rich kid. Looking back, I'm actually thankful that I don't come from money. It's just too much of a corrosive influence, and as strong as I am, I don't think money would bring out the best in me.

On not being sold

Why such an aggressive, "tough shit" approach to giving advice?

Oh, I'm sorry. Was I supposed to be writing copy for eHarmony? Are you reading from a box of Wheaties? Is this all just a media tie-in for the latest indie romantic comedy?

No, asshole. I'm not selling anything. Natalie Portman doesn't play me in the movie. I'm not a manic pixie dream girl or a marketing strategy.

My 'tough shit' approach is the sound your friends would make if they could shoot straight with you, and I don't even think you know the meaning of the word aggressive.

Advertising is aggressive. Lifestyle branding is aggressive. The parking enforcement bureau is aggressive.

Hell, I'm not pushing anything. I'm not even selling t-shirts. This is a hobby. All I'm doing is answering questions with as much brutal honesty as I can muster at any particular hour, and on more than one occasion while I'm absolutely wasted.

Don't get all snippy with me because I don't strap on knee pads and cup your balls and lull you into a fugue state.

Your cock is huge, by the way. You should probably buy those XL condoms.

On taking a guess

Lemmie guess, you're really a nerdy girl who, like many nerdy girls who learn to use makeup, discover (or not) they're actually pretty and then begin to hang out with a less-than-honorable crowd only to realize this in time and, with the help of friends, was able to find a balance between the stuff that you like doing and the stuff that needs doing. Right?

Ugh. You can tell when a guy writes this shit.

Okay, dude. I'll admit, I was an ugly duckling. Gangly as fuck at just the right age where my eventual hotness didn't go to my head the wrong way. I suppose my mother also helped with that. She made sure I understood the limitations of physical beauty. It was never about anything as trite as learning to use make-up. That's an external process, like learning to lace up a boot. Sure, it's useful, but it's not a source of discovery.

Also, I'm not a nerdy girl. I'm an intelligent woman, so we can dispense with the archetypal moment where I took off my glasses, let down my hair, and suddenly everyone started blowing rails off my tits.

As for the less-than-honorable crowd remark, I'd say you haven't been paying attention to what I do here. Of course, I've met more than my fair share of less-than-honorable people, but I know how to spot them, I know how to deal with them, and they never become part of my crowd. Ever.

You got the last part right, though. Finding a balance between the stuff I like doing and the stuff that needs doing with the help of friends, well shit, that's how I live my life every day.

On how it's done

*How do you make any money doing coke/other shit
every day? Are you like a celebrity or something?*

I work my ass off, and I have fun when I've earned it. I sure
as hell don't do drugs every day, and when it comes down to it, I
really don't do all that much blow.

A few lines with friends a few times a month is a less expensive
habit than cigarettes if you're a girl. Hell, a good tab of ecstasy lasts
all night for the price of a couple of cocktails.

Shit, if you want to break down the budget on a wild night of
fun, the real money gets burned on hotel suites and private tables.
It's not about finding good drugs, it's about keeping good company.

And fuck being a celebrity, especially by today's definition. That
shit is nothing but hassle. I'll take a velvet rope over a red carpet
any day of the week.

*I like you but I think that I like you in the same way I
like cheap vodka, an easy way out. Obviously you're
human but seriously your ego and sheer arrogance is
painful to read. I once found your advice to be that of a
big sister that I never had but I've lost the faith. Is it me
or is it you? Both?*
It's not me. It's the voice in your head you hear when you read me,
which is really just a projection of yourself. You're thinking more
critically now, and that's the whole point. I'm glad that you once
found my advice sisterly, but at the same time, I'm just as happy for
you to realize that I'm as completely full of shit as everyone else.

Why do I hate you?
Because something about who you think I am is a threat to your
identity.

You're such a self righteous bitch.
Duh.

you're such a cunt. I bet you're fat and unlovable
Well, now I know your two greatest fears.

Your an idiot!
Well, at least I know the difference between *you're* and *your*.

The quietest people have the loudest minds...what does that make you?
Immune to your clichéd bullshit.

You are the anti-Cupid
That's me. Just walkin' around pulling arrows out of lovesick idiots.

I hate your happy life.
Don't envy something that doesn't even exist.

Where do your authority issues come from?
My authority issues come from consistently being wiser and having more integrity than those in authority.

What is the most interesting thing you've learned from the submissions you receive on here?
We are all exactly the same. Every last one of us.

On being normal

I've been reading your blog now for a month or so and I can't help thinking to myself you're actually a normal human. What I mean by this is that you merely use this as an opportunity to be someone you're not in everyday life. I would bet that you are no where near as brash and politically un-correct. I don't think it is possible to actually live the life you portray here. Or am I wrong?

You're not wrong. You're not right either.

I am actually a normal human being. Beyond that, I can't quite bring myself to accept your premise that a normal human being can't think and act the way I do.

I don't know what it's like where you're from, but bitches like me are a dime a dozen out here. I've just decided to write some shit down. Is it really that hard to believe?

Maybe you're imagining things to be far more fabulous than they appear. Sure, I have my share of fun, but if you bumped into me in a hotel lobby, you wouldn't be magically transported into a Terry Rodgers painting.

Shit man, this is LA. It doesn't matter what side of the velvet rope you're on at night. Come morning, we're all stuck in traffic wishing we spoke more Spanish.

On philosophers and fools

Heartbreak is not inevitable...why are you so bitter? Sure there are hard times but some people who say "forever" mean it. I'm sorry that has not been your experience. Every time I read your articles I end up thinking about you and how miserable your existence must be and what horrible life experiences you must have had. I am so sorry for you!

Sweetheart, I'm not bitter. I'm just not a candy-headed twit. Please save your shallow pity for sad puppies in Sarah McLachlan commercials, because I certainly don't need it.

I'm over here leading a charmed life of self-realized happiness, but you aren't equipped to spot something like that. I'm sure you're a decent enough person – earnest, Wonder Bread wholesome, sweet in a saccharine sort of way – but you couldn't find enlightenment if it was in the rollback bin at Walmart.

That's okay. I don't need you to understand that what you consider bitterness, I consider a healthy dose of pragmatism. What you consider sin, I consider a celebration of the human condition. What you consider bliss, I consider ignorance.

I welcome heartbreak as an inevitability because I have no childish illusions about true love or happily ever after. That doesn't mean I don't love deeply. I do. I just don't need it to be a fairy tale.

And yes, some people who say forever mean it, but forever is a word for philosophers and fools. If you're using it to describe your love life, I'll let you guess which of the two you are.

On the eye of the beholder

I can't help but envy the depth and texture of your life glimpsed through the anecdotes you've shared. It feels like my life choices, or maybe just my nature, have limited my opportunities for adventure and spontaneity. Then I remember conversations where friends or strangers would gape at my own more modest experiences. Is it all in the eye of the beholder? Is there some Rock Star bell curve we all fall onto or is it all in the presentation?

Both. There is a rock star bell curve, and still, it's all in the presentation. There are echelons of heiresses and overachievers who make my minor adventures seem quaint, but I tell a better story than they do. Not that any of it really matters, because you can find depth and texture in any experience – and in anyone's life – if you only bother to look. It's the looking, the examination itself, that reveals the depth and texture.

Don't envy the life you've glimpsed through my anecdotes. Don't compare my life to yours. That feeling you have about your nature, that your life choices are somehow limiting your opportunities, it is the essence of wistfulness. Feeling wistful is a powerful emotion, one that can easily turn into envy and melancholy if you start comparing yourself to others. Resist the urge to compare, and never let the thought of missed adventures bother you.

You and I and everyone else are all inherently limited by our choices. There are an infinite number of adventures that we will never get to experience – some beautiful, some tragic, and some so magnificently transcendent that our tiny brains aren't even capable of imagining them. Every choice we make collapses the possibility of every other, forever limiting our opportunities for all those grand and unknowable adventures, but that's the singular nature of time and the human condition, so fuck it.

We only get one go of it, and the brutal truth is that some people have more fun than others. Some get a few more spins around the sun. Some get a pile of shit and suffering. None of it's fair and none of it matters and the only way to get it wrong is to live an unexamined life.

The most important question you asked me is whether it's all in the eye of the beholder, because that's exactly where it is. All of it. The eye of the beholder is everything, and the sharper your eye, the closer you look at the world, and the deeper you examine your experiences, the more depth and texture you'll reveal about your own life no matter what adventures come your way.